The Wildlife
of the
Thames Counties

THE THAMES COUNTIES
Existing county boundaries
Pre-1974 county boundaries
Salcey Forest
Olney
Newport Pagnell
Whittlewood Forest
Stony Stratford
Milton Keynes
R. Ouzel
Banbury
R. Ouse
Bletchley
Buckingham
Deddington
Winslow
Chipping Norton
COTSWOLD HILLS
R. Evenlode
R. Cherwell
Bicester
BUCKINGHAMSHIRE
Whitchurch
Wychwood Forest
Woodstock
R. Ray
Blenheim Park
Ivinghoe
OXFORDSHIRE
Aylesbury
Burford
Boarstall Decoy
Tring Reservoirs
R. Windrush
Witney
Bernwood Forest
Farmoor Reservoir
Wytham Hill
Wendover
R. Isis
Oxford
Thame
Icknield Way
Bampton
Bagley Wood
Princes Risborough
R. Thame
Great Missenden
Chesham
R. Thames
Chinnor Hill
Cothill Fen
CHILTERN HILLS
R. Misbourne
R. Chess
Faringdon
Abingdon
Watlington
R. Colne
Dorchester
High Wycombe
Vale of White Horse
Beaconsfield
Wallingford
Wantage
Gerrards Cross
Warburg Reserve, Bix Bottom
East Ilsley
Henley on Thames
Burnham Beeches
Goring
Maidenhead
Ridge Way
Eton
Slough
Windsor
Reading
Windsor Great Park
Windsor Forest
BERKSHIRE
Virginia Water
R. Kennet
Hungerford
Wokingham
Bracknell
Newbury
Aldermaston
R. Loddon

The Wildlife of the Thames Counties

Berkshire, Buckinghamshire, and Oxfordshire

Edited by
RICHARD FITTER

ROBERT DUGDALE
in association with
BERKSHIRE, BUCKINGHAMSHIRE AND OXFORDSHIRE
NATURALISTS' TRUST
OXFORD
1985

First published in 1985 by Robert Dugdale,
c/o Corpus Christi College, Oxford, OX1 4JF
in association with
the Berkshire, Buckinghamshire and Oxfordshire Naturalists' Trust

ISBN 0-946976-00-7

Printed in Great Britain by
Thetford Press Limited, Thetford, Norfolk

FOREWORD

When several years ago BBONT was approached by a publisher for a book on the wildlife of the three counties, the Trust turned to its former President, distinguished naturalist and wildlife author, Richard Fitter, who generously undertook to assemble the authors and edit the book.

It has proved a much more prolonged and onerous task than was originally envisaged, and the Trust is immensely grateful to Richard, who persevered and brought the venture to a successful conclusion.

This is the first book ever written on the wildlife of our three counties as a whole, and the first for nearly sixty years about the Oxford area. We hope that it will not only stimulate interest in the great variety of wildlife that survives despite the batterings of recent years, but also lead to a surge of support for BBONT in the crucial task of saving it.

John Phillipson
Chairman, BBONT

BBONT welcomes enquiries about membership, to its office at 3 Church Cowley Road, Rose Hill, Oxford OX4 3JR (Tel. Oxford 775476).

ACKNOWLEDGEMENTS

The Trust is extremely grateful to all those who have helped to make this book possible, especially the authors and photographers, who have most generously given their services free — all royalties go to the Trust — and to Neil Curtis, whose brainchild it was. Particular thanks are due to Gordon Maclean, who not only supplied many black-and-white photographs but generously defrayed the whole cost of the colour cover from his own transparency, and to Maisie Fitter, the Trust's former Chairman and Bulletin Editor, who has done much subbing and acted as honorary art editor.

The book would not have appeared at all if, when the original publisher failed us, Hugo Brunner had not stepped in and organized the private consortium which has actually produced the book. To him especially, and to all other member of the consortium, and to the trustees of the two private trusts whose generous grants bridged a vital financial gap, the Trust's very warm thanks are therefore due.

Dr Woodell wishes to thank Dr T. J. King and Joanna Martin for their valuable comments on his chapter, and the Editor wishes to thank Tim Sands of the Royal Society for Nature Conservation for digging out of the Society's files valuable material for Chapter 12.

James Bateman wishes to thank the following with help for Chapters 5 and 7 and the Museum's appendix: Oxfordshire County Museum's Biological Recording Scheme, and especially John Campbell 'for feeding records to me as soon as they reached him'; Reading Museum and Art Gallery, and H. Carter, whose 1983 paper in the *Reading Naturalist* is frequently cited; Buckinghamshire County Museum, Aylesbury, and Jill Royston; Newbury Museum and A. Higgott; and Elaine Hurrell, who did some of the preliminary research.

Richard Fitter

CONTENTS

A NOTE ON THE COUNTIES

In this book references are to the historic counties of Berkshire, Buckinghamshire and Oxfordshire, whose boundaries have determined the great bulk of the natural history recording which forms the basis of this book. The boundary changes of 1974 fortunately did not affect our outer boundary, while transferring large parts of historic Berkshire, including the escarpment of the Berkshire Downs, to the new Oxfordshire, and a small part of southern Buckinghamshire to Berkshire. Places affected by these boundary changes are therefore referred to as in Berks/Oxon and Bucks/Berks respectively.

THE CONTRIBUTORS

Brian R. Baker is Deputy Director of the Reading Museum and Art Gallery. He was a founder member of the Trust and for many years Berkshire County Secretary.

James A. Bateman is Director of the Department of Museum Services at the Oxfordshire County Museum at Woodstock.

Dr Humphry Bowen is Reader in Chemistry at Reading University and author of the *Flora of Berkshire*. He is Chairman of the Trust's Scientific Policy Committee and has held several other posts on the scientific side of BBONT.

Ursula Bowen is Principal Lecturer in Biology at the Oxford Polytechnic. A former Chairman of BBONT's Education Committee, she was later Chairman of the Education Committee of the Royal Society for Nature Conservation. She has written several nature trails for BBONT and also booklets on freshwater biology and environmental education.

W. D. Campbell is a retired headmaster and a keen field naturalist, well known for his writings in the *Guardian* and elsewhere.

Richard Fitter is an author and naturalist who has specialised in wildlife field guides. A founder member of BBONT and its first Hon. Secretary, he has also served as President and as Chairman of Council. He is now Chairman of the Fauna and Flora Preservation Society.

Chris O'Toole is a technician with the Hope Entomological Collections at Oxford University. A specialist in Hymenoptera, he has made numerous interesting discoveries of rarities on the Trust's reserves.

Vera N. Paul OBE, a retired biology teacher and former Deputy Head of Henley Grammar School, has been the presiding genius of the Warburg Reserve since long before she persuaded the Trust to buy it in 1967. As the Trust's Appeals Director, she was the driving force in raising large sums for the Trust, including the 1974–6 appeal, which raised over £100,000.

John M. Steane is Keeper of the Field Section, Department of Museum Services at the Oxfordshire County Museum at Woodstock.

Dr S. R. J. Woodell is Lecturer in Botany at the Oxford University Botany School and co-author of the *Flora of Oxfordshire* currently in preparation. He was for many years Chairman of the Trust's Scientific Policy Committee.

Dr Margaret E. Varley is Consultant in Biology at the Open University, having retired as Reader in Biology in September 1983.

THE PHOTOGRAPHERS

B. R. Baker: pp. 110, 118.

Richard Fitter: p. 189.

E. A. Janes: pp. 83, 84, 85, 86, 95, 101.

Dr David Macdonald: p. 77.

Gordon Maclean: pp. 2, 5, 11, 27, 53, 59, 61 (nos. 6 & 7), 66 (no. 10), 68, 91, 92, 111, 112, 163, 168, 171 (nos. 5-7), 172, 175, 185, 188 (no. 6).

Nigel Phillips: pp. 61 (no. 5), 66 (no. 9), 75, 79, 98, 116, 117, 135 (no. 5), 182, 186 (no. 4), 188 (no. 5), 190, 191.

Ken Preston-Maffham: pp. 123, 124, 129, 135 (no. 4), 137, 139, 146, 149, 160.

Sally Ann Thompson: pp. 41, 61 (no. 8), 171 (no. 4), 174, 186 (no. 3), 188 (no. 7).

Derek Whiteley: pp. 157, 158, 159.

Dr S. R. J. Woodell: pp. 9, 26, 28, 30, 36, 46.

1 The Physical Background and the Influence of Man

RICHARD FITTER

The wildlife of any region exists within a physical matrix, made up of the rocks, soils, land forms and climate of that region. These determine in large degree the nature and contents of the region's ecosystems. An ecosystem may be defined as a unit of vegetation together with its associated animals, both interacting with their physical environment; the study of the whole is the science of ecology, as distinct from the current popular use of the word. The two other major factors in these ecosystems are the interactions between the animals and plants and the dominant influence of a single animal species—man. This introductory chapter deals with geology, physiography and climate in broad outline, as they affect the plants and animals, and is in no sense a technical account of these subjects.

The three counties of Berkshire, Buckinghamshire and Oxfordshire share many common characteristics. They form the south-western end of the English scarplands, and their underlying rocks have been laid down like a layer cake that has been tilted at an angle, the different strata running north-east/south-west: the oolitic Cotswolds are the bottom layer and the chalk Chilterns and Berkshire Downs the top layer, with the Upper Jurassic clays and limestones and the Lower Cretaceous sands and clays the successive fillings up to the icing on the top represented by the patches of Eocene sands, gravels and clays on the higher Chilterns and much of eastern Berkshire. In this sense the cake is upside down as you look at the geological map, the oolites having been laid down many millions of years before the Eocene.

The Thames is the link, for with the exception of parts of North Buckinghamshire which drain into the Great Ouse system, the three counties comprise the valley of the Middle and Upper Thames. Above its confluence with the Thame at Dorchester the Thames used to be called the Isis. On its north bank it receives successively the Windrush at Newbridge, the Evenlode at Cassington, and the Cherwell, which has itself received the Ray at Islip, at Oxford. All these drain the Cotswolds and their exension north-eastwards into Northamptonshire. The scarplands are drained by the Thame, after which no more rivers reach this bank until after the Goring gap through the chalk, which is a fairly spectacular physical

1. River Thames, at Pixey and Yarnton Meads, above Oxford

feature for the South of England. Only the little River Wye now joins the Thames at Hedsor, before we reach the eastern Buckinghamshire border, which is formed by the River Colne; this with its tributaries the Misbourne, the Chess and the Gade, is the major drainage outlet from the Chilterns.

On the south bank of the Thames the River Cole forms historic Berkshire's western boundary with Wiltshire, after which there is nothing till the River Ock, draining the Vale of White Horse, arrives at Abingdon, and then again nothing till we reach the Kennet at Reading, bringing with it the drainage from the Berkshire Downs. The Loddon, with its tributary the Blackwater, which joins it at Swallowfield, is the only other significant tributary on the south bank of the Thames; between them the Loddon and the Blackwater drain most of mid and eastern Berkshire, and bring the first significant contribution of non-calcareous water the Thames has received since it began its course in the Gloucestershire Cotswolds.

The Great or Bedford Ouse actually rises in Northamptonshire, not so very far from the source of the Cherwell, and flows past Buckingham and Newport Pagnell into Bedfordshire on its way to the Wash, draining as it goes a large part of northern Buckinghamshire. It too is a primarily calcareous river, having no highly acid soils in this part of its catchment.

The highest points in the three counties are 297m at Walbury Hill on the downs along the Berkshire/Hampshire border, 260m at Aston Hill above Halton in the Chilterns, and no more than 221m at Great Rollright in the Oxfordshire Cotswolds (which of course go over 300m across the border in Gloucestershire). Nor are there many stretches of really flat land, although the Thames valley above New Bridge, and Otmoor in the Ray valley south of Marsh Gibbon are exceptions. The countryside is typically rolling, and the succession of small escarpments, created by the differential wearing down of the successive strata, has led to the whole district, together with neighbouring Northamptonshire and Lincolnshire to the north-east, being termed the scarplands. The only major escarpment is that of the chalk, facing north-west in the Chilterns and north in the Berkshire Downs.

Geology

If we start on our north-western boundary, with the oldest rocks in the region, and proceed to eat our layer cake in a south-easterly direction, we come first to some calcareous clays of the Lower Jurassic or Lias around Banbury. The Middle Lias produces the ironstone, which is still mined in parts of North Oxfordshire. Next comes the main stretch of the Great Oolite, which provides most of the Cotswold limestone. This is the stone from which Cotswold villages such as Burford and Shipton-under-Wychwood are built, and includes the famous Stonesfield slates, which are not true slates but narrow bands of sandy limestone that were widely used in the Cotswolds for roofing. The best quarries were at Taynton, right on the Gloucestershire border. The Cotswolds thus have predominantly limy soils, producing limestone grassland, beechwoods and ashwoods, when allowed to do so. Included with the Middle Jurassic or Upper Oolite rocks are two distinctive formations, the Forest Marble, named from Wychwood Forest, which was once used to produce polished 'marble' chimney-pieces, and the Cornbrash, a rubbly limestone so called because it produced well drained 'brashy' or rubbly soils deemed excellent for corn-growing. The oolitic limestones are succeeded, in a belt that passes from the Vale of White Horse through Oxford itself to the Vale of Aylesbury, by the Upper Jurassic or Middle and Upper Oolite strata, constituting a sandwich in which the Corallian limestones come between the Oxford Clay and the Kimmeridge Clay. The Oxford Clay is characteristically blue-grey, but turns brown on exposure, and is the source of the clay used in the brickworks at Calvert, Bucks. The Corallian strata are named from the beds of rubbly coral-rock they contain; they were laid down in shallow water; the famous (or infamous if you regard its wearing quality) Headington stone, which was used to build much of

Oxford, is a Corallian deposit. The Kimmeridge Clay is named from Dorset, as are both the Portland and Purbeck Beds of limestone, which are found only on a few hilltops in this region, notably Shotover and Brill.

The succeeding sandwich layers, of Lower Greensand, Gault Clay and Upper Greensand, mark the beginning of the Cretaceous system, but are nowhere near so clearly marked in our area as they are in the Weald, where an additional layer of the sandwich, Wealden Clay, virtually absent from our region, is found. The Lower Greensand is scarcely visible either, except at Faringdon and one or two places near Aylesbury, such as Stone, where it was once dug for use as moulding sand in metal manufacture. The Gault, however, is well developed, and forms the underlying rock of the flattish area south-east of Thame, the southern end of the Vale of Aylesbury. The Upper Greensand is also rather inconspicuous, though it does have a distinct escarpment looking down on the vale between Watlington and Lewknor. Now we come to the Chalk, which dominates the landscape both along the Chiltern escarpment and along the Berkshire Downs, but on the south-east trending dip slopes presents a very different aspect. The Chilterns are largely covered with a Clay-with-Flints deposit, which has a low enough pH reading to permit such acid-loving plants as heather and rhododendron to grow. This is lacking on the Berkshire Downs, where soils are calcareous even on the plateau; in the Chilterns calcareous grassland in found only on the steep valley sides below the plateau.

The Chalk outcrops in a few places south of the Thames, such as Remenham, Hurley and Windsor Castle, but once the tops of the Chilterns and the lower slopes of the Berkshire Downs are reached, the soils become increasingly neutral or even acid, as the Eocene formations, such as Thanet Sands, Woolwich and Reading Beds and London Clay take over. These produce the Chiltern commons, such as Cadmore End, Moorend and Wheelerend, south-west of High Wycombe, now largely overgrown with bracken, as well as such notable features as the heathlands of south-eastern Berkshire, and Black Park and Burnham Beeches in Bucks. Sarsen stones, which Sherlock defines as 'parts of the sand that have been cemented into hard shapeless masses by percolating waters' are found in the Reading Beds, among other formations. In Wiltshire they are quite common, but there are few in our area, apart from a well-known group at Bradenham, Bucks. The region was just too far south to be affected by the southernmost extension of the ice-sheets of the Pleistocene era, but one or two small valleys such as Coombe Hole near Ivinghoe Aston in Bucks, show the steep-sided, flat-bottomed outline characteristic of glacial valleys, suggesting that very minor glaciers may have existed in the northern Chilterns.

2. Chiltern Escarpment, at Beacon Hill, Oxon, with the M40 motorway

A more notable feature of the Chilterns is the dry valleys, some of which form riverless gaps in the hills, as at Wendover and Princes Risborough. A few produce temporary streams or 'woe waters' (so called because they were believed to presage some public ill) when the water table rises, as it did in the spring of 1979 at West Wycombe for instance. The rest are believed to be a relic of the glacial period, when the melting ice produced a substantial lake that ponded up against the Chiltern escarpment, until its level rose high enough to break through these gaps and create these semblances of broad river valleys. Certainly gravels have been deposited in these valleys at some time in the past.

Down by the Thames three terraces of the river gravels can still be detected, indicating various stages in the fall of the river level as the post-glacial age advanced and the floods produced by the melting ice subsided. The highest is the Boyn Hill Terrace, not very well represented in our area. Next comes the Taplow Terrace, well illustrated by the slight hill on which Taplow Church still stands. Lowest of the three is the Flood Plain Terrace. Much of these gravels has, of course, been quarried away for building and road-making over the centuries.

The net result of our journey, our consumption of the cake, is that the diet has been almost entirely calcareous. Wiltshire is usually credited with being the most calcareous county in Britain. In fact Oxfordshire and Bucks are hardly less so, and if East Berkshire were omitted, the three counties as a whole could make a strong challenge to Wiltshire in this respect. The major impact of the geology is therefore that the predominant plant communities of the area are calcicolous, those adapted to soils with a high alkaline content, while acid soils with their associated heath communities are scarce, and indeed in many districts completely absent. The physiography of the region, lacking any land above 300m, means of course that there are no upland or mountain animal or plant communities. Likewise the lack of any large sheets of water, although there are good river systems and plenty of ponds and ornamental lakes, especially in the Thames valley in Berkshire, means that the animal and plant communities of large water bodies are missing.

The Climate

Fluctuations in their supply of light, heat and moisture are the three main ways in which the climate affects the wildlife of any area. All three are vitally necessary both for plant growth and for the wellbeing of animals, whether these are directly dependent on plants or only secondarily so because they prey on other animals. It is important therefore that our three counties, being located in the South of England, enjoy a mild Atlantic climate.

Light is perhaps the most basic element of all, for it is day-length that triggers the reproductive cycles of many plants and so at least indirectly controls those of many animals. Our area receives about 1,400–1,500 hours of sunshine a year, with a tendency to be sunnier in the east than in the west. Two recent figures, both averaged over ten to fifteen recent years, and kindly supplied by Dr H. R. Oliver, are 1,442 hours at Grendon Underwood (Bucks) and 1,416 hours at Wallingford (Berks); an earlier figure averaged over 1885–1925, is 1,473 hours at the Radcliffe Observatory in Oxford. Obviously most sunshine occurs in the summer half of the year, rising to 209 hours at Wallingford in June, while December can muster only 32.5 hours. There are of course many local variations, but the tendency for smoke to obscure the rays of the sun in town centres, which used to result in some quite sharp reductions, must now be much less marked since the smoke abatement laws became effective. There is no real evidence that atmospheric pollution has affected wildlife in our area, though the disappearance of certain lichens from Bagley Wood has been blamed on sulphur dioxide in the winter air emanating from nineteenth-century Oxford. Smoke abatement has also led to fewer, or at least less dense, fogs, so that the old statistics no longer reflect the current situation. However, one may still see the well-known phenomenon of the hilltops around Oxford and along the Chiltern escarpment standing clear in bright sunshine, while the plains and valleys below are shrouded in thick white mist. At other times, of course, it is the hills that are covered with low cloud, while the valleys, though not sunny, at least have more or less normal visibility.

Variations in temperature within the region are much greater than variations in sunshine, if only because of the 1°C difference between the countryside and the towns with their great store of artificial heat and bricks and stones which hold the summer heat. A similar 1° difference arises as you ascend the Chiltern and the Berkshire Downs escarpments, whose summits are roughly 100m higher than the plains below. This gives the tops ten to twelve days fewer in the length of the growing season; in the Thames valley this is about 250 days, with a dormant period between mid-November and early March, when the average temperature is normally less than 6°. The different flowering times of spring flowers can be quite marked between a village such as Chinnor (Oxon) and its adjacent hilltop. Mean maximum and minimum temperatures at Grendon Underwood and Wallingford respectively range from 13.5 to 4.4 and from 13.8 to 5.2. Though June has the most sunshine, July is usually the warmest month, and in winter February is usually the severest month. Some older figures for Oxford give ninety-one days in the year when ground frosts occurred, the largest number rather surprisingly in March (fifteen). The incidence of frost varies very greatly with height and aspect, and probably the higher ground of the Chilterns has appreciably more than Oxford. Under certain weather conditions, however, katabatic winds produce gravitational flows of cold air from the hills into the valleys, which are thus turned into frost pockets. On clear summer nights temperatures in a Cotswold valley near Leafield (Oxon) have been found to be 2–3° lower than on the nearby hilltops. Gardeners and fruit growers are very conscious of these effects, which must also affect the natural vegetation of such valleys. Humphry Bowen has pointed out that while the July isotherms run broadly east and west through our area, the January ones run north-west/south-east, so that plants needing high summer temperatures, such as hemlock water dropwort *Oenanthe crocata* and Solomon's seal *Polygonatum multiflorum*, can be expected to be restricted to the south of our area, while others which do not like cold winters, such as the golden saxifrage *Chrysosplenium alternifolium* and navelwort *Umbilicus rupestris*, occur only in the south-west of Berkshire. Our three counties are, however, too small for many striking effects of climate on wildlife to be noticeable.

Rainfall is also variable, and greater on high ground than on low. It is noteworthy that Wallingford, at 45m in the Thames valley, has 576mm a year, while Grendon Underwood, only 22m higher in altitude, has 626mm. The Chilterns, Cotswolds and Berkshire Downs all have appreciably more rain than these two stations, but not really enough to produce major differences in the vegetation. Since these hills are all calcareous, there is no question of their higher rainfall producing bog conditions, as it might do if they were in the North of England. At Wallingford, November with 61mm is the wettest month and February (despite its fill-dyke reputation due to the melting snows) the driest with only 30.4mm. July and August rank as the two next wettest months, but owing to the much greater evaporation in summer, waterlogging of the soil is always much more marked in winter. Bowen points out that in Berkshire the rainfall is rarely so decisive a factor as the geology in determining plant distribution. Rushes *Juncus* spp, for instance, are much commoner in poorly drained soils in low rainfall areas in the valleys than in the well drained high-rainfall areas on the chalk downs. He notes only a few species, such as herb paris *Paris quadrifolia* and spiked star of Bethlehem *Ornithogalum pyrenaicum* whose distribution can be correlated with high rainfall, or contrariwise, as with pale toadflax *Linaria repens* or cotton thistle *Onopordum acanthium* with low rainfall.

Snow is not a serious factor affecting wildlife in our area, although Oxford has an average of seventeen snow days in a year. Nor are such vagaries of the weather as hailstorms and thunder, interesting though they may be to the meteorologist. It is doubtful whether these three factors have any effect on the distribution of any animal or plant in our area.

The Influence of Man

If the physical factors of soil, land form and climate were the only factors that determine the nature of our wildlife, that wildlife would be very different from what it is today. Two thousand years ago our three counties still largely consisted of forest, marsh, thicket and swamp, and were still relatively unaffected by the primitive agriculture described in the next chapter, although much of the downs must already have been bare. Today there is literally not a square metre of our area that has not been affected both directly and indirectly by the activities of man. True, much of it would revert to woodland if allowed to do so—and the increasing likelihood of large-scale nuclear disasters makes it more possible than was once thought conceivable that this will one day happen—but the new ecosystem thus produced would be very different from that of 2,000 years ago. For the foreseeable future, however, we are stuck with the man-made and man-influenced wildlife we

3. Plateau beechwood near West Wycombe, Bucks

have today. To be convinced that our farmland could indeed revert to woodland, it is only necessary to stray a few miles over the Hertfordshire border to the Rothamsted Experimental Station, and see the portion of the Broadbalk Field that was left uncultivated over a hundred years ago. It is now an oakwood, indistinguishable from other oakwoods the layman would imagine to be immemorial and natural. In fact none of the seemingly immemorial woods in our area are more than semi-natural. Almost the whole of the Chiltern beechwoods appear to have been planted for the High Wycombe chair trade in the eighteenth century, replacing, it is believed, oakwoods that were destroyed over the centuries to provide firewood for London. Even such a beechwood as Bledlow Great Wood in the Bucks Chilterns, which was recorded in Domesday Book, is unlikely to be entirely natural; it has probably been felled and replanted or allowed to regenerate more than once. Indeed the whole of our three counties is a deliberately landscaped countryside, the work of eighteenth-century landowners, who wrought better than they knew, and were probably hated by their peasant contemporaries for destroying the immemorial treeless open landscape of medieval agriculture.

Today there are many other ways than agriculture and forestry in which man's use of the land has influenced the vegetation and animal life of our area. Industrial activities, from cement works to motor factories create huge areas of bare ground which are colonized by such hardy weeds as mugwort *Artemisia vulgaris*, spear thistle *Cirsium vulgare* and evening primrose *Oenothera erythrosepala*. Our network of roads and railways provides both waste ground and strips of grassland which are often the only semi-natural grassland remaining in the district. The display of meadow cranesbill *Geranium pratense* on the roadsides of the minor roads in the Cotswold part of Oxfordshire, for instance, is one of the features of that district. Gardens and parks are enormously important, especially for birds, and rooks have a well-known predilection for nesting in or near churchyards, presumably at least partly because the Church frowned on rook shooting on its premises. Additional wetlands have been provided by man in the form of reservoirs and flooded gravel-pits, which are of the highest importance in providing habitats for aquatic and marshland birds and other animals. Indeed much of the diversity of habitats in our area is the accidental by-product of human activity and nothing to do with the survival of patches of semi-natural habitats from the pre-industrial and pre-agricultural area.

Man has also exercised his often harmful influence in more direct ways. Game preservation, for instance, has strongly affected certain animal populations. Not only have several completely new species, such as the pheasant, red-legged partridge and rainbow trout, been introduced for people to shoot or fish, but existing stocks of other game animals, such as common partridge, mallard, and many freshwater fish, have been so heavily reinforced by fresh stock, either bred at home or imported from the Continent, that it is doubtful how far the present stocks can be considered as native. Moreover, to protect these animals, gamekeepers have killed off many predators. Pine marten, polecat, buzzard, kite and raven have all long gone from our counties, all largely as a result of this anti-predator campaign by keepers not by farmers. By way of grim compensation the animals they might have preyed on, rats, rabbits, woodpigeons and grey squirrels (three out of the four being introduced species), have vastly increased in the countryside and become pests.

Some of the animals have been introduced for purely amenity reasons: thus have the Canada goose, little owl, grey squirrel, fallow deer and muntjac been added to our fauna. At one time our area boasted a small population of coypus, at the sewage farm on the outskirts of Slough, and now in our rivers we have the mink, both escaped from fur farms. In a limited area of the Chilterns the fat dormouse, liberated just over the Hertfordshire border at Tring, has established itself. The brown rat and the house mouse arrived as unwanted visitors in human baggage or stores aboard ship, and eventually made their way to our inland counties. The

4. Oxford ragwort by roadside, Besselsleigh, Berks/Oxon

house mouse came a very long time ago, probably with our Neolithic ancestors. Innumerable invertebrate pests have also arrived in this way, among them the woolly aphis of apple trees and various longhorn beetles and cockroaches.

Nor is our native flora uncontaminated by the hand of man. Besides many more or less ephemeral plants that came in with impure seed corn and now grow in cornfields and on waste ground, there is a host of plants that have escaped from gardens, such as winter heliotrope *Petasites fragrans*, hedge bindweed *Calystegia silvatica*, Himalayan balsam *Impatiens glandulifera*, giant hogweed *Heracleum mantegazzianum* and red valerian *Centranthus ruber*. Most famous of all in our area is Oxford ragwort *Senecio squalidus*, a native of Sicily, which has colonized all England after escaping from the Oxford Botanic Garden. Its spread was aided by the railway, whose trains blew its aerial seeds along the cinder tracks which closely resembled its native habitat, the volcanic slopes of Mount Etna. Some very common weeds, such as common field speedwell *Veronica persica*, pineapple weed *Chamomilla suaveolens* and hoary cress *Cardaria draba* are introduced, the last-named supposedly arriving in Kent with the bedding of soldiers returning from the Napoleonic wars. Some of our commonest trees too are introduced: European larch in the seventeenth century, sycamore in the Middle Ages, and common elm perhaps in the Iron or even the Bronze Age. So the native British credentials of many a common animal and plant are very questionable.

2 Land Use History

JOHN M. STEANE

The landscape of the three counties cuts across a series of geographical regions. It includes the broad winding river valley of the upper Thames and the narrower valleys of the Cherwell and the Ock. It is bounded by the high limestone Cotswold hills to the west and the two great ridges of chalk downland, the Chilterns and the Berkshire Downs, with their intervening clay vales, to the south-east and south. This area has been settled by man for the last ten thousand years. The present landscape contains visible elements of successive and increasingly effective attempts of man to control this environment. The following essay presents in extreme summary form the main stages in this story. If it emphasizes the prehistoric aspect this is because important archaeological work on the landscape has been done recently. Also the post-medieval scene is comparatively well recorded and will be more familiar to readers.

During the third millennium BC colonists from the European mainland arrived in Wessex. Known as Windmill Hill people, from a type site near Avebury, Wilts, these Neolithic farmers brought with them agricultural skills and equipment and lived as nomadic tribal groups, driving flocks and herds wherever there was pasture and water and practising a slash-and-burn arable cultivation. They left three enduring marks on the landscape of southern Britain—causewayed camps, flint mines and earthen and chambered long barrows—whose distribution shows that the Windmill Hill people almost exclusively chose the chalklands for their first phase of colonization, other groups subsequently moving into the Cotswolds and further north. The one excavated causewayed camp site in the upper Thames valley, however, is at Abingdon, Berks/Oxon, on the gravels about a quarter of a mile to the east of the present town. Such camps were probably designed primarily for the impounding of stock at an annual round-up; the presence of pottery from a number of far-flung areas suggests that they also served some market function. Two flint mines, probably supplying axe factories, were found at Peppard Common in the Oxfordshire Chilterns. Neolithic chambered long barrows and other sites of religious or ritual significance are more common in the three counties.

Particularly noteworthy is the number of sites around the confluence of the rivers Ock and Thames at Abingdon. On the chalk downland there are two well-known Neolithic burial monuments on the Berkshire Downs: The Lambourn long barrow, which now consists only of a few sarsen stones protruding from the ground, and, on the Ridgeway three miles to the north, Wayland's Smithy long barrow, its great sarsen façade dramatically framed by an eighteenth-century beech clump.

Air photography and fieldwork on the Berkshire Downs over the past 25 years have gradually revealed a picture of extensive field systems dating from the Bronze and Early Iron Ages and representing great efforts in land clearance by these early farmers. The other aspects of the Bronze Age landscape which have survived are religious monuments and burial mounds. The largest single barrow group on the Wessex chalkland is the Seven Barrows cemetery in the Lambourn valley where a total of forty-six barrows has been recorded and many can still be seen as swollen grass-covered tumuli at the bottom of the dip slope below wedges of beech woodland. Twelve miles to the north, in the flat flood plain of the Thames, are the remnants, now shredded by gravel extraction, of one of the most important prehistoric landscapes in Britain—the Devil's Quoits at Stanton Harcourt, Oxon. Yet a third great concentration of ring-ditches within the region is near the Big Rings sacred complex at Dorchester, Oxon, now almost entirely quarried away.

It seems certain that the gravels of the Thames valley were densely and continuously farmed from the Bronze Age until the end of the Romano–British period. It is less easy to tell whether the neighbouring clay vales and Corallian ridge were similarly populated, as their soils are less conducive than the gravel to the formation of crop marks.

In the upper Thames valley three basic types of Iron Age settlement are found: permanent sites, seasonally occupied temporary sites, and densely occupied, more permanent sites. Examples of all three have recently been excavated. The type site of the first is Ashville, now an industrial estate in the western suburbs of Abingdon, where the economy seems to have been almost exclusively devoted to cereal production. Two temporary sites are the settlements at Farmoor in north Berks/ Oxon and at Mingie's Ditch, Hardwick, Oxon, on the flood plain of the river Windrush. Here the house sites and enclosures were subject to flooding and were only occupied temporarily (presumably seasonally) for a few years; a preponderance of cow bones suggests that dairying was the main basis of the economy.

By 500 BC hill forts were steadily increasing in number. The close proximity to one another of the forts at Rams Hill, Uffington Castle, and Hardwell, Berks/Oxon, makes it very unlikely that all were occupied at the same time. The enormous area occupied by some hill forts becomes more understandable if they are viewed as huge cattle and sheep corrals. That pastoralism was an important element in the Iron Age economy on the chalk downland is also indicated by the long, linear, non-defensive ditches which run between the scarp slope of the chalk and the Lambourn river and its former tributaries, dividing the downland into blocks. Rams Hill and Alfred's Castle (fig. 1) sit in the middle of such large strips while other hill forts such as Uffington Castle lie against or even astride the limits of the ditches. The Berkshire Grim's Ditch was similarly connected with livestock, and it seems to have been dug by the prehistoric peoples living on the chalk downland to demarcate a grazing zone and to obstruct rustlers from the north. These huge ranches must have required herder riders. The horse was important in Early Iron Age society; ten horses have been found buried with ceremony at Blewburton hill fort, and an even more dramatic reminder of the horse's prestige is the gigantic tribal emblem sculptured into the chalk down below Uffington Castle.

During the first century AD the Oxford region was a thinly populated frontier area and as such was easily overrun by the Roman armies between AD 43 and 47. The Romans founded two small walled towns in Oxfordshire, Alchester and Dorchester, and there were further large settlements at Abingdon and at Swalcliffe, Oxon. Romano-British farmers exploited three areas within the three counties: central Oxon, the south-eastern Chilterns and the Vale of White Horse. In central Oxon fourteen farms, of which Shakenoak and North Leigh are the best-known examples, grew up alongside Akeman Street which was driven through the limestone region across the centre of the county. Their siting suggests that their owners preferred to settle near two or more different soils (fig. 2). In the Chiltern valleys the Romano-British villas are evenly spaced at intervals of just under two Roman miles: Latimer, Saunderton and High Wycombe, all in Bucks, being among the most prominent. Analysis of bone, plant and cereal remains and excavation of farm buildings at Shakenoak suggest that crops would have been spelt, club or bread wheat, barley and possibly rye with a likely flock of about 200 sheep used for breeding, wool, and milk. Several buildings and enclosures suggest that during the fourth century the villa was changing to a predominantly cattle-raising economy. At Latimer villa in the Chilterns livestock rearing seems to have been more important than cereal growing.

The first Anglo-Saxon settlers, invited over and given the task of defending small towns such as Silchester and Dorchester from infiltrators and other invaders,

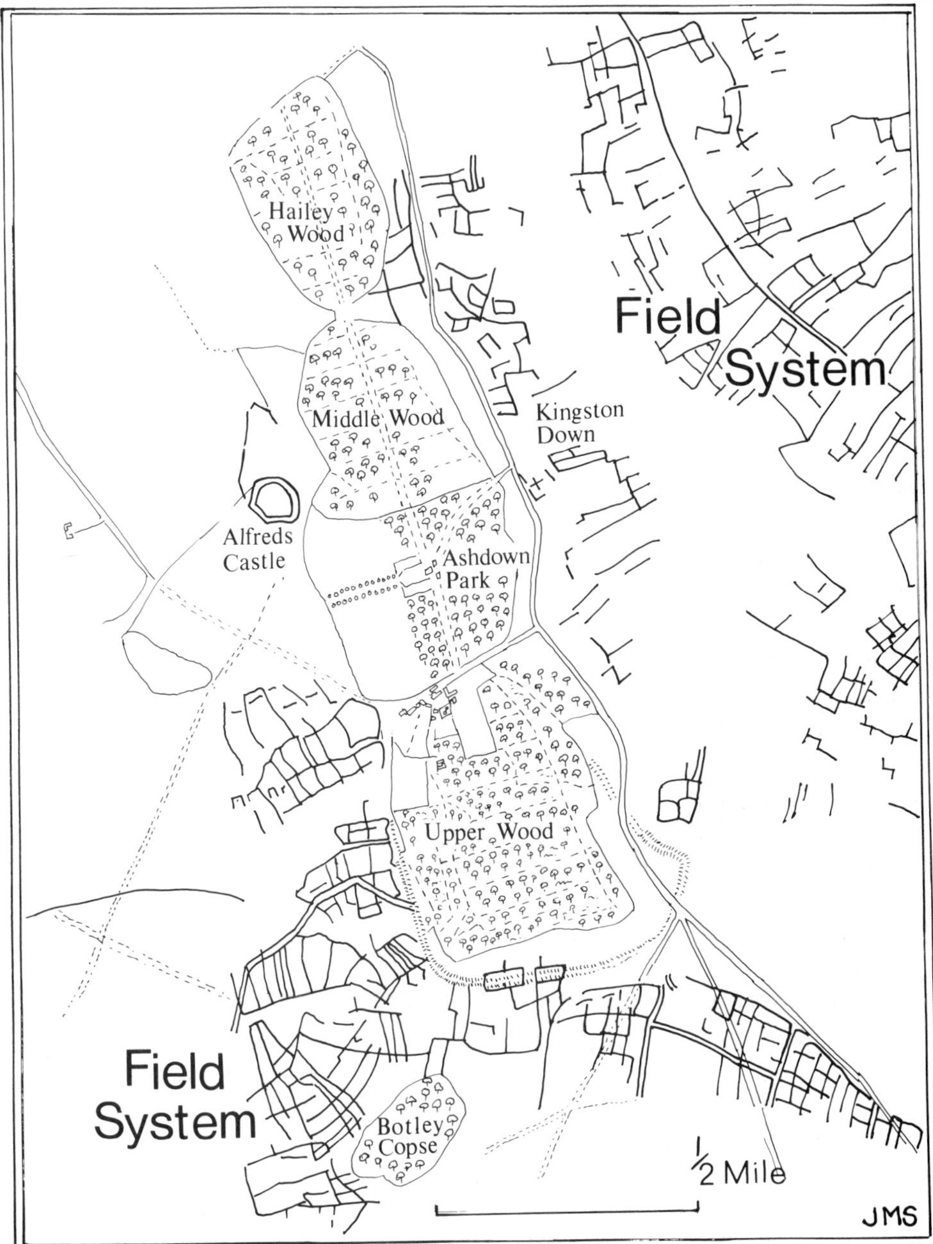

Map 1. Prehistoric and Romano-British field systems around Ashdown, Oxfordshire. This map is compiled from aerial photographs in the Sites and Monuments record of the Oxfordshire County Museum. Two additional aspects of land use are the medieval deer park of the Abbots of Glastonbury and the seventeenth-century landscaping in the woodland around the Earl of Craven's house, Ashdown Park.

penetrated Britain during the fourth–fifth centuries AD when the province was still nominally under Roman authority. Later influxes of settlers arrived in the region by means of the Icknield Way, perhaps the River Cherwell and certainly the Thames. To begin with the newcomers left the Chilterns alone, and a Romano–British enclave survived there for at least two more centuries. Recent studies stress continuity and peaceful co-existence between Romano–British and Anglo–Saxon farmers and it has been suggested that some large estates, such as those centred on Blewbury and Lambourn, actually survived intact from prehistoric times through the Roman period and the upheavals beyond. At other sites, such as Barton Court near Abingdon, the Roman buildings were systematically demolished by the newcomers.

From the tenth century onwards documentary records begin to supplant

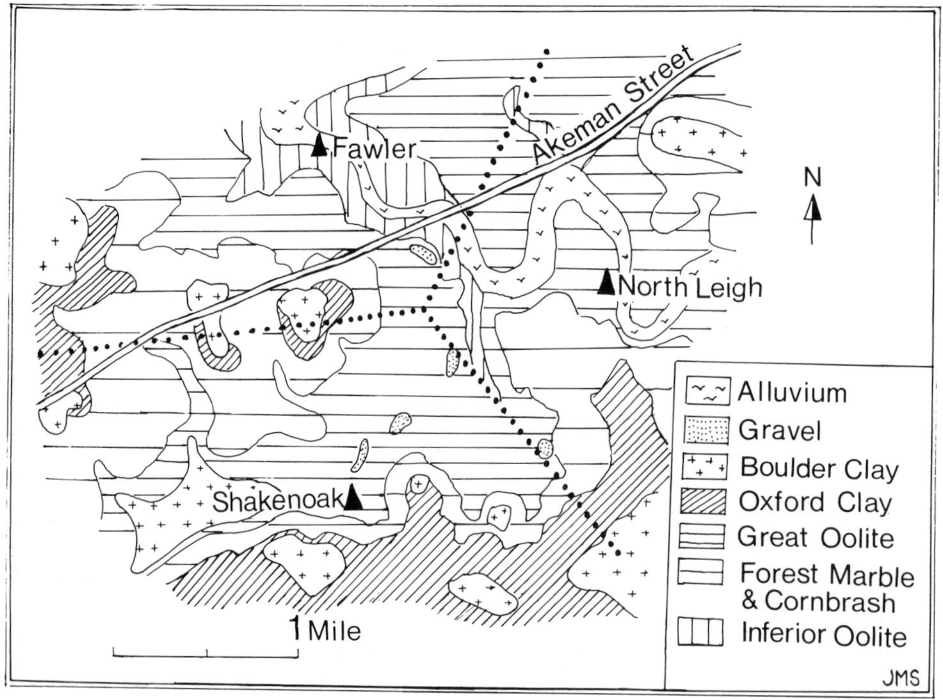

Map 2. The siting of the Roman villas of Fawler, Shakenoak and North Leigh in Central Oxfordshire. Each is found on either side of the Roman road, Akeman Street. Each is surrounded by a varied series of soils which would have provided a diverse land use. Geological information is simplified from sheet 236 1 inch to 1 mile Geological Survey (Witney).

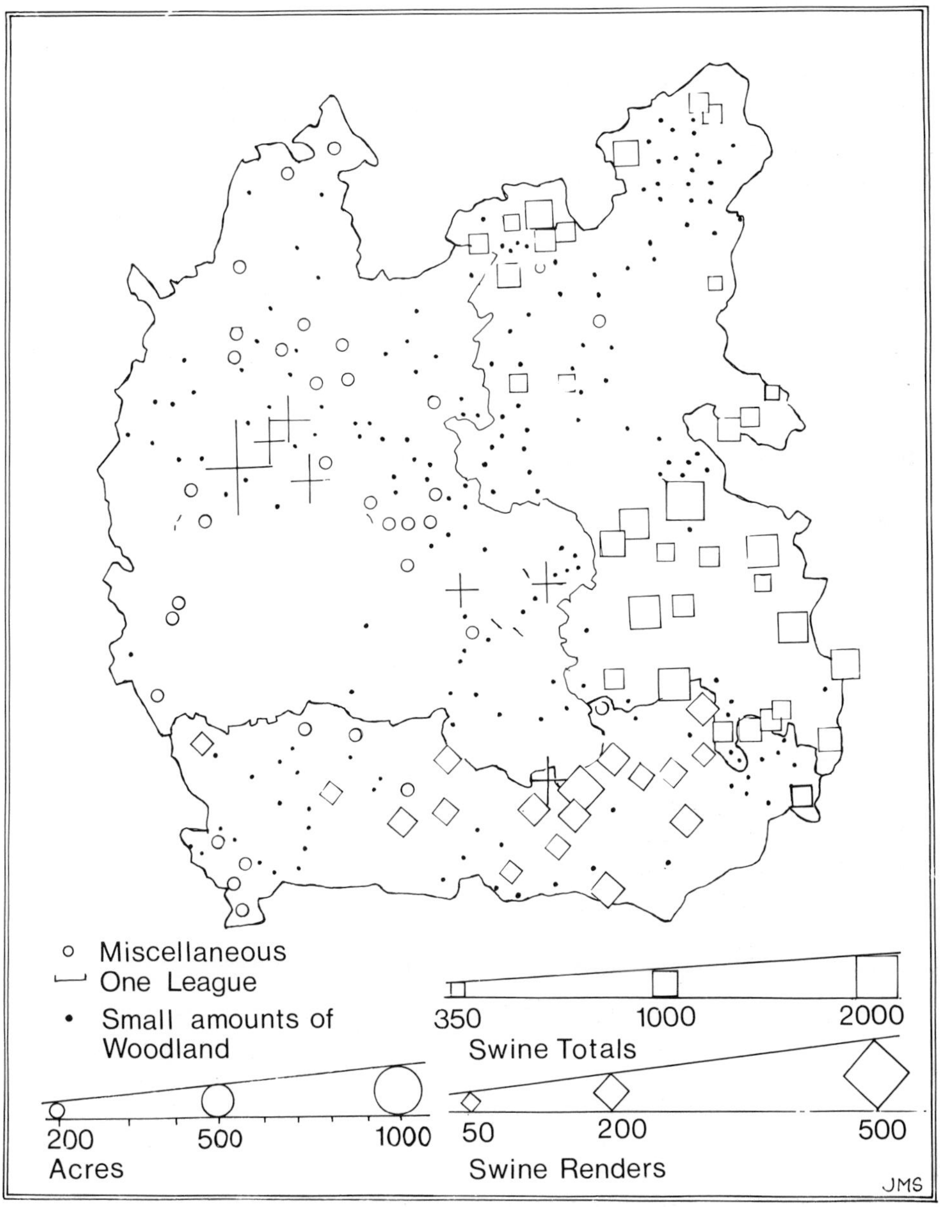

Map 3. Domesday woodland in Oxfordshire, Berkshire and Buckinghamshire (redrawn from Fig 72 in Darby H. C. *Domesday England* 1977, with permission). Woodland is recorded by Domesday Book in several different ways, lineal measurements, acreage and swine totals. When plotted the entries are dispersed in four main groups, central Oxfordshire (Wychwood and Shotover), north Buckinghamshire (Forest of Salcey), the Chilterns and eastern Berkshire (Forest of Windsor). The Vale of the White Horse is conspicuously devoid of woodland.

archaeology. Charters and surveys such as Domesday Book give a clear view of the early medieval landscape, with an intensively cultivated arable countryside in south-west Oxon and west Berks and much slower clearance in the Chilterns. Domesday Book reveals in addition the extent of woodland in the region. In Oxon the Forest of Wychwood lay to the west with Bernwood Forest, Bucks, to the north-east. Practically the whole of east Berks was in the Forest of Windsor, and Wychwood was part of a belt of royal forest which approached the very walls of Oxford by way of Headington, and merged into the Forest of Bernwood (fig. 3). During the early Middle Ages the largely forested nature of the Chilterns was gradually reduced by cultivation. By the eleventh century most of the region north of the chalk was being farmed as arable land in multitudes of strips held from nucleated settlements. On the chalk hills and their southern environs clearings appeared as a large number of relatively small fields, the holdings lying close to their respective farmsteads.

During the medieval period the foundation of monasteries was a major influence on the development of the man-made landscape. In the three counties eighteen out of thirty-five religious houses in Berks and twenty-nine out of fifty in Oxon (including twenty in Oxford itself) were sited on or near the Thames. These included the oldest and wealthiest of the houses and implied a considerable and largely river-borne trade in building materials. Fine quality stone came from Taynton near Burford, Oxon, other stone came from Wheatley or the coral rag of Cumnor, while clay tiles for roofing and paving were obtained from Nettlebed in the Chilterns which also supplied New College, Oxford, and sent bricks to Stonor Park, Oxon. The monastic houses were early and vigorous clearers and enclosers of waste and woodland. Large abbeys such as Abingdon acquired an enormous congeries of estates entailing the setting up of granges and outlying administrative centres. Monastic farm buildings in the form of large barns and dovecotes can still be seen at Northcourt, Bisham and Hurley, with earthworks at Cumnor and a stone solar wing at Charney Bassett. The most impressive surviving monastic building in the three counties is the tithe barn at Great Coxwell, Berks, built *c* 1300.

This dynamic economy was supported by a steadily growing population which reached its peak by the beginning of the fourteenth century and was fuelled by experiments to improve arable production in the cultivation of only marginally viable arable land such as the cold boulder clays of north Bucks. Without a corresponding increase in livestock and consequently in manure these techniques led to progressive soil exhaustion, and harvest failures in turn produced a cycle of malnutrition, vulnerability to plague, heavy mortality and the desertion or shrinkage

Map 4. The distribution of medieval parks in Oxfordshire, Buckinghamshire and Berkshire. It is noteworthy that parks are denser in distribution in some of the areas which were formerly Royal Forest. Information on parks from Sites and Monuments, records in the Oxfordshire and Buckinghamshire County Museums, and lists provided by Professor L. Cantor deposited at Woodstock and Aylesbury. The boundaries of Royal Forests are from Bazaley M. L. 'The Extent of the English Forest in the 13th Century', *Trans. of Royal Historical Society,* 4th series, iv, 1921, pp. 140-72.

of many villages (fig. 4). At the same time the greater profits connected with sheep farming brought about a change in land use from arable fields divided into thousands of strips into a few large pastures enclosed by hedges and, by calling for fewer workers, hastened the decline in population. The villages themselves went down to grass. A number of these villages have been excavated at Milton Keynes, Bucks, and one, Seacourt, Oxon, was dissected by archaeologists in advance of road works in the early 1960s. Areas not heavily dependent on a corn husbandry were relatively immune from the agrarian contraction of the late Middle Ages. Consequently in the Cotswolds and the Chilterns there were hardly any deserted villages.

By the sixteenth century a sheep–corn husbandry had emerged throughout the limestone region of Oxon and the chalk downland of Berks and the Chilterns, while the western half of the Vale of White Horse was a dairying economy and most of the rest of Oxon and the Vale of Aylesbury was under the plough. From the late sixteenth century onwards enclosure made its mark on the landscape as 'improving' landlords and gentlemen set out to rationalize the farming of their holdings. Most of Berks was enclosed between 1780 and 1830, largely by general enclosure acts, while in 1813 Arthur Young remarked of Oxon: 'proportionately to the extent of it, more land has been enclosed since I first travelled in it, which is about 40 years ago, than in any county in England.' Padbury, Bucks, provides a classic example of an open field landscape, known in detail from a superb sixteenth-century estate map, overlain by the rigid ruler-straight hedges of the parliamentary enclosure commissioners of 1796. Improving farmers were also quick to make use of new implements such as the seed drill invented by Jethro Tull, born and buried (1741) at Basildon, Berks, and farming at Prosperous Farm near Hungerford, Berks.

The Vale of White Horse was still famed for the excellence of its dairying and improvements in the drainage of floodable pasture were being made by landowners such as Edward Lovedon at Buscot, Berks/Oxon. Large quantities of the local single Gloucester cheeses were sent to London annually from Buscot wharf up to the middle of the nineteenth century when, with the coming of the railway, cheese began to give way to milk.

The drainage of the upper Thames valley was continued in the mid-nineteenth century. Damp common lands in the so-called Bampton Polderland were enclosed by William Bryan Wood, creating splendid rich meadows between Newbridge and Radcot, and Otmoor was enclosed and drained despite fierce opposition.

The three large areas of woodland within the region saw great changes during the eighteenth and nineteenth centuries. The Chilterns saw a considerable extension of beech (heavily used during the Second World War for rifle butts and plywood for aircraft). Wychwood, used as a Crown reservoir of timber and coppice woods, was not disafforested until 1857, when seven new farmsteads were created out of the Crown allotments. Only the Forest of Windsor in east Berks retained something of the status and size of a royal forest up to the twentieth century, and even here the stockbroker belt has begun to intrude. Another area where trees added a memorable visual element to the landscape was the Berkshire Downs, where beech clumps were extensively planted during the eighteenth century. Lord Wantage, for example, trimmed his 20,000-acre estate around Ardington and Lockinge with hedges and decorated it with tree plantations. Downland sheep pasture has been largely replaced by arable since the great plough-up of the Second World War, but there are a few areas of grassland left such as Kingston Warren and White Horse Hill, used as racehorse gallops, and training establishments and stud farms exist at Letcombe, Childrey, Lambourn, Ilsley and Compton.

The future of the landscape of the three counties is uncertain. Oxfordshire has long been a producer of sand and gravel and in 1974–76 output averaged 2.4 million tonnes a year. Mineral extraction is necessary for the continuation of a concrete-dominated architectural environment. It threatens archaeological sites and areas of natural history importance and scientific interest. Large parts of the rich pastures of the Thames flood plain have become a derelict landscape of flooded gravel pits interspersed with islands and grassy and weed-covered mounds. Elsewhere the thunder of lorries proclaims the continuing presence of the gravel extraction industry. Modern agricultural techniques also pose a threat. All over the region farms are getting larger, their syndicate owners more faceless, hedges are obliterated, wildlife is threatened and soil structures are deteriorating under impaction and gigantic doses of artificial fertilizer. Both ecological and archaeological voices cry out for conservation, but at present they are too often crying in a wilderness.

3 Vegetation

S. R. J. WOODELL

Berkshire, Buckinghamshire and Oxfordshire could be regarded as a microcosm of inland lowland England. They contain a major river basin, a variety of parent rocks, though mainly base-rich or calcareous, and they are intensively farmed. Their area of semi-natural vegetation is small in total and is made up of isolated sites scattered through a matrix of arable land and intensively managed grassland. Nevertheless there is much of interest. Woodland, scrub and various kinds of grassland occur in some quantity, and there are small but significant areas of open water, fen, heath, bog, and marsh. In addition some man-made sites carry interesting patches of vegetation.

As a background to present-day semi-natural vegetation it is essential to know something, however brief, of its developmental history, since this more than anything has determined what we find now. In an area occupied for so long by people, and so much used by them, nothing remains of the original natural vegetation, but the remnants, much modified, do give some impression of the original.

During the last thirty-five years or so the development of techniques for the study of recent, subfossil remains has enabled botanists to build up a remarkably complete picture of the changes in vegetation that have occurred in the last million years (Godwin 1977). The last 10,000 or so are what concern us most, i.e. the period since the last glaciers melted. The most useful single source of information is fossil pollen which occurs in organic sediments and lake deposits and which can be analysed by the careful sequential sampling of layers in the peats or muds. The counting and identification of the highly decay-resistant pollen grains is supplemented by the identification of larger remains such as twigs, leaves, fruits, molluscs, insects, small vertebrate bones, and the debris around old habitations.

Unfortunately pollen preservation is less good in areas of limestone or other base-rich soils and the record is incomplete, but some data are available and can be supplemented by that from further afield. It is possible to produce a picture of the kinds of vegetation that were probably here before human disturbance began, and of some of the early changes that took place. The 'original' vegetation was itself the product of a long sequence of natural changes over the previous few thousand years and was still changing under the influence of a different climate. When human interference began the climate was relatively warm and dry. From about 5,000 BC it remained warm but became wetter and remained like that until about 3,000 BC. Mesolithic peoples, being mainly hunter-gatherers, had little effect on the vegetation.

At this point most of Britain was covered by climax vegetation, the most complex that can develop in an undisturbed area. Climax vegetation is not static, but is in a state of stable equilibrium: climatic changes and sometimes other factors can disturb this and result in vegetative changes but essentially it is stable. Climax vegetation is usually rich in plant and animal species, and the interrelations between the organisms are numerous and complex. The changes wrought by human interference have led to a decrease in species richness and in complexity.

The forests that occupied most of lowland Britain then were primarily mixed, broad-leaved types, with oak predominating over large areas. The two native species, pedunculate oak *Quercus robur* and sessile oak *Q. petraea*, grow on a wide variety of soils: the former is commoner on base-rich and/or heavy soils and so is present over most of our region, the latter prefers lighter, well-drained soils, and though it occurs in some places locally is more typical of northern and western Britain. It is unlikely that pure oakwood occurred, but we can envisage a mixture of forest types in which oak was usually abundant. On drier base-rich soils elms (probably wych elm *Ulmus glabra*), small-leaved lime *Tilia cordata* and some ash *Fraxinus excelsior* were present. In the Chilterns, beech *Fagus sylvatica* was common but neither so abundant nor so exclusive as now. In the poorly-drained clay vales alder *Alnus glutinosa* was always present and was sometimes very common indeed. In fact in the humid conditions of high forest it was not confined to poorly drained soils. Thus our three counties were covered by high forest, mainly a mixture of oak, alder, elm and lime, with beech locally, and other less common trees here and there, including common whitebeam *Sorbus aria*, ash, wild service tree *Sorbus torminalis*, and field maple *Acer campestre*. These forests had tall straight-trunked trees and much standing and fallen dead timber, unlike the tidy woodlands of today. Beneath the tree canopy hazel *Corylus avellana*, hawthorns *Crataegus monogyna* and *C. laevigata* and many other shrubs formed a lower canopy. Birches *Betula* spp must have occurred here and there, and may have acted as pioneers in some places where fallen mature trees left gaps.

Neolithic peoples, with axe and fire, rapidly changed the relative abundance of the trees; elm and alder declined, perhaps the faster because of a simultaneous climatic deterioration. Though Neolithic clearances were temporary at first, based on shifting cultivation akin to that in the tropics today, the forest that reoccupied the cleared areas was richer in ash and birch. Elm was probably selectively felled even beyond the clearings as the leaves made good fodder for cattle, and in the Chilterns the removal of oak and subsequent impoverishment of the soil on steep chalk slopes probably gave beech its chance to establish itself as a dominant species over larger areas. (Godwin 1976; Dimbleby 1967).

Today everything we see is the result, fully or partly, of the changes wrought by human interference, especially woodland clearance from Roman times and through extensive social changes and their effects on land use. Only a few fragments of ancient forest remain in Great Britain in places where it was physically difficult or totally uneconomic to remove them; none are in the three counties. Even areas of ancient royal forests, such as Wychwood in Oxfordshire are much modified by management. The great grassland areas which we accept as so characteristic of our hills are completely secondary, and of course are still undergoing change, often rapid, as a result of the changing demands of agriculture. It is important to realise that all the so-called natural habitats we are trying to conserve are in fact modified habitats: modified, that is, by our own activities. This is not to say that we should not conserve semi-natural vegetation, only to remind ourselves what we are dealing with.

Although grassland is the predominant type of vegetation I deal first and most fully with woodland, as the closest to the original natural vegetation, then consider the varied and diverse grasslands, and finally discuss rather briefly the other vegetation types, none of which is common in the area, though some are interesting and valuable, and some are under great threat and so perhaps claim a disproportionate part of the attention of conservationists, who must protect the most threatened habitats as a matter of urgency.

Woodlands

Woodlands are unevenly distributed through the three counties, the Chilterns being among the most wooded areas of southern England. Most of the Cotswold woodlands are in Gloucestershire. On the clay there are numerous woods, many being fragments of old royal forests, but this intensively farmed area also has large tracts with little or no semi-natural woodland, only scattered plantations of little ecological interest.

Though I deal with woodlands in terms of their dominant trees, there are many intermediate types. In fact variation in vegetation is continuous and drawing clear boundaries is impossible except where sharply defined physical boundaries occur. Thus although some woods are dominated by one species—often planted—more often there is a mixture of dominant trees. Oakwood grades on the one hand into beechwood, on the other into mixed deciduous woodland—oak, ash, elm, lime, wild cherry *Prunus avium*, wild service tree. Beechwood is more exclusive, but mixed beech–oak and beech–ash–oak woods occur. Much of what can be said about the understorey vegetation of oakwood applies to mixed deciduous forest.

The picture is further complicated by the fact that in any one area there may be a complex mosaic of woodland types on different slopes, aspects, drainage types and soils, as well as a variety of past and present management and mismanagement. Most of the woodland of today, apart from plantations, occupies sites that have been woodland continuously since before man came on the scene. Their diversity of plants and animals must in part be a consequence of this fact. The relatively few species in plantations result from the slow colonization across intervening agricultural land. Where a site has been woodland for thousands of years, even though it has been modified and managed, the original stocks of plants and animals have often persisted surprisingly well.

Oakwoods and mixed deciduous woodland

Of the former forests that have been increasingly stripped of their timber by man only fragments remain. Remnants of high oak forest occur on three major soil types in our region: acid sands and gravels, brown earths and clays, and very wet clays. Probably there was never any pure oakwood but oak may have ranged from being the most important species, especially on well-drained acid soils, to being a minor component in mixed deciduous woodland. Most of what follows refers to mixed deciduous woodland.

On acid soils a characteristic oakwood occurs, either with a fairly open canopy or with tall slender trees. Birch often grows associated with the oak, sometimes reaching the canopy. The field layer is dominated by bracken *Pteridium aquilinum*, bramble *Rubus fruticosus* and honeysuckle *Lonicera periclymenum*. Often associated with the bracken are bluebell *Hyacinthoides non-scripta* and creeping soft-grass *Holcus mollis*; each of which exploits different parts of the forest floor at different times of the year. The field layer tends to be poor in species, but often rich in individuals, so that one species may dominate large patches, typical herbs being wood anemone *Anemone nemorosa*, wood sage *Teucrium scorodonia* and cleavers *Galium aparine*. The ground layer of mosses is sparse, since the deep, slowly decaying bracken litter suppresses it. This acid kind of oakwood occurs in Bagley Wood, parts of Windsor Forest and Tubney Wood, all Berks. Naphill Common, Bucks, has both oak species mixed with beech. Holly *Ilex aquifolium* and wild cherry are abundant; elder *Sambucus nigra*, rowan *Sorbus aucuparia* and willows *Salix* spp are common, indicating somewhat more nutrient-rich soil. The bramble–bracken–honeysuckle mixture is widespread, accompanied here and there by heather *Calluna vulgaris*.

Small patches of heathy oakwood also exist, with both species of oak and plentiful birch, for example in Burnham Beeches, Bucks. This may be a stage in succession to mixed oak–beechwood, from heath in which heather, sheep's fescue *Festuca ovina*, wavy hair-grass *Deschampsia flexuosa* and common bent *Agrostis capillaris* are characteristic. This type of woodland is rare in our region, though no doubt if some of the Berkshire heaths were permitted to go through natural succession a woodland of this type would develop eventually.

The most typical oakwoods occur on the heavier, less acid, more basic rich loams and clays, often merging into mixed deciduous woodland. Here we may find ash,

1. Oak-birch woodland with heather *Calluna* understory, Burnham Beeches, Bucks

elm, birch, service tree, field maple, aspen *Populus tremula* all in the canopy, together with a wide variety of shrubs, including holly, crab apple *Malus sylvestris*, hazel, hawthorn, blackthorn *Prunus spinosa*, dogwood *Cornus sanguinea*, elder, wild privet *Ligustrum vulgare*, guelder rose *Viburnum opulus*, spindle *Euonymus europaeus* and various willows and roses, plus honeysuckle and ivy *Hedera helix* as climbers. The field and ground layers are very species-rich.

One of the most striking features of these woods is the abundance of spring-flowering herbs, which exploit the light phase before the trees leaf out, and often form pure stands over large areas. Dog's mercury *Mercurialis perennis*, wood anemone, wood sanicle *Sanicula europaea*, lesser celandine *Ranunculus ficaria*, and primrose *Primula vulgaris* are among the most widespread and typical. In some woods enchanter's nightshade *Circaea lutetiana*, ground ivy *Glechoma hederacea*, wild strawberry *Fragaria vesca* and yellow archangel *Lamiastrum galeobdolon* also form these local patches or societies. Some spring-flowering plants die back early, while others persist throughout the summer, the primrose through the year.

This woodland type is found throughout the clay vales. Perhaps the largest

2. Oak-ash woodland

area is the remaining part of the ancient forest of Bernwood, spanning from the eastern edge of Oxfordshire through Bucks to the Northamptonshire border. Much of it is modified, some is old coppice, some is derelict, but some areas are still very rich in plant and animal species, e.g. Waterperry Wood and Stanton Great Wood, Oxon, parts of Shabbington Wood, Bucks, and those further north. These are entomologically very varied and interesting. Wychwood has patches of oakwood on clay, again much modified but still rich. Similar woods occur elsewhere, too numerous to list. Wytham Wood, Berks/Oxon, for instance, is a complex of woodland types including some areas of good oakwood.

Much oakwood that remains owes its survival to coppice with standards management, which was for centuries an integral part of the rural economy. Oaks (the standards), planted at about thirty per hectare, acquire the characteristic 'stag-headed' appearance of oak trees grown wide apart, and beneath their light shade hazel and ash (the coppice) are grown in close stands and cut back to short 'stools' every ten years or so. Beneath these are abundant herbs and mosses, which get an enormous boost from the increased light intensity each time coppicing occurs, and

3. Old coppiced oakwood, Burnham Beeches, Bucks

give the wonderful displays of spring flowers associated especially with this kind of management. Every hundred years or so the oaks are felled and replaced.

Unfortunately most coppice has been neglected as the demand for poles has declined. Some woods are still coppiced for paper pulpwood and a few for conservation purposes. Much of the local oakwood that has not been replaced by exotic softwoods has fallen into neglect, following indiscriminate felling during two wars, often followed by grazing. On the other hand pheasant raising and fox hunting have helped preserve some woods, albeit often in a poor state. A few, however, retain their beauty and value, such as Salcey Forest on the Bucks/Northants border, fragments of Bernwood, Tubney Wood, Brasenose Wood, Oxon, and small patches of Bagley and Wytham Woods.

On wetter soils, oak woodland grades into oak-alder and finally alderwood on waterlogged areas. Few oakwood herbs can survive waterlogging, although some species thrive, notably creeping buttercup *Ranunculus repens*, common nettle *Urtica dioica*, meadowsweet *Filipendula ulmaria* and various sedges, such as *Carex pendula* (pendulous sedge), *C. strigosa* (thin-spiked wood sedge) and *C. remota* (remote sedge). Other plants often found in such woods are tufted hair-grass *Deschampsia cespitosa*, ragged robin *Lychnis flos-cuculi*, marsh thistle *Cirsium palustre*, wild angelica *Angelica sylvestris* and creeping jenny *Lysimachia nummularia*. Some of these, together with a few others including adder's tongue fern *Ophioglossum vulgatum* and water avens *Geum rivale*, are more characteristic of wet meadows. Parts of Noke Wood, Oxon, for instance, and Whitecross Green Wood, Bucks/Oxon, both on the edge of Otmoor, are of this wet oakwood type.

Despite the depredations and neglect of the last few centuries there are still significant patches of oakwood and mixed deciduous woodland in our three counties, some of them fortunately in nature reserves. Others are disappearing fast, often being replaced by conifers. There is an urgent need to save more. They are extraordinarily rich in both flora and fauna and still retain many features of primeval woodland.

Beechwoods

Beechwoods, with their smooth, grey-trunked trees, and spaciousness resulting from an absence of shrubs are unlike any other native British woodlands. They are the great glory of the Chiltern Hills yet it is suspected that this kind of beechwood was not at all widespread before Neolithic times. Beech, though native, was probably a subordinate member of the woodland canopy before clearance of the oak enabled it to spread. Even now beech is exclusively dominant only on certain soil types, an artificial monoculture which biologically would be much more interesting with a greater diversity of trees, making it like what once occupied large areas of the Chilterns.

The Chiltern beechwoods are managed mainly for the furniture industry. Until the Second World War much small furniture manufacture took place actually in the woods, and relics of coppiced beech exist at the Warburg Reserve, Bix Bottom, Oxon, for example, which testify to this form of past usage.

Beech favours well-drained soils and avoids wet and waterlogged clays. It is found on three main soil types in the Chilterns: the shallow rendzinas of the chalk escarpment, the deep loams of the plateau, and the acid silty loams and sands also on the plateau and in the London Basin. The escarpment woods, so prominent a feature seen from the clay vale to the west, are the most exclusively beech-dominated. Little else can compete in these shallow chalk soils, but beech's spreading shallow root system is well adapted to these conditions, and has a high demand for water at the surface. A few ash and whitebeam trees reach the canopy, which is not very high, as beech on these soils does not grow much above 20–25

4. Escarpment woodland in spring, Whiteleaf, Bucks, with beech in leaf and wild cherry in flower

metres. Wild cherry is sometimes a conspicuous constituent of these woods in spring.

Holly and yew *Taxus baccata* are the only shrubs found frequently; others occur only in gaps, since they are excluded by the combination of heavy shade and root competition. Mature escarpment woods have quite a varied field layer. A good example is the very steep Whiteleaf Hill at Monks Risborough, Bucks, where dog's mercury is abundant at the top but is replaced by sanicle as the slope steepens and the soil becomes shallower. Here we find not the large, exclusive patches of one species that are typical of the clay oakwoods or the plateau woods, but a more scattered cover. The other common plants include wood anemone, wild strawberry, enchanter's nightshade, bugle *Ajuga reptans*, herb robert *Geranium robertianum* and, in the Whiteleaf woods, woodruff *Galium odoratum*, hairy woodrush *Luzula pilosa*, wall lettuce *Mycelis muralis* and the early dog violet *Viola reichenbachiana*. Several grasses are scattered on the woodland floor, notably false brome *Brachypodium sylvaticum*, hairy brome *Bromus ramosus* and the delicate wood melick *Melica uniflora*.

Almost all the escarpment woods have some orchids, notably the broad-leaved helleborine *Epipactis helleborine* and the honey-brown bird's-nest orchid *Neottia nidus-avis*, hard to see in the beech litter. The white helleborine *Cephalanthera damasonium* (p. 61) is very abundant in some woods notably in the Lewknor Copse, Oxon, nature reserve (the little beechwood at the foot of Beacon Hill) where it is mixed with numerous plants of spurge laurel *Daphne laureola*. Other, less common, orchids include the violet helleborine *Epipactis purpurata* and the fly orchid *Ophrys insectifera* (p. 171).

Mosses are patchy, mainly in the open spaces swept clear of leaves that accumulate in hollows and among the taller herbs. Even planted woods may come to possess many of the characteristics of the typical escarpment woodlands. On the Corallian limestone reef forming Wytham Hill are very large planted beeches about 150 years old, and the understorey has the same shrub-free and patchy vegetation, though it is only on a gentle slope. Dog's mercury, enchanter's nightshade and a few brambles form the only large patches in the field layer, and they trap the leaves swept from the rest of the woodland floor. This wood is extremely rich in soil invertebrates, possibly remaining from whatever woodland originally occupied the site, though it has also once been arable land.

The escarpment wood soils are of course highly calcareous, with fragments of chalk appearing right up to the surface. On the plateau the soils are deeper and all traces of chalk at the surface are lost. Many of the hilltops have a clay-with-flints deposit which is more acid but still nutrient-rich. The woods around Great Hampden, Bucks, are of this type, in which beech reaches its maximum height in Britain, occasionally exceeding thirty metres. On the gently undulating plateau oak can grow as tall as beech and is often found with it in the canopy. Wild cherry and whitebeam are present, but otherwise these woods have no woody plants apart from a few scattered holly bushes and patches of shrubs in clearings. They are very rich in herbs, though again rarely with complete cover. The exception is the abundance of bramble that covers much of the ground in many plateau woods. In addition to the herbs of the escarpment woods, others such as wood sorrel *Oxalis acetosella* and bluebell are common, together with several grasses, creeping soft-grass and such striking tall species as giant fescue *Festuca gigantea*, wood millet *Milium effusum*, hairy brome and wood barley *Hordelymus europaeus*, this last rather a Chiltern speciality. The beech litter is much more continuous and mosses are scarce. These Chiltern plateau woods give the area much of its distinctive character and it is to be hoped that many of them will remain in their present state.

On the more acid podsols of the sands and gravels beech is again a dominant. Lodge Wood, not far from Prestwood, Bucks, is a good example. The trees are more slender and less tall, and oak reaches the canopy, even overtopping the beech at times. Birch is abundant, and mountain ash scattered in open spots. Beech has regenerated freely and forms great thickets. The field layer is sparse, the most obvious plant being the wavy hair-grass. Creeping soft-grass, common bent and pill sedge *Carex pilulifera* occur, and in a few spots heather remains. Two mosses, *Polytrichum formosum* and the great yellowish cushions of *Leucobryum glaucum*, carpet areas of the soil, and the stag's-horn clubmoss *Lycopodium clavatum* may still remain.

In this woodland type, as a result of the extreme acidity of the soil and the consequent paucity of soil organisms, litter breakdown is very slow and the fallen leaves become compacted, passing below into a layer of raw humus above the mineral soil, which is strongly leached, with redeposition of the iron salts at some depth to form a typical podsol. The best known beechwood of this kind is at Burnham Beeches, on Tertiary sands and plateau gravels of the London Basin. Here the beeches used to be pollarded, but since this has ceased the branches have grown huge, giving the trees their familiar gnarled and stunted appearance. The field layer is similar to that of Lodge Wood, but more heathy in character, with bracken and heather as well as the wavy hair-grass.

Fungi abound in all these beechwoods especially in autumn, some characteristic of different beechwood types. Beech, like almost all trees, has mycorrhiza (fungi which are associated with the roots in a symbiotic relationship beneficial to both tree and fungus) and if one exposes the young roots in the litter and humus, the fungal mycelium can be seen as a felt over the roots' surfaces.

Succession to beechwood depends on soil type. On the escarpment juniper *Juniperus communis* scrub was a major precursor, but hawthorn is also common; on the plateau, beechwood is preceded by a more mixed type of scrub, and on the acid sands by birchwood.

Apart from plantations the remaining woods of the three counties are fragmentary. A few scattered patches of yew wood give some idea of the conditions that exist under yew—bare soil resulting from the deep shade. Some clumps at Watlington Hill, Oxon, show this well. Similarly boxwood *Buxus sempervirens* is scarce—the only patch on the Chilterns is near Little Kimble, Bucks, on the Chequers estate. It too casts a heavy shade and little grows beneath it.

Ashwood is confined to the Cotswolds in our area, and it is much more extensive over the border in Gloucestershire. Ash is often found in oak and beechwoods, either as a constituent of the canopy or, more often, as a stage in succession. Along the Evenlode valley in Oxfordshire ash forms 'hanging' woods on the steep slopes, mixed with oak and wych elm. Hazel is abundant, along with other deciduous shrubs, and toothwort *Lathraea squamaria* is a common parasite on the hazel. There is a carpet of dog's mercury, bluebell, wood anemone and ramsons *Allium ursinum*, and in early spring also patches of moschatel *Adoxa moschatellina*. These woods also have a rich bryophyte flora, presumably favoured by the very humid conditions on the riverside slopes.

Alderwoods are scattered and occur either as fringing strips along streams or on fen peat. At Cothill Fen, Berks/Oxon, and a few other patches of fen, there are fragments of alderwood on waterlogged peat with the water table at or above the surface. Silver birch *Betula pendula* and various willows, especially grey willow or sallow *Salix cinerea* are associated with the alder, and the great tussock sedge *Carex paniculata*, which forms huge tussocks, is a characteristic feature. Other sedges occur, along with meadowsweet, common comfrey *Symphytum officinale*, nettle, hemp agrimony *Eupatorium cannabinum* and many other flowering plants, as well as numerous mosses. Alderwood of this kind, on fen peats which result from the filling in of open fens, is called carr and is really only a stage, sometimes prolonged, in the gradual succession to oakwood, which will normally invade when the soil level rises above the water table. Because of its susceptibility to drainage alderwood has declined very rapidly indeed.

Though birch and pinewoods are not stable climax woodland in the south, extensive areas of the Berkshire heaths have nevertheless been colonized by birch, sometimes accompanied by pine, which forms temporary woodlands. Again these would eventually pass to oakwood, but often they burn and heath returns. Incidentally birch shows its wide tolerance by occurring not only on these highly acid soils but on base-rich clays (it is common in Bernwood) and even on shallow soils over chalkland limestone—it colonizes freely on some patches of Corallian limestone at Wytham.

I have ignored plantations which are often of fairly recent origin, particularly nineteenth-century. They are floristically poor and uninteresting, often with only half-a-dozen herbaceous species, usually including many nettles, and occasionally ivy creeping over the ground. They add visual diversity to the landscape but are ecologically dull.

Scrub

I have already pointed out that the natural stable vegetation of lowland England is forest. We have replaced it with grassland or arable crops. If either is abandoned the land will rapidly be colonized by shrubs and other native plants. Most of the scrub in our area has resulted from the cessation either of sheep grazing for economic reasons, or of rabbit grazing as a result of myxomatosis. The former happened mainly in the 1930s depression and some old successional scrub is a relic of that time, the latter in the mid-1950s from which much of the extensive scrub on the Chiltern chalk and Cotswold limestone dates. Another type of scrub occurs along disused railway lines since the regular burning was stopped.

Yet another type of scrub occurs in cleared woodland that was never replanted. This is really 'thicket scrub', and there are patches in Bernwood and Wytham. Thicket scrub also sometimes grows on abandoned arable land on heavy soils. In our area it tends to be dominated by one or both species of hawthorn, blackthorn and various roses. The shrubs grow to 5–7 metres, and often there is a tangled mass of dead and dying spinous shrubs beneath the canopy making it almost impenetrable. The heavy shade suppresses most herbs except for a few scattered nettles, bugle, dog's mercury and mosses. Interestingly in some places the remains of anthills can be found; some at Wytham still have depauperate individuals of plants normally found on such hills in grassland. Probably their slight elevation prevents the accumulation of leaf litter which would otherwise smother the herbs. Thicket scrub is dull, but it gives cover to some mammals and birds, and some of the shrubs are important food plants for scarce insects. It tends to persist for a long time since colonizer trees cannot easily become established in the deep shade beneath it.

On some well drained acid soils another type of thicket scrub develops, dominated by gorse *Ulex europaeus* and broom *Cytisus scoparius*, with a similar dearth of herbs beneath their dense shade. Patches of this type of scrub occur in a few places, for instance Cumnor Hurst, Berks/Oxon. Although prone to fire, it tends to persist once established because gorse can regenerate from the roots. Again, given time this would eventually develop into woodland.

Much more widespread is successional scrub, which is rapidly taking over the formerly extensive grassland on the Chiltern escarpment. As soon as grazing pressure is relaxed shrubs begin to spread. Some can survive grazing and in grassland one can often find stunted individuals; this is especially true in those areas dominated by taller grasses such as upright brome *Bromus erectus*. Most of the shrub species involved have animal-dispersed fruits, and since birds perch on isolated shrubs the scrub tends to spread from centres which began as individual song-posts. On the shallower, steeper slopes juniper occurs, though much less abundantly than formerly. Fine examples of juniper scrub are at Aston Rowant NNR, Oxon, and Aston Upthorpe on the Berkshire Downs. Juniper protects other shrubs developing beneath it, so it is often found at the centre of a spreading patch, but eventually it gets overshaded and dead or dying bushes can be found in the middle of older scrub.

Much more common is scrub dominated by hawthorn, accompanied and often preceded by roses. Once it is established, other shrubs enter, including privet, spindle, wayfaring tree, dogwood, hazel, elder and buckthorn *Rhamnus catharticus*, and soon saplings of woodland trees become established, protected from grazing by the scrub. Ash, whitebeam, oak and beech are the usual invaders, and eventually if left to itself the succession will proceed to typical Chiltern beechwood. Examples of every stage from the beginning of scrub development to the establishment of woodland, can be seen at Aston Rowant NNR, Grangelands, Bucks, and Chinnor Hill, Oxon, to name but a few. In the mid 1980s most of the Chiltern scrub is between twenty and thirty years old, and at a stage when woodland will rapidly take over, and when the grassland beneath it has changed almost beyond recognition or redemption. Scrub poses one of the region's most difficult and long-standing conservation problems.

This generalized pattern of scrub development has imposed upon it variation depending on location, proximity of parent shrubs, slope, aspect and past management. Much of the Chiltern chalk grassland was ploughed during the war, but few or no crops were planted. The abandoned fields rapidly reverted to a herb-rich grassland; examples can be seen at Aston Rowant where the characteristic shrub

5. Chalk grassland and scrub, and beechwood with whitebeam, Pulpit Hill and Grangelands, Bucks

dominant is dogwood, which spreads rapidly by underground stems to form dense patches that are a pretty sure indicator of past ploughing. Many of the shrubs and young trees on these abandoned ploughlands die when they are a few metres tall, probably from nutrient deficiency, especially phosphate. Such areas would take a very long time to go through to woodland (Lloyd and Pigott 1968).

Beneath scrub all but a few shade-tolerant grasses and herbs are shaded out and replaced by marginal species that can tolerate less light. The hairy violet *Viola hirta* is one of the survivors from grassland, and soft brome and ground ivy are particularly successful invaders. But beneath old hawthorn scrub even they have difficulty in persisting; the combination of shade and litter accumulation is too much for them.

Though scrub is essentially a successional community, it is an important part of the present-day landscape as a habitat for many birds and insects that would otherwise be much scarcer. Conservation management should include the maintenance of some scrub as part of the diversity of semi-natural vegetation.

A truly man-made habitat that is best included in a consideration of scrub is the hedge. Hedgerows are linear woodland margin/scrub habitats which occupy many thousands of hectares and link areas of more continuous cover, providing refuge for many species of plant and animal, whose numbers would otherwise be much smaller. Though hedges have recently been destroyed to an alarming extent, they are still a major feature of our landscape, and as well as having great historical interest they are biologically valuable. Most are composed of several shrub species and some are very diverse in shrub and tree species (Pollard, Hooper and Moore 1974). Some shrubs are found almost exclusively in hedges; the barberry *Berberis vulgaris* is one such that is still found in some local hedges, especially in the Otmoor region. However, even the single-species hedge provides some shelter both for other plants and for animals. Though hedges harbour some pests, they also hold animals beneficial to the farmer. On balance, apart from the actual space they occupy, they are probably agriculturally neutral. Their value for conservation in general cannot be overemphasized (Elton 1957).

Grasslands

Lowland neutral grassland

Most grassland has been 'improved' either by the heavy fertilization of old pasture to favour palatable species, or more often by ploughing and reseeding with a mixture of grass species such as perennial ryegrass *Lolium perenne*, cocksfoot *Dactylis glomerata* and timothy *Phleum pratense*, usually mixed with white clover *Trifolium repens*. The few other plants which may come in are regarded as weeds. Though agriculturally productive, these improved grasslands are biologically dull. In the clay vales they have replaced a diverse and interesting series of neutral grasslands, which survive only where farmers have for one reason or another maintained traditional management practices. The soils range from the drier, well-drained loams, where most have been cultivated, to the seasonally flooded riverside meadows. Though some species occur in all, different areas have quite different sets of communities. The Thames Valley has the most important neutral grasslands remaining in Britain.

The composition of neutral grassland depends not only on soil type and drainage but on management, which may include either grazing, or cutting for hay, or both. A consistent well-managed grazing regime produces a turf of strongly tillering grasses, with a mixture of perennial herbs that grow low enough to survive grazing. Hay meadows have taller grasses with less tillering and often a great diversity of herbs which are intolerant of grazing. Some meadows are cut for hay once and then grazed late in the season, which produces great species diversity and returns some nutrients to the fields as manure, but is not much practised nowadays. In all these grasslands management is crucial. There are differences between grazed and hay meadows, and also in grazing techniques and in the grazing behaviour of animals that can profoundly affect the composition of pasture. Moreover grazing by sheep, rabbits, cattle and horses all produce differing swards which are the result both of the mode of grazing and the mechanical effects of the different animals. Mowing has yet different results. Much lowland grassland has in the past been undergrazed in summer and overgrazed in winter, a consequence of the attempt to maintain a herd of more or less constant size through the year. This causes the pasture to deteriorate, leading to an increase of unpalatable weedy species and to poaching in winter by the hooves of the stock. Some of the resulting thistle and dock-infested pasture can still be seen.

Although traditional hay-cutting followed by grazing returns some nutrients to the soil, there is still a net loss, some of which is replaced by dung from the cowsheds. But dung is deficient in some nutrients and lime and phosphate have to be added. Today mixed artificial fertilizers are used, and their excessive use again reduces species diversity. In meadows annually flooded by rivers the nutrients are replenished by silt, and some Thames-side meadows have been maintained on this plus added dung for centuries without further supplements.

It is difficult to categorize grasslands precisely. In areas of varied topography and drainage they grade into each other to such an extent that on quite a gentle slope one may pass from dry meadow at the upper end to wet meadow at the lower. In the widespread 'ridge and furrow' meadows of the Thames Valley relics of medieval farming can still be seen: strips of strikingly different vegetation types occur every few metres. In some places, where drainage is poor, the furrows may remain wet throughout the year and species characteristic of wet alluvial meadows occur cheek-by-jowl with dry meadow species on the ridges. Another difficulty is that neutral grasslands can be classified in at least three dimensions: nutrient-richness, moisture, and management, with results too complex to deal with adequately here.

The most widespread type of neutral grassland is probably the nutrient-poor 'dry meadow', some of which is very old. Dry meadows develop on well-drained soils, either when re-sown meadows are allowed to revert, or when more species-rich meadows are fertilized. The dominant species include crested dogstail *Cynosurus cristatus*, cocksfoot, perennial ryegrass, white clover, daisy *Bellis perennis*, common knapweed *Centaurea nigra*, creeping thistle *Cirsium arvense* and meadow buttercup *Ranunculus acris*. Many hectares of species-diverse dry meadow (and other neutral grasslands) survive as roadside verges, commons, village greens, churchyards and the like. These provide a reservoir, unfortunately a vulnerable one, of neutral grassland of a more or less natural type.

Several of the other neutral grasslands are biologically much more interesting. So-called 'damp' and 'wet' meadows still exist in somewhat moister areas. Wet meadows have impeded drainage, and characteristically, tufted hair-grass, hard rush *Juncus inflexus* and creeping jenny *Lysimachia nummularia* are found in them. In damp meadows soft rush *J. effusus*, Yorkshire fog *Holcus lanatus*, rough meadow-grass *Poa trivialis* and buttercups abound. The nutrient-rich meadow types include some of the most interesting. Some are especially well represented in our three counties, others survive only as little patches; all are scarce. At the wet end of the range grassland merges into marshland and even fen.

Base-rich marshes persist along calcareous streams and around springs, and have such well-known plants as marsh marigold *Caltha palustris*, ragged robin *Lychnis flos-cuculi*, common marsh bedstraw *Galium palustre*, jointed rush *Juncus articulatus*, and several sedges, including long-stalked yellow sedge *Carex lepidocarpa* and tawny sedge *C. hostiana*. Marsh helleborine *Epipactis palustris* is common. Some grasses are abundant in these marshes, especially purple moor-grass *Molinia caerulea* and meadow foxtail *Alopecurus pratensis*. Such communities occur on Otmoor and in parts of north Oxfordshire and Bucks along the River Ray, though they are all rapidly disappearing because of efficient drainage.

Otmoor has some sedge-rich meadow and there are little patches of it elsewhere, as at Menmarsh, and in some of the Bernwood woodland rides. These are characterized by a predominance of sedges, especially common sedge *Carex nigra*, tawny sedge and carnation sedge *C. panicea*, often accompanied by purple moor-grass, meadow thistle *Cirsium dissectum*, creeping soft-grass, sweet vernal-grass *Anthoxanthum odoratum* and a few other herbs. Sedge-rich meadows have a very distinct appearance, the sedges often giving them a bluish tinge.

One grassland type of which there are superb examples in Oxfordshire is the alluvial meadow. This develops in river floodplains, where every winter the river overflows (though this too may be modified by river management). These meadows are the main habitat for that speciality of our area, the fritillary *Fritillaria meleagris*. The two hay meadows of Pixey and Yarnton Meads, which are cut once a year and then grazed, provide a striking contrast with the continuously-grazed Port Meadow (Baker 1937). All are species-rich and beautifully illustrate the results of different management. All have been managed in the same way for several centuries, although Port Meadow has had its disturbances including some ploughing during the Civil War and the presence for a short while of an airstrip. The species composition of the two meadow types overlaps considerably, but also many species can be found only in one or the other. One of the most conspicuous plants on the meads is the great burnet *Sanguisorba officinalis*; other species intolerant of grazing include common meadow rue *Thalictrum flavum*, pepper-saxifrage *Silaum silaus*, adder's tongue fern, ragged robin and yellow rattle *Rhinanthus minor*. These meads also harbour several very rare dandelions which are confined to such habitats. Port Meadow contains strongly tillering grasses in abundance, and in addition many prostrate herbs that cannot survive the shading in the tall meadow. Among the larger herbs on the Meadow several thistles are prominent, including the handsome woolly thistle *Cirsium eriophorum*, and unfortunately, common ragwort *Senecio jacobaea* has become very abundant in places, probably because of winter overgrazing. The meads and Port Meadow together form one of the most interesting groups of grassland sites in Europe.

The neutral grasslands also include some calcareous pastures. Calcareous clays have a plant mixture familiar to anyone who knows the meadows along the River Ray and on Otmoor, but again many have gone as a result of drainage. Their mixture of grasses commonly includes creeping bent *Agrostis stolonifera*, sweet vernal grass, crested dogstail, meadow fescue *Festuca pratensis* and red fescue *F. rubra*, together with ribwort plantain *Plantago lanceolata* and red clover *Trifolium pratense*, together with abundant yellow rattle, common knapweed, betony *Stachys officinalis*, quaking grass *Briza media*, Yorkshire fog, great burnet, pepper saxifrage, adder's tongue fern and cowslip *Primula veris*.

Some of the best calcareous pastures are in and around Otmoor, their diversity enhanced by the fact that many of them are ridge-and-furrow grasslands with the variations in water table that this produces. Some should be conserved both as examples of a fascinating and little studied grassland habitat and as living documents of past land-use.

Finally there are the true water meadows, which no longer exist except as relics in areas such as the Kennet Valley. These meadows were deliberately flooded by an intricate series of gullies, and, since the water was base-rich, again had a rich flora. Some may still be flooded and retain a few of their original plants.

These calcareous meadows and their drier counterparts on loam (only fragments of which remain, mainly in churchyards and similar places) have many plants also found in dry calcareous grassland, which is the other major grassland type for which our area is famous.

Chalk and limestone grassland

Along the Chiltern escarpment and in places on the Berkshire Downs there used to be extensive stretches of chalk grassland (Smith 1980). Much has been lost to scrub colonization and arable farming but enough remains to give a good idea of what this habitat is like. Similar but less well known and studied grasslands occur on the Jurassic limestones of the Cotswolds, and on the Corallian around Oxford as well as on some calcareous grits. All show floristic similarities and also some subtle differences which depend on rock type, on geographical location and on such factors as slope, aspect, chalk purity, and past management or neglect. The overall similarity derives from the abundance of many species.

Almost all these grasslands are floristically rich—indeed this is the source of their interest and biological value, since they are also rich in animals. Paradoxically the richness may derive from nutrient poorness. Though there is abundant calcium, other nutrients (especially phosphate, nitrogen and potassium) are in short supply, and the tall growing grasses which might otherwise become abundant are sufficiently restricted to allow the less competitive herbs to flourish. A striking series of nutrient-addition experiments carried out on one Chiltern grassland has demonstrated just how rapidly an increase in major nutrients can impoverish the flora by favouring coarse growth and excluding the less competitive herbs.

6. One of the Chequers box combes, Great Kimble, Bucks

Dry calcareous grassland owes its existence over such a large area to sheep grazing since Neolithic times and latterly to rabbit pressure. The decline in sheep grazing and the onset of myxomatosis were the main reasons for its decline. Sheep grazing produces a short and compact turf; rabbits in great numbers reduce it so much that weedy species such as ragwort (which are a normal component of the grassland) become very abundant. Sheep also produce parallel horizontal tracks on the steep slopes, and on these and the slopes above them, as well as in rabbit scrapes, plants which are poor competitors can survive.

Although the differences between dry calcareous grasslands are subtle, a few main types can be easily distinguished. On much of the Chiltern escarpment and the north slope of the Berkshire Downs the grassland is dominated by sheep's fescue and red fescue, which are characteristic of well-grazed pasture. Some chalk and limestone grasslands, where grazing is relaxed or absent, are notable for dense stands of upright brome, which give a quite different appearance to the vegetation, although it is still somewhat open and other species can grow mixed with it. Both Warren Bank and Sydlings Copse, two BBONT reserves in Oxon, have fine examples of this. In some limestone areas a much more dominant grass is tor grass *Brachypodium pinnatum*, a rhizomatous, very tough and unpalatable plant that spreads rapidly and suppresses many herbs, resulting in a rather uninteresting uniform vegetation; Wytham has some good examples of this.

On deeper and disturbed, more nutrient-rich soils, especially towards the foot of the Chiltern escarpment, false oat-grass *Arrhenatherum elatius* sometimes forms dense tall stands, the lower growing herbs are again suppressed, and grasses such as cocksfoot come into the canopy. Other grasses regularly associated with the shallower soils and especially the fescue sward include downy and meadow oat-grasses *Avenula pubescens* and *A. pratensis*, yellow oat-grass *Trisetum flavescens*, crested hair-grass *Koeleria cristata* and quaking-grass.

It is, however, the herbs that give the dry calcareous grasslands their characteristic appearance, and make the hills so attractive with their abundance of flowers in summer. A dozen or so are frequent: salad burnet *Sanguisorba minor*, glaucous sedge *Carex flacca*, small scabious *Scabiosa columbaria*, wild thyme *Thymus praecox*, dwarf thistle *Cirsium acaule*, burnet saxifrage *Pimpinella saxifraga*, fairy flax *Linum catharticum*, common birdsfoot trefoil *Lotus corniculatus*, rough hawkbit *Leontodon hispidus*, red clover and ribwort plantain. One of the great pleasure of exploring this kind of grassland is the sheer abundance of species, many of them uncommon and attractive: autumn gentian *Gentianella amarella*, Chiltern gentian *G. germanica*, wild carrot *Daucus carota*, wild basil *Clinopodium vulgare* and marjoram *Origanum vulgare*. On bare chalk or very shallow soils wild candytuft *Iberis amara* is conspicuous. On the numerous anthills made by the yellow ant *Lasius flavus* which are such a feature of these pastures, poor competitors such as the early forget-me-not *Myosotis ramosissima* and parsley piert *Aphanes arvensis* survive. On the Berkshire Downs one of the loveliest plants is the pasque flower *Pulsatilla vulgaris* which grows at Aston Upthorpe. Several orchids, some of them rare, are found in chalk turf.

In places where there are very distinct aspect differences, such as Watlington Hill with its steep south and north-facing slopes, one can see how much the flora is affected. Rockrose *Helianthemum nummularium* is abundant on the south-facing slopes, but on the north-facing slopes taller herbs, such as wild parsnip *Pastinaca sativa*, and also several mosses, especially *Pseudoscleropodium purum* and *Dicranum scoparium*, are common.

Though it has been well studied, there is still a lot to learn about dry calcareous grassland, especially on the limestone. Whether much will survive outside nature reserves is doubtful: indeed its survival inside reserves is a matter of hard work and considerable expense. This is one problem which naturalists' trusts such as BBONT, with responsibility for substantial areas of calcareous grassland, have to face unless it is all to go to woodland.

In a few places at the top of the Chiltern escarpment, the deep loams or clay-with-flints are leached and somewhat acid, all effects of the chalk being lost. Here a grassland can be found with common bent and smooth meadow-grass *Poa pratensis* very abundant. Heather sometimes occurs, together with gorse and other species intolerant of calcareous soils. On the edges of these areas, where they grade into chalk grassland, one can find a mixture of acid-tolerant species rooting in the shallow loam and chalk species whose roots penetrate to the calcareous soil below. Such a community is known as chalk heath.

Heath, Bog and Fen

In a few places where very acid soils are uncolonized by woodland there are patches of heathy vegetation where grasses are the most conspicuous species. On the Greensand at Cumnor Hurst, Berks/Oxon, there are small areas of very acid, nutrient-poor soil, with very few species indeed: Yorkshire fog, brown bent *Agrostis canina*, heath bedstraw *Galium saxatile* and sheep's sorrel *Rumex acetosella* are the only common herbs, with a little catsear *Hypochaeris radicata* here and there. The two mosses *Dicranum scoparium* and *Polytrichum formosum*, together with several lichens, mainly *Cladonia* spp, make up the rest of the vegetation.

The grass heath mentioned above is one end of a spectrum of communities passing through true heath to wet heath and finally bog, along a gradient of increasing moisture. The only significant areas of heath are in southern Berkshire, with only scattered patches elsewhere, as at Burnham Beeches. These are part of the heath that formerly covered the areas of Greensand and Bagshot Sands in south-eastern England, much of which has been lost to farming, housing and military use. A few good areas remain, notably at Snelsmore Common and Owlsmoor, both Berks. Heath is relatively poor in higher plant species; heather and dwarf gorse *Ulex gallii* are most prominent and bell heather *Erica cinerea* common in places. Bryophytes and lichens are numerous. The soil is podsolised with a shallow layer of raw humus over the heavily leached sand below, and redeposition of the leached iron and aluminium salts below this in an 'iron pan'. The humus is colonized by various lichens, especially *Cladonia* species, and rather few mosses, two important ones being *Pleurozium schreberi* and *Hypnum cupressiforme* var *ericetorum*. On the better-drained areas bilberry *Vaccinium myrtillus* is sometimes very frequent; bracken is widespread on many heaths, but is often almost excluded from the most vigorous stands of heather. A few grasses are scattered here and there, especially wavy hair-grass *Deschampsia flexuosa* and sheep's fescue, but in undisturbed heath, at least until trees invade, heather is almost totally dominant. These heaths are rapidly invaded by birch, and unless burned frequently they become woodland.

On deeper, damper soils, heather still predominates, but here cross-leaved heath *Erica tetralix* and purple moor-grass are mixed with it, giving a tussocky terrain. In still wetter areas, bog-mosses *Sphagnum* spp, accompanied by deer grass *Scirpus cespitosus* and tormentil *Potentilla erecta* are the most important species. This gradation from dry to wet heath can be clearly seen down a slope from the flat plateau to a little stream at Snelsmore Common. This stream is naturally dammed and behind the dam the valley is filled with a well-developed bog, into which the wet heath grades. One of the very few bogs in the three counties, this contains several species of *Sphagnum*, in places forming quite deep peat. Associated with it are several sedges, round-leaved sundew *Drosera rotundifolia*, bog asphodel *Narthecium ossifragum* with its conspicuous yellow flower spikes, and heath milkwort *Polygala serpyllifolia*. The whole heath-bog complex here and in some other sites, such as Owlsmoor and others in south Berkshire, is a gradual transition, and a fascinating example of the difficulty of drawing hard and fast boundaries between communities.

At the other wetland extreme from bog is fen, its vegetation determined by a base-rich, usually calcareous, water supply in contrast to the nutrient-poor acid water of bog. Fen occurs in areas where peat has accumulated as a result of poor drainage and where the water supply is base-rich. It grades into marsh, which is found in wet areas of mineral soil, for example along rivers and around ponds. Both these vegetation types have declined drastically in the last fifty years. True fen is restricted to a few small, but still surprisingly good patches scattered through the region. Cothill Fen, Berks/Oxon, is one of the best known, and even in the city of Oxford the very restricted area of Cowley Marsh (Bullingdon Bog) in the Lye Valley, still retains many interesting fen plants.

Fen develops where little silt accumulates: the level of the ground is the result of the gradual accretion of plant remains which do not decay in the waterlogged humus. The calcium in the water keeps the peat alkaline. At Cothill one can see the complete succession from open water through fen to fen carr, though the present open water is the result of a deliberate attempt to maintain a diversity of habitats in this nature reserve. Fen peat used to be extracted, and on Parsonage Moor, part of the Cothill complex, there is a series of different levels as a result of past cutting. The vegetation here varies with the level of the peat surface above the water table. In some fen areas (but not here) reeds *Phragmites australis* are also cut, thus introducing yet another human disturbance into the fen system.

Some of the typical fen species have already been mentioned in the account of alder carr. At Cothill the open water is colonized by blunt-flowered rush *Juncus subnodulosus* and various sedges, which form a floating mat of vegetation that gradually thickens and fills in the pool until it is sufficiently stable to be colonized by willows and alders. Reeds are often important at one stage in this succession. None of the fens in our counties is large enough or sufficiently undisturbed to demonstrate the full open water-woodland succession, but by piecing together little bits from here and there one can see most stages. Fen is a fragile habitat easily damaged by public pressure; it also requires careful management to maintain its full diversity.

Riverside marshes have been sadly depleted by drainage and dredging, but here and there some remain, especially along smaller rivers and streams, and even in places along the Thames. Not that one can find anything as good as those that used to exist, such as Hagley Pool, Berks/Oxon, and the photographs in Church (1922) indicate something of what has been lost. Marshes have a greater variety of plants than fens, being usually less calcareous, but they have many in common with them.

Open waters

These are very scarce. The number of small ponds has declined everywhere, though efforts have been made to save some of the better ones. Around farm ponds there is often a characteristic group of plants, almost always including the celery-leaved buttercup *Ranunculus sceleratus* and one of the water starworts *Callitriche* spp. Many farm ponds, however, are polluted by nitrogen fertilizers or cattle droppings, and their flora is limited. Large bodies of open water are few. Tring Reservoirs on the Bucks/Herts border have some submerged species and also good fringing vegetation in spots. Some other reservoirs, such as that at Weston Turville, Bucks, also have fine reedbeds. Some ponds in Wychwood NNR, Oxon, are highly calcareous. Open waters of this kind—or marl lakes as they are called—often have a number of plants which are uncommon elsewhere, and these include the Characeae, the evil-smelling, calcium-depositing group of algae that grow in calcium-rich waters.

7. The pond in the Henry Stephen/C. S. Lewis Reserve, Risinghurst, Oxon, with fringing reeds and floating vegetation

There is tremendous potential for the creation of new open-water areas apart from reservoirs, where conflicting demands on the water use often prevent the establishment of much vegetation. Gravel and clay pits are the prime example, and though many are filled with rubbish of some kind, others are being kept open. Calvert brick pits, Bucks, may develop into an interesting area, and the complex of gravel pits that adjoins Stony Stratford, Bucks, has potential. Though the main interest in all these may be ornithological, aquatic plants are likely to colonize rapidly and among them may be some of the more uncommon ones.

Artificial habitats

Ponds and gravel pits are artificial, but they develop kinds of vegetation that resemble that in natural waters. Other kinds of artificial habitat also develop interesting vegetation, but sometimes it is unlike any natural types. However, a few such habitats provide refuges for plants that otherwise would have nowhere to grow in a lowland area. They are also refuges for many introduced and naturalized plants.

Most farmland is poor wildlife habitat; agriculture inevitably destroys most of the native vegetation and the animals that depend on it, but brings an interesting weed flora, especially in cornfields. Weeds, like any other group of plants, have individual environmental preferences. Different soils exert their effect, and such other as past land use history, present farming methods and herbicide resistance all play a part in determining which grows where.

Most farms have little patches of uncultivated land—corners of fields, wet spots, farmyards themselves—and each of these may have interesting plants. When collecting records for the new Flora of Oxfordshire we found many plants surviving in tiny fragments of disturbed ground on farms. Farm ditches, like ponds, are also sometimes of value.

The three counties are blessed with a network of canals and other man-made or modified linear aquatic and semi-aquatic habitats that harbour numerous interesting plants, and, despite the intensive management of them practised by water authorities and the pollution from fertilizers and herbicides, some still remain as islands of this type of vegetation in the sea of agricultural land.

Another linear habitat is the railway embankment or cutting. Active railway lines must have their banks managed and this has traditionally been by fire, creating yet another habitat type. Disused railway lines have not only the embankments but also the old tracks which are no longer sprayed to keep down vegetation. These railway tracks offer several interesting possibilities, even for casual observation, of the effect of physical environment factors on vegetation. Examine the plants on the banks of an east-west line and you will see very clearly the effects of aspect: the south-facing bank has much drier soil, and there are often distinct groups of plants on the two opposite banks. Unfortunately too many disused lines are rapidly becoming scrub-covered and this will result in the loss of interesting grassland habitats and a consequent decline in many insect populations. Another interesting factor introduced by railways is that the ballast often comes from some distance and results for instance, in the presence of heather and other acid-tolerant plants on some railway embankments in the calcareous clay area of north Oxfordshire.

Railway yards, with their variety of buildings, substrata and past history also offer refuges for many plants: some, such as the small toadflax *Chaenorhinum minus* are almost confined to such places. Old airfields and military establishments with their areas of decaying concrete similarly repay study for their developing vegetation.

Walls provide a refuge for many common plants as well as for many which have little or no other lowland habitat; they extend the cliff and rock-face environment into our countryside and towns. Not only boundary walls, which of course have their best development in the Cotswold and oolite limestone region, but also garden walls—especially good in Oxford—churchyard walls, and even churches themselves, harbour many plants. Several ferns are particularly good at exploiting walls: the aptly named wall-rue *Asplenium ruta-muraria*, black spleenwort *A. adiantum-nigrum*, maidenhair spleenwort *A. trichomanes*, rustyback. *Ceterach officinarum* and harts-tongue *Phyllitis scolopendrium* are the best known of these. Other characteristic wall plants are the ivy-leaved toadflax *Cymbalaria muralis* and several little annuals such as common whitlow-grass *Erophila verna* and thyme-leaved sandwort *Arenaria serpyllifolia*. Walls also provide excellent places in which to study the micro-environmental effects of, for instance, substratum, aspect, dampness and many other variables.

Many of these artificial habitats are under threat because of drainage, hedge-grubbing, herbicides, wall-cleaning and general 'tidying up'. There is a strong case for encouraging plants on walls, and similar cases can be made for other artificial habitats (Woodell 1979). The fact that these are more man-made than other habitats makes them no less interesting.

Conclusions

A short account of the habitats of a region as large and diverse as Berkshire, Buckinghamshire and Oxfordshire must inevitably restrict itself to the highlights, and these occupy only a small proportion of the total area. Further, they are fragments scattered through the intensively managed agricultural and urban landscape. This need not depress us too much: from this and other chapters it will be evident that there is plenty of interest left—plenty to see and a great deal to learn. If the semi-natural vegetation is properly integrated into the agricultural background, with adequate give-and-take on both sides, there is little reason why much of what we have should not be conserved, maintained and even enhanced. This requires goodwill and hard work, as well as money, and BBONT has to act as a focus for active conservation in the three counties.

Finally, we must remember that the vegetation is only one part of a complex ecosystem, but it is an essential part—the foundation on which all else, animal populations, both invertebrate and vertebrate, stands. Conservation must begin and end with the habitat: once that is established the rest should be assured.

4 The Flora

H. J. M. BOWEN

Seed Plants and Ferns

About a thousand native vascular plant species have been found in the region, together with about half that number of aliens, though relatively few of these are well established. The native flora consists mainly of widespread European plants with a few Atlantic and Southern species, but has no Arctic–Alpine species and very few Mediterranean and Oceanic Northern species. From a European point of view there are only four uncommon species in the region, namely creeping marsh-wort *Apium repens* (one or a few sites), early gentian *Gentianella anglica* (several sites on the chalk and one on limestone), wild parsley *Petroselinum segetum* (once frequent, now rare in arable fields), and pillwort *Pilularia globulifera* (one lake). If we take the definition of current rarity given by Perring and Farrell, the region has thirty-two very rare British species, plus a further fourteen believed to be extinct here. All the extant rarities are mentioned in the survey which follows.

Since comprehensive county floras are available for all three counties in the region, and new floras are in preparation for both Oxfordshire and Bucks, this account concentrates on the more interesting species and localities, subdividing the region into nine areas as follows, with larger towns given in brackets.

North Bucks (Bletchley, Milton Keynes)
Mid-Bucks (Aylesbury)
Chilterns (High Wycombe)
South Bucks & East Berkshire (Slough, Windsor)
Mid-Berkshire (Reading)
West Berkshire (Newbury)
Berkshire Downs (Wantage)
Mid-Oxfordshire and Upper Thames Valley (Oxford, Abingdon, Faringdon, Witney)
North Oxfordshire (Banbury)

North Bucks

This area was covered with oak forest until comparatively recently, but relatively little of botanical interest survives on its heavy clay soils. Both Whaddon Chase and the Bucks portion of the Forest of Whittlebury have been almost completely converted to farmland, but about one square kilometre of Salcey Forest remains. This has been extensively replanted with conifers, but retains a good woodland flora with midland hawthorn *Crataegus laevigata* as a prominent undershrub, and herb Paris *Paris quadrifolia*, fritillary *Fritillaria meleagris*, violet helleborine *Epipactis purpurata* and greater burnet saxifrage *Pimpinella major* as scarce herbs. Wood smallreed *Calamagrostis epigeios* is a characteristic grass which forms dense stands along rides. Stowe Park is a fine landscaped park with a small wet wood, kept as a nature reserve, containing the golden saxifrage *Chrysosplenium oppositifolium*. There are also old records for moonwort *Botrychium lunaria*.

The most interesting part of the region is the area of woods and heaths on acid soil near the Brickhills, on the Bedfordshire border. There are old records for climbing corydalis *Corydalis claviculata*, lily of the valley *Convallaria majalis*, and yellow star of Bethlehem *Gagea lutea* from the woods, in which both native oaks occur; marsh fern *Thelypteris palustris*, royal fern *Osmunda regalis* and bog asphodel *Narthecium ossifragum* from valley bogs; and an ephemeral flora on the sand which included shepherd's cress *Teesdalia nudicaulis*, lamb's succory *Arnoseris minima*, smooth catsear *Hypochoeris glabra* and red-tipped cudweed *Filago lutescens*. How much of this remains is uncertain, for apart from agricultural and forestry pressures, this corner of Bucks receives much fluoride pollution from local brickworks. A remarkable alien bellflower, *Downingia elegans*, colonized margins of man-made lakes near Milton Keynes.

Mid-Bucks

Once again the native oak forest survives only as relics, here of Bernwood Forest, as at Waterperry Wood, Oxon, Shabbington Wood, Rushbeds Wood and Whitecross Green Wood. These have a flora similar to Salcey Forest's, and their current interest is more for the entomologist than the botanist. Wild service tree *Sorbus torminalis* is frequent in Waterperry Wood. There are old records for the rare green houndstongue *Cynoglossum germanicum* near Mentmore.

A century ago there were several tiny patches of fen on the clay plain, with such plants as grass of Parnassus *Parnassia palustris* and common butterwort *Pinguicula vulgaris*. Now only one such patch is known to survive, at Stoke Hammond, where it has some protection from BBONT. Its flora is not very rich, but it does have cottongrass *Eriophorum* sp. and marsh helleborine *Epipactis palustris*.

The surroundings of the large artificial reservoirs in this area harbour several interesting plants, such as asarabacca *Asarum europaeum* and broad-leaved ragwort *Senecio fluviatilis* (actually in Hertfordshire), both introduced. The mud of Boarstall Decoy used to have golden dock *Rumex maritimus*, but this dock requires regular disturbance and is sporadic if not transient. Greater spearwort *Ranunculus lingua* has been seen in a disused branch of the old canal near Buckingham, now a BBONT reserve.

Chilterns

This relatively waterless area of chalk hills rises from the plain to a height of nearly 300 metres. A glance at the map will show the high proportion of woods in the area compared with all other parts of the region. Much of this is planted beech woodland, but oak and holly are common. Two dry valleys near Chequers have abundant native box *Buxus sempervirens*, associated in one spot with musk orchid *Herminium monorchis*.

The Nature Conservancy Council have recently had the invidious job of grading the Chiltern woods on inadequate scientific data. They rate Bradenham Woods and the Chequers box woods, both in Bucks, as Grade 1, and Aston Wood, Oxon, and Windsor Hill, Bucks, as Grade 2. From a botanical standpoint, this grading is of questionable value, as it fails to emphasize the large number of other woods containing interesting plants.

There are several Chiltern woodland rarities whose localities will not be given beyond mentioning that the three orchids are protected by BBONT. Coralroot *Cardamine bulbifera* forms small colonies in woods around High Wycombe, with one record from Bisham Wood, Berks. Green houndstongue is now restricted to a single site under oak near Watlington, Oxon. Ghost orchid *Epipogium aphyllum* is a shy-flowering plant known from two localities, but there are old records from other woods where it may survive. It is a saprophyte, deriving its nutrient from rotting vegetables, and its requirements are more those of a fungus than a vascular plant, as it grows in pockets of deep litter in very shaded places. Red helleborine *Cephalanthera rubra* also tolerates deep shade, but it now rarely if ever flowers in its only locality. Military orchid *Orchis militaris* used to be widespread, but is now restricted to three sites, in scrub or clearings, but the seedlings seem to need bare, shaded soil to establish themselves. Lady orchid *O. purpurea* persisted for a few years in a wood near Whitchurch, Oxon. Two uncommon grasses, lesser hairy

1. Chiltern gentian

2. Downy woundwort

brome *Bromus benekenii* and wood barley *Hordelymus europaeus*, occur in many of the older woods. There are still at least four sites for the shrub mezereon *Daphne mezereum*.

Chalk grassland sites in the Chilterns have also been graded by the NCC, who gave their National Nature Reserve at Bald Hill and Beacon Hill, Oxon, Grade 1 status; this has (or had) matgrass fescue *Vulpia unilateralis* and wild candytuft *Iberis amara* and is used for grazing experiments. Ivinghoe Beacon and Pitstone Hill, Bucks, which have pasque flower *Pulsatilla vulgaris* and field fleawort *Senecio integrifolius*, and Coombe Hill, Bucks, have Grade 2 status. A number of BBONT reserves contain good chalk grassland, such as Aston Clinton pits, Buttlers Hangings, Dancers End, Grange Lands, Holtspur Bank and Winchbottom, Bucks, and Chinnor Hill, Hartslock and Warren Bank, Oxon, as do the National Trust lands at Watlington Hill and Christmas Common, Oxon. Among the rarest species are monkey orchid *Orchis simia*, which has one site in the Goring gap, and man orchid *Aceras anthropophorum*, with a single unprotected site at Ipsden, Oxon. Early gentian *Gentianella anglica*, unknown in Europe, occurs in short turf and is commoner on the Berkshire Downs, while Chiltern gentian *G. germanica* flowers late in the season among longer grass with bare patches. Great pignut *Bunium bulbocastanum* grows on the edges of arable fields around Ivinghoe, which is its western limit. At Fingest dragon's-teeth *Tetragonolobus maritimus* is established in some quantity on a road verge, but it may not be native.

Where leached, acid soils occur on the Chiltern ridge, as at Coombe Hill, Shirburn Hill, Oxon, and many of the commons, a heath vegetation may develop with abundant heather *Calluna vulgaris*. No unusual heath plants are known from such sites. The aquatic flora of the Chilterns is restricted by lack of water, but the alien waterweed *Crassula helmsii* has established itself in a pond at Cholesbury, Bucks and curly water-thyme *Lagarosiphon major* at Stone.

South Bucks and East Berkshire

This area is a complete contrast to the last in that most of its interesting sites are on acid or very acid soils, and the aquatic flora is well represented, but it has suffered from suburbanization and pollution. It has two fragments of ancient forest, Windsor (Grade 1), Berks, and Burnham Beeches (Grade 2), Bucks. Windsor has plenty of wild service tree, and the eyebright *Euphrasia anglica* grows in its rides, while Burnham Beeches is noted for its ancient pollard trees, both species of oak, and the rare bladderseed *Physospermum cornubiense*. Burnham also has yellow bartsia *Parentucellia viscosa* as a recent colonist, but both royal fern *Osmunda regalis* and common butterwort *Pinguicula vulgaris* appear to be extinct there. Royal fern has been seen near Crowthorne in the last few years. Other woodland plants of note, all in Berks, are lily of the valley at Englemere Pond, green-flowered helleborine *Epipactis phyllanthes* from Tower Hill, and common wintergreen *Pyrola minor* at Ascot and in Wellington College grounds. The low shrub *Gaultheria shallon* is well naturalized near Englemere Pond.

Some heath vegetation survives around East Burnham Common, but Iver Heath in Bucks has gone. However, extensive heaths with much dwarf gorse *Ulex minor* remain on very acid soils in east Berkshire, together with bogs in shallow valleys, as at Caesar's Camp, Englemere, Owlsmoor and Tower Hill. Sweet gale *Myrica gale*, white beak sedge *Rhynchospora alba* and the sundews *Drosera intermedia* and *D. rotundifolia* are characteristic plants of these bogs, while marsh clubmoss *Lepidotis inundata* and crested buckler fern *Dryopteris cristata* are extremely local. The Berkshire heaths closely resemble the Surrey heaths, but have a poorer flora: for example, slender cottongrass *Eriophorum gracile* is absent from Berkshire. Where the heath has been ploughed, lamb's succory *Arnoseris minima*, should be looked for; it is very rare and sporadic, and was last seen in a rhubarb field near Easthampstead.

A good example of the Thames marshland flora has been preserved by the

National Trust at Cock Marsh near Cookham, Berks. This has knotted pearlwort *Sagina nodosa* and the aquatics frogbit *Hydrocharis morsus-ranae* and hair-like pondweed *Potamogeton trichoides*. The old goose-green vegetation once found on Littleworth, Naphill and Gerrards Cross Commons, Bucks, has probably disappeared, although star-fruit *Damasonium alisma* lingered on one of these sites until 1960. Chaffweed *Anagallis minima*, common chamomile *Chamaemelum nobile*, pennyroyal *Mentha pulegium* and small fleabane *Pulicaria vulgaris* have gone from the sites mentioned, but brown galingale *Cyperus fuscus*, which used to grow on mud at Dorney Common, Bucks, was found on Cock Marsh in 1982. However, both coral necklace *Illecebrum verticillatum* and six-stamened waterwort *Elatine hexandra* occur sporadically in and around acid ponds in south Berkshire. A mature gravel pit near Sandhurst, Berks, has the waterwort and a lawn of needle spikerush *Eleocharis acicularis* kept grazed by Canada geese, as well as two North American aquatics, the blue-flowered pickerel weed *Pontederia cordata* and an arrowhead which is probably *Sagittaria platyphylla*. Another American alien, the skunk cabbage *Lysichiton americanum* is established in swamps at Black Park, Bucks, and Virginia Water, Berks, while the bur marigold *Bidens connata* has colonized the Grand Union Canal near the Middlesex border.

Mid-Berkshire

Although some of the London Clay soils of this area have a dull flora, it has a great variety of other soils and habitats. Woods on the chalk include Sulham Woods with clumps of stinking hellebore *Helleborus foetidus*; a small wood near Streatley where green hellebore *H. viridis* is abundant; and Bisham Woods with a rich flora including coralroot, yellow birdsnest *Monotropa hypopitys* and birdsnest orchid *Neottia nidus-avis*. There are also wet woods on more acid soils as at Moor Copse (a BBONT reserve) and Padworth, which have abundant common Solomon's seal *Polygonatum multiflorum* and two uncommon sedges, *Carex laevigata* and *C. strigosa*. Padworth also has the rare sedge *Carex elongata* and a hybrid St John's wort *Hypericum x desetangsii*. Among the aliens, Cornelian cherry *Cornus mas* and Austrian yellow-cress *Rorippa austriaca* are established at Caversham. Purple toothwort *Lathraea clandestina* is abundant on sallow roots in a Reading park, while the foreign grasses *Festuca heterophylla* and *Poa chaixii* are established in old plantations at Whiteknights Park, Reading and elsewhere. Yellow eyebright *Odontites jaubertiana*, unknown elsewhere in Britain, may have arrived from Europe during the Second World War, and has survived for at least fifteen years near Aldermaston.

A small chalkpit near Hurley, protected by BBONT, has an extraordinarily rich flora including Chiltern gentian, wild candytuft and many orchids. In contrast, south-west of Reading there is good heath and bog vegetation around Mortimer and Wokefield Common. Here common and dwarf gorse *Ulex europaeus* and *U. minor* grow together, and plants which may be hybrids are being studied. Near here the beech fern *Thelypteris phegopteris* was found in 1892 but has not been seen since. A patch of the very rare sedge *Carex montana* used to occur near Wokingham, but was destroyed by recent roadworks.

The Loddon river gives its name to two rare plants which still occur along its banks despite gravel extraction along the lower reaches. The Loddon lily is a plant of wet alder and willow holts whose bulbs can survive the destruction of woody cover; its other name is summer snowflake *Leucojum aestivum*. Loddon pondweed *Potamogeton nodosus* is locally abundant in the stream itself. Coleman's Moor, bordering the river, is no longer of much botanical interest, but tower mustard *Arabis glabra* may survive in a suburban lane. There is a meadow full of fritillaries *Fritillaria meleagris* where the Loddon crosses the Hampshire border. At Southlake the aquatic fern pillwort grows in an acid lake with blunt-leaved pondweed *Potamogeton obtusifolius*. Slightly more eutrophic lakes at Bearwood and Whiteknights have fine displays of fringed waterlily *Nymphoides peltata*, which has disappeared from the Thames because of damage by motorboats. Two aquatics recently found in this region are golden dock *Rumex maritimus* and dittander *Lepidium latifolium*.

West Berkshire

This well watered and unpolluted area in the Kennet valley has a varied flora but no NCC graded sites. It is fairly well wooded, with one fragment of old forest at Hamstead Park with its huge oaks, and ancient hazel hangers such as Rivar Copse. Woods on the chalk often have herb Paris and spiked star of Bethlehem *Ornithogalum pyrenaicum*, though neither is common. On acid soil around the old commons, climbing corydalis and wild daffodil *Narcissus pseudo-narcissus* are scarce, while common Solomon's seal is often abundant. Both oaks occur at Fence Wood, a well-managed wood which has a small patch of stagshorn clubmoss *Lycopodium clavatum*. Much of the common land at Bucklebury, Crookham, Greenham, Snelsmore and Inkpen still has extensive heaths with bogs in the valleys. These heaths have much dwarf gorse together with bristle bent *Agrostis setacea*, whose very different distribution patterns just overlap. Rare species are the upright chickweed *Moenchia erecta* from Snelsmore and Greenham, and the pale dog violet *Viola lactea* which is now protected by BBONT at Inkpen. Spreading bellflower *Campanula patula* and yellow figwort *Scrophularia vernalis* are of somewhat irregular occurrence near Bucklebury.

The marshes and water-meadows bordering the Kennet are the main stronghold of water avens *Geum rivale* in the region. Two booklets have been produced by Mr and Mrs Frankum on the natural history of Freeman's Marsh, near Hungerford, which has knotted pearlwort, cottongrass, flat sedge *Blysmus compressus* and whorl grass *Catabrosa aquatica*. Not far off, near Shalbourne, Wilts, but actually in Berkshire, is the only site in the region for green figwort *Scrophularia umbrosa*, which grows by an unpolluted stream. A high chalk ridge rises in the extreme south-west of the area near Walbury, where BBONT helps to protect a small site for the musk and other orchids.

Several alien plants have become established. The best known is probably the spring crocus *Crocus purpureus*, which occurs in tens of thousands in an old pasture near Inkpen. Giant butterbur *Petasites japonicus* is reported from three sites along the Kennet, where the native plant *P. hybridus* is frequent. Near Membury, crown vetch *Coronilla varia* and yellow restharrow *Ononis natrix* have recently appeared in old grassland. Railway banks near Hungerford are a good place to see the hawkweed *Hieracium arvorum*, while near Newbury Caucasian beet *Beta trigyna* has persisted for many years, and there is a record for the rare toadflax hybrid *Linaria purpurea x repens*. Field eryngo *Eryngium campestre* was found on a railway bank at Hermitage in 1934, but has not been seen since.

Berkshire Downs

This area has a similar flora to that of the Chilterns, though it has far less woodland, and beech does not appear to be native except around the Goring gap. The only scarp woodland left is an ashwood at Britchcombe with impressive lianes of traveller's joy *Clematis vitalba*, and herb Paris and fly orchid *Ophrys insectifera* in its ground flora. Ashridge Wood on the dip slope has a mass of common Solomon's seal, spiked star of Bethlehem and meadow saffron *Colchicum autumnale*. Near Aston Upthorpe are some fine stands of juniper *Juniperus communis*.

Probably the best chalk grassland remaining in this area occurs at White Horse Hill, where numerous orchids, including musk orchid, as well as field fleawort and early gentian are found. Patches of old grassland also survive around Aston Upthorpe (Grade 1) and the Fair Mile, where there are two sites for pasque flower, as well as matgrass fescue, wild candytuft and burnt orchid *Orchis ustulata*. Other fragments may be found at Moulsford Downs, Knollend Down, East Hendred Down, Kingstone Down and Seven Barrows. At Segsbury Camp, Chiltern gentian has been known to hybridize with autumn gentian *Gentianella amarella*. Dragon's teeth is at one site near Streatley. Lizard orchid *Himantoglossum hircinum* has been found in two places, but is probably extinct in both. The native purple milkvetch *Astragalus danicus* has been ploughed out near Chilton, and the bugle *Ajuga genevensis*, probably introduced with pheasant food near Churn, is also gone.

The arable fields on the chalk can support a rich weed flora, now sadly reduced by herbicides. However, pheasant's eye *Adonis annua*, the rare fumitories *Fumaria vaillantii* and *F. parviflora*, corn goosegrass *Galium tricornutum* and broad-fruited cornsalad *Valerianella rimosa* still occur sporadically. The two umbelliferous weeds wild parsley and spreading hedge parsley *Torilis arvensis* have similar habits, and were last seen off the chalk in a fallow near Appleford. Thorow-wax *Bupleurum rotundifolium* occurred at Cholsey as late as 1954, while corn cockle *Agrostemma githago* disappeared about 1958.

Alien plants established at the foot of the chalk scarp include wild tulip *Tulipa sylvestris* which flowers regularly near Challow, yellow anemone *Anemone ranunculoides* and creeping comfrey *Symphytum ibiricum* near Childrey.

Mid-Oxfordshire and Upper Thames Valley

This large area includes the Vale of White Horse, the Oxfordshire Cotswolds, Otmoor and the Upper Thames valley. Wychwood Forest (Grade 1) has a rich flora which must have been still richer before its fragmentation. Stinking hellebore, chaffweed *Anagallis minima* and small-flowered buttercup *Ranunculus parviflorus* are all present. Its outliers on limestone have green hellebore (at Wilcote) and yellow star of Bethlehem in Whitehill Wood by the Evenlode; wood vetch *Vicia sylvatica* occurs sporadically. Cogges and Singe Woods are outliers with leached soils and this accounts for the presence of durmast oak *Quercus petraea* and climbing corydalis there. Another ancient wood occurs on the west side of Blenheim Park, which has the most extensive stand of venerable oaks in the region, and large-leaved lime *Tilia platyphyllos* as a likely native tree; nearby green houndstongue persists in a hedgebank. Bagley Wood, south of Oxford, is also ancient, and is the only site in the region for the tiny ivy-leaved bellflower *Wahlenbergia hederacea*. Mezereon has been found in several woods, most often in Appleton Lower Common.

Limestone grassland sites have been sadly reduced by ploughing. Pasque flower is probably extinct in this area, as it has not been seen at Wychwood for many years, though it may survive at Cherbury Camp, Berks. Late spider orchid *Ophrys sphegodes* was once widespread, and survived until 1920 near Stanton St John. Old

3. Meadow clary

4. Fritillary, includding a white specimen

limestone pits and field boundaries sometimes retain rare species, for example purple milkvetch and downy-fruited sedge *Carex filiformis* near Burford, grape hyacinth *Muscari atlanticum* near Chadlington, bulbous meadowgrass *Poa bulbosa* near Stonesfield, which appears to have been lost following afforestation, and the three Cotswold specialities meadow clary *Salvia pratensis*, downy woundwort *Stachys germanica* and perfoliate pennycress *Thlaspi perfoliatum*. Although these last three are rare in Britain they are quite common in south Europe. Meadow clary is found in a number of sites, in one of which there are over 10,000 plants. The other two prefer recently bared soil, and are sporadic. Downy woundwort is not seen at all in most years, and will then turn up in a new site, so it is a most difficult species to protect.

There are several classic neutral grassland sites in this area. Port Meadow is one of the few localities for creeping marshwort, and mudwort *Limosella aquatica* occurs sporadically there. Nearby Pixey Mead has some extremely rare dandelions, such as *Taraxacum fulgidum* and *T. tamesense*. Most fritillary fields have been ploughed up or grazed to near extinction, but where preserved, as at Magdalen Meadow, Oxford, or near Ducklington, the colonies make a splendid show in April and May. A few wet fields and woods near Otmoor, now protected by BBONT, have two rare sedges *Carex filiformis* and *C. vulpina* and the hybrid violet *Viola canina x persicifolia* with much else of interest. Marsh sowthistle *Sonchus palustris* once occurred in a ditch in this area, but seems to have gone.

The outstanding fen in the area is at Cothill (Grade 1), where the list of over 300 species includes common butterwort, grass of Parnassus, the bladderwort *Utricularia neglecta*, fen pondweed *Potamogeton coloratus*, marsh helleborine, the marsh orchid *Dactylorhiza traunsteineri*, broad-leaved cottongrass *Eriophorum latifolium* and black bogrush *Schoenus nigricans*. Other, somewhat less rich, fens occur at Wootton, Marcham and Frilford, Berks, and at Latchford Combe, Headington Wick and Bullingdon Bog, in Oxon. Great fen sedge *Cladium mariscus*, whose remains have been found in buried peat at Cothill, is now restricted to a few sterile clumps near Hatford, but variegated horsetail *Equisetum variegatum* is a new arrival in young fen at Dry Sandford pit. Fens by the Thames at Wytham and Abingdon once had water germander *Teucrium scordium*, which survived until 1934 at Wytham, and greater spearwort, which is still at Wytham but was destroyed by building at Abingdon. The records for narrow-leaved water dropwort *Oenanthe silaifolia* from local fens need re-investigation. Near Marcham there is a salt spring, the only one in the region and difficult to locate. Salt-tolerant plants such as wild celery *Apium graveolens* and sea clubrush *Scirpus maritimus* are—or were—found nearby.

Wherever they have been left relatively undisturbed, the wet meadows and ditches near the Thames have a rich flora, but the main channel of the river is kept clear of vegetation by the excessive number of powered boats. Loddon lily occurs on many islands and holts downstream from Nuneham Park, and greater dodder *Cuscuta europaea* is a frequent but inconspicuous parasite of nettles. Greater water parsnip *Sium latifolium* is now rarely seen, mostly by very wet ditches. The rarer pondweeds, which are mostly transient, are *Potamogeton compressus*, *P. friesii* and *P. pusillus*, while water soldier *Stratiotes aloides* is found sporadically at Abingdon and Kennington.

True heaths are scarce near Oxford. By far the most interesting is the heath at Frilford, where the calcareous subsoil allows common rockrose *Helianthemum nummularium* to grow side by side with heather. The flora recalls that of Breckland, and such plants as shepherd's cress *Teesdalia nudicaulis*, smooth catsear, maiden pink *Dianthus deltoides*, striated catchfly *Silene conica*, matgrass fescue, loose silky bent *Apera interrupta* and the hybrid fleabane *Conyza canadensis x Erigeron acer*. Other heaths at Hurst Hill, Shotover and Clifton are much less interesting, but North Leigh Heath is the only site in the region for western gorse *Ulex gallii*.

5. White helleborine

6. Southern marsh orchid

7. Ghost orchid

8. Male fern and great horsetail

Apart from the transient plants associated with rubbish from Oxford city, some established aliens are worth mention. Birthwort *Aristolochia clematitis* has been known for centuries from an incongruous site, the ruins of Godstow Nunnery. Martagon lily *Lilium martagon* is established in plantations in several places; at Marsh Baldon it may have been introduced by the philosopher Jean-Jacques Rousseau. The invasive cock's eggs *Salpichroa origanifolia* grows among nettles in Nuneham Park. Eynsham Park has many aliens near the lake, among which are spring snowflake *Leucojum vernum* and spring cyclamen *Cyclamen coum* in quantity. The large snowdrop *Galanthus elwesii* is naturalized under trees near Longworth, Berks. Sporadic aliens include caraway *Carum carvi*, once found at the BBONT reserve at Sydlings Copse; Breckland speedwell *Veronica praecox*, which maintained itself for a few years in gravel workings near Standlake; and stinking goosefoot *Chenopodium vulvaria*, noted in the Abingdon area in 1890, 1914 and 1955. Oxford Botanic Garden is the original site from which Oxford ragwort *Senecio squalidus* spread over England. Ivy broomrape *Orobanche hederae*, the hawkweed *Hieracium amplexicaule* and the fern *Pteris vittata* are established there at present, while alien plants on other old walls in Oxford city include Cheddar pink *Dianthus gratianopolitanus*, fairy foxglove *Erinus alpinus*, the rampion *Phyteuma scheuchzeri* and the toadflax *Asarina procumbens*. The alien teasel *Dipsacus strigosus* appears sporadically by the Cherwell at St Catherine's College. An old rubbish tip near Stanton Harcourt had another rare teasel *Dipsacus laciniatus*, together with a yellow milfoil *Achillea ageratum* and a rayless mayweed believed to be *Matricaria decipiens*, in 1978 and 1979.

North Oxfordshire

There are few outstanding sites in this area, which is mostly calcareous farm land, with substantial deposits of iron ore. Bruern Wood in the west resembles outliers of Wychwood with acid soil, so that hard fern *Blechnum spicant* and climbing corydalis are found. Near Ardley there is a small site for meadow clary, and dragon's teeth has established itself around Ardley Quarry. Large parks, as at Wroxton and Great Tew, contribute to the landscape more than to the flora. At Heythrop Park one plantation has plenty of the alien Abraham, Isaac and Jacob *Trachystemon orientalis*, and broad-leaved ragwort has been known for many years at Hanwell Castle grounds.

At one time Tadmarton Heath, now a golf course, had a heath flora which included shepherd's cress, but this has not been seen lately. However, a fine stand of heather has invaded the railway banks near Fernhill Farm, and more acid-loving plants may colonize this site.

Bryophytes: Mosses and Liverworts

About 350 species of mosses and liverworts have been recorded from the region, and Dr E. W. Jones has produced an admirable bryophyte flora of Berkshire and Oxfordshire, from which I have drawn freely in what follows. Compared with most of Britain, apart from East Anglia, the region has a low rainfall and relative humidity. This is probably why so many bryophytes which are common in west Britain, such as *Dicranum majus*, *Frullania tamarisci* and *Rhytidiadelphus loreus* are extremely rare and confined to unusually humid sites in our region.

As with the bark lichens described below, several bark-living mosses, such as *Leptodon smithii*, are becoming very rare in the region, and others, such as *Antitrichia curtipendula*, *Orthotrichum obtusifolium* and *O. striatum* are now extinct. On the other hand *Dicranoweisia cirrata*, now common on bark and wood, was apparently rare in the nineteenth century, and *Herzogiella seligeri*, recently seen on logs in Bagley Wood and in Cogges Wood, Oxon, may be spreading. The best sites for bryophytes growing on bark (e.g. *Lejeunea ulicina*, *Neckera pumila*, *Orthotrichum* spp, *Ulota* spp, *Zygodon* spp) are either in ancient forests, wooded ravines such as Taynton Bushes, Oxon, or fen carr as at Cothill, Berks, and Latchford, Oxon. Of particular interest are *Platygyrium repens* from Wychwood and several old woods near Oxford, *Zygodon baumgartneri* from Wychwood and *Z. forsteri* from Burnham Beeches, all of which are rare elsewhere.

A much greater area of old grassland survives along the chalk ridge of the Chilterns and Berkshire Downs than on the limestone of the Oxfordshire Cotswolds. Both habitats have similar bryophytes, including *Barbula acuta*, *Ditrichum flexicaule*, *Entodon concinnus*, *Fissidens cristatus*, *Pleurochaete squarrosa*, *Rhodobryum roseum*, *Scapania aspera*, *Thuidium abietinum* and its subspecies *hystricosum*, *T. philibertii* and *Tortella tortuosa* in favoured sites. Good spots exist at Cherbury Camp, Berks and Wytham Hill, Berks/Oxon, and Stonesfield and Taynton, Oxon on the limestone, and at Ivinghoe Beacon and Ellesborough Warren, Bucks, Watlington Hill and Aston Rowant, Oxon, and Aston Upthorpe and White Horse Hill, Berks, along the chalk scarp. The stubblefield flora is poor on the Cotswolds, but much richer on the chalk, where *Dicranella schreberi*, *Phascum floerkeanum*, *Pottia* spp, *Pterygoneurum ovatum* and *Weissia sterilis* may be found.

The clay soils of the Vale of White Horse in Berkshire and much of north Oxfordshire and north Bucks are bryologically boring, except when the clay has become acid and nutrient-poor by leaching, or on the margins of reservoirs and gravel pits with fluctuating water levels. The former situation occurs in woodland rides in some of the outliers of Wychwood, such as Bould Wood, Cogges Wood, Singe Wood, North Leigh Heath and Ramsden Heath, where acid-loving plants such as *Fossombronia caespitiformis* and *Weissia multicapsularis* have been seen. The exposed mud of the reservoirs near Halton, Bucks and Wilstone, just across the Herts border, have a good ephemeral flora in autumn, while liverworts such as *Blasia pusilla*, *Preissia quadrata* and *Riccia cavernosa* have recently colonized the margins of wet pits near Oxford.

The dry heaths of south Berkshire have few outstanding bryophytes apart from the only 'Atlantic' species of the region, *Leptodontium flexifolium*, which is on Greenham Common and elsewhere. *Buxbaumia aphylla* and *Ditrichum pusillum* have both been found on top of Hurst Hill, a small patch of heath south of Oxford. A rich bryophyte community develops in shallow valley bogs surrounded by heath, as at Chawley pits under Hurst Hill, and in south Berks at Snelsmore Common, Bucklebury Common, Broadmoor Bottom, Owlsmoor and Tower Hill. In association with some of the fourteen species of *Sphagnum* found in such bogs are rarities such as *Cephaloziella elachista*, and *Cryptothallus mirabilis* may be found buried in peaty tussocks of *Molinia*. Some of the cushions of *Leucobryum glaucum* near Rapley lake are 2 metres in circumference and 50 cm high.

Mosses can precipitate calcium carbonate and so give rise to tufaceous deposits around springs in limestone areas. Such deposits occur at Taynton Bushes, Wychwood and Blenheim Park, and are often associated with *Cratoneuron commutatum*, *Eucladium verticillatum*, *Gyroweisia tenuis*, *Philonotis calcarea*, *Riccardia pinguis* and *Solenostoma triste*. Cothill Fen is on outstanding site for bryophytes of wet calcareous situations, such as *Campylium elodes*, *Drepanocladus revolvens*, *Rhizomnium pseudopunctatum* and many others. In this fen, acid-loving mosses such as *Sphagnum palustre* and *S. subnitens* occur in the old peat diggings. Similar, but poorer, fens may be seen at Frilford, Marcham and Wootton, Berks and Bullingdon Bog, Headington Wick, Latchford and Weston-on-the-Green, Oxon.

The mosses of dry limestone walls and roofs in the Cotswolds are less interesting than the lichens. However, a rich flora has developed on rock ledges in some old stone pits, as at Holton, Wytham and Stonesfield, and notably on shaded limestone exposures in hanging woods by the River Evenlode. The latter have *Lejeunea cavifolia*, *Mnium stellare*, *Platydicta confervoides*, *Seligeria* spp, and *Taxiphyllum wissgrillii*, but lichens are shaded out. Submerged limestone in the Thames has two uncommon mosses, *Barbula nicholsonii* and *Octodiceras fontanum*, both of which occur within Oxford city limits, while shaded, fast-flowing streams in north Berks provide a habitat for *Rhyncostegiella curviseta*. The sarsen stones near Ashdown are the only sites in the region for *Grimmia decipiens*, *G. laevigata*, *G. trichophylla* and *Hedwigia ciliata*, some of which may now be lost, together with the liverwort *Frullania tamarisci.* Several species of *Rhacomitrium* are colonizing old slag on railway banks at Mortimer and Twyford, Berks, and Hook Norton, Oxon, often associated with the lichen *Stereocaulon vesuvianum*.

Fungi, including Toadstools and Mushrooms

About a thousand species of fungi have been recorded from the region, but the smaller Ascomycetes and rust and smut fungi are certainly underworked. Frequent forays have been made in the following localities, where the larger fungi are fairly well known: Burnham Beeches, Bucks; Bagley Wood, Bradfield, Buckland Common, Mortimer, Virginia Water and Windsor Park, Berks; and Bix, Crowell Wood, Kingwood Common and Wychwood Forest, Oxon. The appearance of fruiting bodies is often irregular, and may be correlated with particular chemical stimuli, as has been shown by Dr F. B. Hora in experiments near Mortimer.

The outstanding site for fungi in the region is undoubtedly Windsor Park and its environs, which has been thoroughly worked for many years. The flora includes forty-four species of *Boletus* (*sensu lato*), thirty-eight species of the difficult genus *Cortinarius*, nineteen species of *Inocybe* and six of *Hydnellum*. Particular rarities are *Boletus rubinus*, *Pisolithus arrhizus*, *Russula pelargonia* and four species recorded here for the first time in Britain: *Agaricus luteomaculata*, *Inocybe leptocystis*, *Mycena maculata* and *Psathyrella multipedata*.

The long list of species from acid heaths and woods near Mortimer includes the very rare *Lepiota permixta* and *Micromphale cauvetii*. A total of 326 species has been identified from the less acid woodland around Kingwood Common, Oxon, notable among which are *Clitocybe houghtonii* and *Phaeolepiota aurea*; College Wood, nearby, is the source of the fourth British record for *Lactarius mairei.* Many unusual species of *Cortinarius*, *Inocybe* and *Russula* have been reported near Bradfield, while the scarce *Amanita solitaria* occurs near Pangbourne. The relatively dry, mixed woodland in the BBONT Warburg Reserve at Bix has *Hygrophorus lucorum* along rides, and two fungi associated with larch, *Boletus tridentinus* and *Hygrophorus subglobosus*. Extensive beechwoods near Crowell have *Mycena crocata* and the striking *Strobilomyces floccosus*.

Nearer to Oxford the old woodland at Bagley has *Lactarius britannicus*, *Russula carminipes* and a fungus associated with Douglas fir, *Clitocybe ditopus*. Wytham

9. Shaggy cap or lawyer's wig
Coprinus comatus

10. *Volvariella surrecta*

Woods, on calcareous clay, have a different range of species including *Cystoderma superbum*, *Inocybe auricoma*, *Naucoria centunculus* and *Psathyrella orbitarum*. Both woods are remarkable for the number of fungi growing on wood. On the sandy soil of north Berkshire, *Agaricus bresadolae* and *Tricholoma constrictum* are notable rarities from Kingston Bagpuize, while Tubney Wood has the second British record of the ascomycete *Thumerella britannica*; at Buckland Warren, the parasitic *Volvariella surrecta* has been found growing on old *Clitocybe nebularis*. Blenheim Park is one of the few sites where *Boletus satanas* has been seen, and deserves more study. Before 1939 many unusual species were recorded from Wychwood Forest, among them *Conocybe pygmaeo-affinis*, *Lepiota setulosa*, *Mycena hiemalis* and *Russula maculata*: the record for *Lactarius pterosporus* is doubtful.

Lichens

About 400 species of lichens have been recorded from the region, 80 per cent of which have been seen recently. Pre-twentieth-century records from a few sites (Banbury, Oxford, Oxon; Stowe, Stokenchurch, Bucks; Windsor, Berks) show that significant extinctions have occurred among bark lichens, owing to pollution of the atmosphere by sulphur dioxide and other causes. The least polluted parts of the region are those furthest from London (west Berkshire, north-west Bucks and north Oxfordshire), and here the larger trees bear a base-rich *Xanthorion* community with *Buellia* spp, *Diploicia canescens*, *Physcia* spp, *Ramalina* spp and *Xanthoria parietina*. Woodland trees may have a *Parmelion* community with *Evernia prunastri*, *Parmelia glabratula*, *P. sulcata* and *P. subrudecta*, but *P. perlata* is very rare. The pollution-sensitive *Lobarion* community of old forests, which herbarium records show to have persisted at Bagley Wood, Berks, and Stokenchurch, Bucks, in the early nineteenth century, is now extinct in the region. Of the thirty bark lichens listed as characteristic of old woodland by Francis Rose, the region has eleven, plus five thought to be extinct. Wychwood Forest, Oxon, retains eight; Blenheim Park, Oxon, and Burnham Beeches, Bucks, four each; Windsor Park, Berks, three; Bix, Oxon; Bucklebury Common, Hamstead Park, Snelsmore Common, Berks; and Salcey Forest, Bucks two each. This evidence pinpoints Wychwood as the site with greatest ecological continuity with primeval forest.

One of our most local bark lichens is *Catillaria bouteillei*, which has been seen on leaves and twigs of box *Buxus sempervirens*, near Chequers, Bucks and Hinton Waldrist, Berks. *Parmeliopsis ambigua* is not uncommon, but may be invading the region from the north, as there are no old records. The same may be true of *Bryoria*

11. Lichens on blackthorn

fuscescens and *Pseudevernia furfuracea*, both scarce, but which may be colonizing bark rendered acid by pollution. Although the region does not possess the lichenological interest of west Britain, a plant found on elm bark near Burford, Oxon, in 1976 is a species of *Ramonia* new to science.

Lichens that grow on the soil are uncommon except on the most acid heaths in south Berkshire, such as Snelsmore Common, Bucklebury Common and the large area around Crowthorne, where numerous *Cladonias* occur, including the rare *C. glauca*. Lichen heaths are sometimes seen elsewhere, as on the acid summits of Shotover, Oxon, and Hurst Hill, Berks, and the cinder tracks of old railways. Our chalk grassland is usually too dense for lichens, but a good lichen sward is found on shallow soil in old limestone quarries, as at Dry Sandford and Wytham Hill, Berks/Oxon and Taynton, Oxon. The pit at Wytham is the only locality in the region for the rare and conspicuous *Psora decipiens*.

Although natural limestone exposures are of doubtful occurrence in the region, there is a well-marked group of limestone lichens with a distribution over the 'Cotswold' area of north-west Oxfordshire and north-west Berkshire, but largely absent elsewhere. These are to be found on dry limestone walls, in old churchyards and on the Stonesfield slate roofs of old farm buildings. They include *Acarospora glaucocarpa*, *Acrocordia conoidea*, *Aspilicia prevostii*, *Caloplaca flavirescens*,

C. lactea, *C. velana*, *Dermatocarpon* spp, *Lemmopsis arnoldiana*, *Leptogium* spp, *Opegrapha persoonii*, *O. saxatilis*, *Petractis clausa*, *Rinodina bischoffii*, *Solenopsora candicans*, *Staurothele* spp, *Thelidium* spp and *Toninia lobulata*. The most notable is perhaps *Staurothele catalepta* from Wolvercote, as all other British records are from Ireland.

There are a few natural sandstone boulders or sarsen stones around Ashdown and Lambourn in west Berks, on which several species occur which are known nowhere else in the region, though some are common in north and west Britain, e.g. *Aspilicia caesiocinerea*, *Buellia saxorum*, *Candelariella corallorhiza*, *Fuscidea cyathoides*, *Lecanora rupicola*, *Parmelia conspersa*, *P. ioxodes*, *Pertusaria pseudo-corallina*, *Ramalina siliquosa* and *Rinodina atrocinerea*. One or two of these occur on puddingstone boulders at Bradenham, Bucks. The remarkable occurrence of the highland lichen *Stereocaulon vesuvianum* on slag by the railway lines at Twyford, Berks and Hook Norton, Oxon is also worth mention. The related *S. pileatum* has recently colonized old brick walls in Oxford and Reading and is believed to have an affinity for lead.

Freshwater Algae and Stoneworts

Freshwater algae have received very little attention in the region. The calcareous stoneworts *Chara* and *Tolypella* spp are mostly rare and transient inhabitants of shallow ponds and gravel pits with hard, phosphate-poor water; only *Chara vulgaris* is at all common. Species of *Nitella*, which are not encrusted with lime, have been seen in acid pools near Ufton Nervet and Sandhurst, Berks.

Three accounts of the microscopic algae of the Thames have been published in the last seventy-five years. The dominant species in the spring bloom is the siliceous diatom *Stephanodiscus hantzschii*: other diatoms and green algae such as *Scenedesmus acuminatus* are often abundant, while yellow-green and blue-green algae are much less common. Some minor changes in the algal flora of the Thames may be correlated with increasing richness in nutrient salts. For example, the concentration of phosphate in the river rose from 0.3 mg/litre in 1935 to 2.4 mg/litre in 1968.

5 Mammals

JAMES A. BATEMAN

Forty species of mammals have been recorded in Berkshire, Buckinghamshire and Oxfordshire in recent times, but one or two of these are unlikely to be found now. Absence of a record does not of course necessarily mean the absence of a species, but where there are also known distributional trends it leaves no great hope for survival.

None the less, it is essential to point out that the distribution and status of mammals could appear distinctly odd in many instances if we were to rely entirely on established records. For many creatures our recent records are not so much an indication of the territory occupied, as evidence of the presence of recorders and the local activity of the institutions from which they operate. It follows that one will expect concentrations of records around centres such as Reading and Oxford with their universities and Woodstock and Aylesbury with their museum-based biological record centres. True distributional patterns can be established only by employing conjecture and intelligent expectation based upon the habits of the animals, together with whatever verified records are available.

Distributional records also follow fashions and current interests, and clearly some mammal groups are less popular than others, sometimes because their habits and behaviour make observation difficult. Bats are a good example of this but the use of new identification techniques such as the analysis of ultrasonic wave records, can now make their distribution easier to study. The mammals mentioned here are not solely native British species but include a number of introductions.

Natural barriers such as the high ground of the Chilterns, the Cotswolds and the Berkshire Downs, and the river valleys of the Thames and Cherwell, can limit the spread of some species and provide areas of containment for others.

The hedgehog *Erinaceus europaeus* is common in all three counties. In Oxfordshire, large numbers are reported from the Vale of White Horse west of Wantage and from the Chilterns down to Sonning and Caversham. They extend into Berkshire where, although undoubtedly present in rural areas, Carter (1973) suggested that they might be commoner in suburban areas from the numbers of road casualties reported, but this is more likely to be the result of a higher pressure from traffic in suburbs. They can certainly be seen at night crossing roads within and between villages.

Moles *Talpa europaea* are not found on very high ground and few are recorded from the tops of the Cotswolds and Chilterns, where the soil may be too shallow for burrowing. In central Oxfordshire there are large numbers, as there are also in the north-east of the county and in the Vale of White Horse. Similarly, they are common in the south-east and on into Berkshire, being well recorded around Reading and to the west of the county. The evidence of moles is usually the presence of molehills, but occasionally there are road casualties and records of captures by cats. Moles may be flooded out of their tunnels and found dead on the surface during very wet weather. An absence of molehills need not imply an absence of moles, since once a tunnel system has been established in untilled land fresh hills will seldom appear.

Since the common shrew *Sorex araneus* frequents mainly uncultivated land with tree cover or rough grassland it is not surprising to find it unrecorded in the large areas of the counties where arable farming is practised. It is found scattered in central Oxfordshire between the Chilterns and the Cotswolds, but is more abundant in central Berkshire. Records are from trapped specimens, from skeletal remains in bottles and tins, and from owl pellets. Captures by cats provide frequent indications. By comparison, numbers of the pygmy shrew *Sorex minutus* appear to be lower. A survey of Wytham Woods, near Oxford, in 1954 allowed Southern to give a ratio of pygmy to common shrew of 1:7, but this could be an underestimate for grassland. The pygmy shrew is found more commonly in central Oxfordshire than elsewhere in the county, but there are records from Henley. Similarly, Carter has suggested that these shrews are less numerous than common shrews in Berkshire, particularly in the Reading area. Reports for 1971 from the Newbury Environmental Study Group indicated its presence in south-western Berkshire. Here again records are usually based on trapping surveys, finds in discarded bottles and cans, road casualties, and owl pellets. The water shrew *Neomys fodiens* is a shy and elusive animal and likely to be more numerous than records suggest. Seven recent records from Oxfordshire include a specimen trapped in Wytham Wood, one at Aston Rowant NNR in 1977 and an interesting instance of one found in a domestic trap in Woodstock. Although, as the name suggests, they are usually found near water, they are also not infrequently found in drier areas; they have been taken on both the dry Berkshire Downs and on the Chilterns. R. C. Lougher reported water shrews trapped in Wytham Woods, half a mile from water, and in tawny owl pellets at Wytham one in every thirty shrews was a water shrew.

Ten species of bats are recorded from the area. Carter (1973) mentions a mouse-eared bat *Myotis myotis* from the Reading area in 1933, considered to be a vagrant. There have been no other records of this rare British bat since in the area. One of the rarer bats recorded recently is the whiskered bat *Myotis mystacinus*, but there are still only two records in the Oxfordshire County Museum Record: one was seen basking in the sun with a pipistrelle on the chalet roof at Wytham, the other, in September 1979, was from Ducklington. A record near Reading appeared in the *Reading Naturalist* for 1966. There is a probable record for Natterer's bat *Myotis nattereri* seen at close range by Fitter in 1956 at Chinnor, Oxon. A single record from near Maidenhead, Berks, was reported in the *Reading Naturalist* for 1965. Daubenton's bat *Myotis daubentoni* has not recently been recorded from Oxfordshire, but it was seen over water near Windsor, Berks, in the 1930s. South of Reading a locality for it is listed in the *Reading Naturalist* of 1975 and the Newbury Environmental Study Group Report for 1975 has an unconfirmed report for the Newbury area. The serotine bat *Eptesicus serotinus* was recorded at Broughton Poggs, Oxon, in September 1979 on the basis of a combination of flight behaviour observed in a farmyard and ultrasonic wavelength analysis of sound emissions recorded at 40 kilohertz. There is also an unconfirmed report in the *Reading Naturalist* for 1976 of one west of Reading. Leisler's bat *Nyctalus leisleri* has been reported in the area only in the 1971 report of the Newbury Environmental Study Group, from Newbury. There are five recent records in Oxfordshire for the noctule *Nyctalus noctula*, three in central Oxfordshire, including one at Wytham Woods and one near the River Glyme at Woodstock. One recorded by Reading Museum was at Emmer Green and another at Sonning Eye. Carter (1973) noted that is was relatively common and had been seen near water, and that records existed for Windsor, near Reading, and undetailed reports from near Newbury.

The commonest species in the area is the pipistrelle *Pipistrellus pipistrellus* and, at any one place, it is likely to be the most numerous. It is frequently seen in flight between trees and above hedgerows, but also close to buildings. Recent records suggest that it is restricted to the centre of Oxfordshire, although this may not be its real distribution. It has been recorded during surveys by Oxford University at Wytham Woods (pre-1970) and there are records at Reading Museum from the Sonning area and Caversham. There have been continuous records from the Windsor area since the early 1970s and more recently it has figured in reports of the *Reading Naturalist* for the Reading area. In Oxfordshire there are only two recent records of the barbastelle *Barbastella barbastellus*, one being from the 1960 survey of Wytham and the other a specimen found by R. S. R. Fitter at Nettlebed in June 1961. This bat has also been recorded near Maidenhead by the Middle Thames Natural History Society. The long-eared bat *Plecotus auritus* is fairly common and easily identified when not on the wing by its exceptionally long ears. Except for one record by Fitter at Chinnor, the remainder for Oxfordshire are from the central area. In 1979 one was caught at Wilcote and one was found dead in a garden at Wootton by Woodstock. Two were recorded in a survey of Wytham Woods and, also west of Oxford, two more were caught in mist nets and later released. It is common in the Reading area, but has also been recorded from the Windsor area, Wokingham, and Bracknell. In west Berkshire there are records from the Newbury and Hungerford districts.

The brown hare *Lepus capensis* occurs most frequently in open country and is seen particularly during the spring in fields of young cereal crops. Both rabbit and hare populations appear to vary on a cyclical basis, probably over a period of four to five years, in all three counties. Hares are particularly numerous in central Oxfordshire within the area between Chipping Norton, Witney, and Bicester, but they also occur in the south-east from Chinnor down to Sonning. They have been recorded from most parts of Berkshire, except the south-east. Records have been established mainly from sightings of single animals or groups; indeed, a group of ten was seen feeding on corn in a field near Charlbury in April 1977. Inevitably they fall foul of the motor car and many records are from adult and juvenile road casualties.

The rabbit *Oryctolagus cuniculus* seems largely to have recovered from the severe attacks of myxomatosis during 1954–5, but outbreaks still occur from time to time and exert a check on local populations. Though rabbits are numerous in many areas, there are still places where they are scarce. Like hares, rabbits in Oxfordshire are most numerous in the central area, but large numbers do occur in the south between Abingdon and Wantage. They are rare in north Oxfordshire around Banbury. Around Reading they are said to be numerous in heathland and woodland fringes, but numbers decline towards Newbury and Hungerford. They are sporadically numerous in Bucks where, as in the other counties, local outbreaks of myxomatosis take their toll. Sightings, road casualties, and active warrens provide information for records.

The sad saga of the disappearance of our native red squirrel *Sciurus vulgaris* from much of Britain is now well documented. Carter has written it off for Berkshire and the same might apply in Oxfordshire where the last record was in spring 1964 at Magdalen College, Oxford. Bucks has no recent records. In Oxfordshire the grey squirrel *Sciurus carolinensis,* which came from North America, is common in areas with broad-leaved trees, but less so in coniferous forests, over the central region of the county between the Cotswolds and Chilterns, and in the north around Banbury. It is also common in the south-east and over the border into Berkshire, and is found in suburban areas and large private gardens, often close to houses. Records are established from live sightings, from numerous road casualties, and from the evidence of chewing patterns on nuts. It is usually considered a pest and trapped or shot by foresters and gamekeepers.

The attractive dormouse *Muscardinus avellanarius* is sporadically distributed. Carter suggests that its dependence upon hazel nuts as a staple article of diet in Berkshire at least, limits it mainly to large stands of fruiting hazel. Within Berkshire there are records from around the Reading area and southwards to the Hampshire border, also in the west around Newbury and northwards across the border into south-east Oxfordshire, where most sightings have been around Nettlebed, in the Warburg Reserve at Bix, on Chinnor Hill and in the Aston Rowant NNR. Elsewhere in Oxfordshire the only other sightings have been in Wychwood Forest. They occur in south-west Bucks and records include one at Lane End in 1968 and one brought by a cat into a house at Saunderton in 1977. The fat dormouse *Glis glis,* a Continental species, was introduced into Hertfordshire, and when it was released at Tring in 1902 it soon spread so that an inquiry by H. V. Thompson in 1951 showed it occupying a territory of 100 square miles within a triangle between Luton, Aylesbury, and Beaconsfield. There is little evidence to suggest much expansion since. Besides being larger than the native species, it has a less restricted diet and a wider habitat preference.

In the British Association Report of 1954 on the Fauna of the Oxford Region the harvest mouse *Micromys minutus* was described as very rare. A renewed interest in its distribution, stimulated by the recent work of Harris, suggests that it is not so rare as was supposed although it may occur more commonly among reeds than in cereal crops. In this context Carter reports that in Berkshire it is most numerous in reed beds along the River Kennet. In Oxfordshire the most northerly records are from Blackthorn in the east of the county and Ascott-under-Wychwood in the west. They have been seen in the Oxford area and around Watlington and one was recorded in the Aston Rowant NNR. Some records are from trapped specimens but most come from the discovery of nests.

The wood mouse *Apodemus sylvaticus* is the commonest and most numerous mouse in Britain and is generally distributed throughout the three counties, although it seems to be absent from some of the higher exposed areas of the Cots-

1. Wood mouse at larder in old blackbird's nest

wolds and Chilterns and is less common in the northern areas of Oxfordshire and Bucks. The usual habitats are woodland and scrubland, but it is frequently found in hedgerows and may well enter domestic premises and other buildings. In rural and suburban areas the wood mouse is probably commoner in houses than the house mouse. Records have come from live-trapping, sightings, owl pellet analysis, skeletal remains in discarded bottles and cans, and from chewed nuts showing typical tooth patterns. Although the slightly larger yellow-necked mouse *Apodemus flavicollis*, occupies similar habitats, it has never been so numerous nor so widespread, usually occurring in small groups, scattered throughout the three counties. One such pocket occurs in the Newbury area and isolated records have come from the Oxfordshire/Berkshire border, south of Blewbury, the Warburg Reserve at Bix and from the Oxford city and Cholsey areas.

The house mouse *Mus musculus* appears less often in the plague proportions once common with this species and no longer associates mainly with buildings. Carter suggested that modern building techniques and materials may discourage colonization and probably newer packaging and storage techniques also contribute to the decline, but some buildings remain infested: for example, in 1973 Carter noted large numbers still in Reading Town Hall; restaurants also find them a problem.

The brown rat *Rattus norvegicus* is widespread, associated more particularly with suburban and rural areas, especially farms with stores of grain and animal feeding stuffs. Because of their pestilent competition with man for stored food, farmers, horticulturists, and gamekeepers constantly wage war on these rats. There are numerous records from the three counties and it is unlikely that many areas are free from them. They are frequently sighted during the daytime and often become road casualties; they are caught by dogs kept for the purpose and of course they are trapped. Apart from being in farming areas, brown rats now habitually scavenge at rubbish tips. From records they appear to be less common on higher ground and this applies especially to the Cotswolds and to a lesser extent the Chilterns.

The diurnal bank vole *Clethrionomys glareolus* is often seen in its usual habitats but untrained observers may have difficulty in distinguishing it from the field vole *Microtus agrestis*. It commonly occurs in undisturbed river valley woodland, where it often becomes the dominant small mammal. In Oxfordshire it is mostly recorded from the central triangular area between Witney, Chipping Norton and Woodstock, but other records show its presence in the Vale of White Horse and in the Chinnor area to the south-east of Oxford. Berkshire records refer mainly to the area around Reading, but there are some from the south-western area around Newbury. According to Moore (1967), observations in the Milton Keynes area of north Bucks suggest that bank voles can colonize disused railway lines, such as those around Newport Pagnell and Wolverton, but they are also found among the vegetation of hedgerows and ditches. The water vole *Arvicola terrestris* is commonly seen along the banks of streams, rivers, and reservoirs, often grooming its fur on a sunny day. In Oxfordshire records have come from the Rivers Glyme and Evenlode, the Oxford and Woodstock canals, water meadows near Cholsey and pools at Sutton Courtenay. In Berkshire they are found along the banks of the Kennet and the Thames and at the edges of lakes and water-filled gravel pits. In Bucks they are recorded from the Rivers Ouse and Thames and along the Grand Union Canal.

The field vole, recognized from its short tail, is found more particularly in grassland, but has proved a pest in young forestry plantations because it nibbles bark from seedling trees and frequently destroys them. It inhabits hedgerows where the grass verge is left uncut and similarly invades disused railway lines, where the grass grows tall. As a common species there are few areas in the three counties where this vole cannot be found and records come from live-trapping, captures by cats, from owl pellets, and from skeletal remains in discarded bottles and cans found around the countryside.

There are few areas in the three counties where foxes *Vulpes vulpes* are not found.

2. Fox cubs

In Oxfordshire the central area between the Cotswolds and Chilterns is thick with records but, although they do occur on the hilltops, there are fewer records from such locations. In Bucks, Fraser (1956) noted that fox numbers were increasing in urban fringes where the animals enjoyed greater protection from hunting. This is a trend elsewhere and foxes have also taken to scavenging food from dustbins on domestic premises. Carter noted that north of the Thames calling foxes were spaced one to every two kilometres, but he also found that suburban populations were even more concentrated. Zoologists at the University have recently been carrying out research on the large urban fox populations of Oxford city. Apart from sightings many records came from road casualties and, in some instances, evidence is provided by an obviously occupied earth. Total numbers either remain constant or increase, even though there are fluctuations in numbers of rabbits and hares, an important food group for foxes.

The numbers of stoats *Mustela erminea* probably vary in response to seasonal fluctuations in rabbit populations, because stoats, unlike foxes which are more omnivorous, depend more heavily on rabbits for their food. In Oxfordshire records indicate a heavy concentration of stoats within the area between Chipping Norton, Witney, and Steeple Aston. There are records from the south-east and also in the north, but higher levels of the Cotswolds and Chilterns seem to be without records, probably because stoats tend to prefer lower ground where they inhabit hedgerows and stone walls as well as woods. They appear to be common around Reading and also in west Berkshire around Newbury and Hungerford. The distribution pattern for the weasel *Mustela nivalis* follows closely that of the stoat but, since weasels have a wider range of prey, their population numbers may remain more constant and the total quantity probably is often double the number of stoats. Both species occupy similar habitats, but again the much smaller weasel can make use of more restricted cover. The wild or feral form of the domesticated polecat/ferret *Mustela putorius furo* turns up from time to time. In the polecat/ferret cross form it could easily be misidentified as a polecat but, in our area such sightings are almost certainly ferret crosses, since the eastward spread of true polecats from Wales is still some distance from the west Oxfordshire border. Crosses have been recorded from the Combe Wood area of Oxfordshire and near Hopcroft's Holt Inn at the Steeple Aston turn on A423. Reading Museum has a record of one from Caversham in 1951, and doubtless ferrets will continue to escape from their owners.

Since the American mink *Mustela vison* was introduced to Britain for fur farming and subsequently escaped, it has rapidly spread through our river valleys. It is uncertain whether or not its presence has influenced the decrease of the otter, but

3. Stoat at rabbit kill

its ability to colonize rivers and breed readily has marked it as a pest to river bailiffs and fishermen. Although rigorously trapped it seems impossible to eradicate it. In Oxfordshire mink have been killed in Cornbury Park near Charlbury, at Ashford Mill on the River Evenlode, and there has been trapping in Blenheim Park. One was killed on the road near Weston Turville reservoir, Bucks in 1967 and it certainly occurs elsewhere in the county. Carter noted its presence in the Kennet and Pang valleys.

The badger *Meles meles* occurs in large numbers in the three counties, but is probably less uniformly distributed than the fox, because it has quite specific environmental requirements when constructing a set. It prefers the cover of woodland especially when on a well-drained slope into which it can burrow. The Chilterns are clearly favoured, except for parts of the clay plateau. Sets in Dyson's Wood, Crosscroft Wood, Turner's Farm, and Gravel Hill, all in south-west Oxfordshire, are recorded at Reading Museum from before 1970. More recently a set has been recorded in Glympton Wood and one killed on the A423 near Hopcroft's Holt Hotel in March 1980, together with bedding noticed by E. J. Glenton in March 1978 as having been carried across a stream at Tackley, all point to the presence of sets in the area between Woodstock and Lower Heyford. The carriage of soiled bedding across a stream confirms the fastidiousness of the badger in keeping its set clean. There are numerous records from Berkshire, particularly in the central and south-western areas, but few sets are recorded from the Cotswolds.

The present-day concern for the status of the otter *Lutra lutra* is amply justified if the records in the three counties are to serve as a guide to the national situation. There are only five post-1970 records in Oxfordshire. These include a sighting by R. Cool of one swimming across the River Cherwell near Tackley in 1975, one at Swinford Bridge (near the Rose Revived inn), one in the River Evenlode at Ashford Mill in 1977, and one by R. C. Lougher at South Stoke on the Thames. Carter considered that there were no residents in the Reading area, but there are records from the Newbury district. New records should be checked nowadays to ensure that there has been no confusion with mink.

No red deer *Cervus elaphus* have been recorded recently in Oxfordshire, but Carter noted that in 1973 two were sighted by an experienced deer watcher at Padworth and one must speculate whether or not there might have been any spread from there. The Sika deer *Cervus nippon*, an introduced species, has only been recorded from two sites, Kingswood in central Oxfordshire and Wychwood Forest. Suggested records appeared in the *Reading Naturalist* for 1975 and 1977 respectively north-east and south-west of Reading. The fallow deer *Dama dama* is not a native but it has a long history and is probably better established in Britain than any other deer. It occurs wild in many woodland areas of the three counties, where it generally rests up during the daytime, emerging at dusk to feed on field and sometimes garden crops. There are records from central and south-eastern Oxfordshire including Glympton Wood in 1980 and from Wychwood Forest in the west. They occur in and around Holton Wood, Stonor Deer Park, and the Warburg Reserve at Bix. Records in the Reading Museum show them to occur in central and western Berkshire and also in south Bucks. The native British roe deer *Capreolus capreolus* was once common all over the country and is now spreading again through the three counties. Carter suggested that it had appeared in 1972 at Mortimer near Reading, after being seen in 1971 at Virginia Water. It has been recorded in the south and east of Oxfordshire. Four were seen at Buckland Warren and odd ones have been recorded in Wychwood Forest, at Aston Rowant and Kingswood. The most successful of our introduced deer must be the muntjac *Muntiacus reevesi*. It is well established in all three counties, being found broadly around Oxfordshire, particularly in the Chilterns, the central area, Wychwood Forest and Blenheim Park. It also occurs in Windsor Great Park, as well as extensively in the Reading area. Carter reported two Chinese water deer *Hydropotes inermis* in Berkshire, one on the border near Silchester and one at Marsh Benham near Newbury, and noted that this species had adapted to dry habitats.

6 Birds

W. D. CAMPBELL

These three Thames counties are a typical slice of lowland England and as such have the birds that are typical of a mainly agricultural countryside: Berkshire has the remains of its heaths, Buckinghamshire has its beechwoods, Oxfordshire its Cotswold limestone; all three have the chalk grassland of the Chilterns and the Berkshire Downs. But none of these habitats has any really unusual regularly breeding birds, except for the few stone curlews that still breed on the downs, the handful of dippers in Cotswold Oxfordshire, and the small colony of firecrests in Bucks. The birds that birdwatchers go out to see in the three counties are those that they might see over a wide stretch of England south of the Trent: great crested grebe and tufted duck on the pits and ponds, grey heron and kingfisher by the waterside, woodcock, sparrowhawk and nuthatch in the woods, and corn bunting and the two partridges on the farmland.

The maps in *The Atlas of Breeding Birds of Britain and Ireland* (1976) reveal an interesting connection between topographical features and species in the area. The northern limits of the Berkshire downs and the Chilterns form a boundary separating the known breeding sites of curlew and dipper (north of the line) from the far more numerous species (woodlark, stonechat, wood warbler, nightjar, stone curlew and cirl bunting) now almost entirely confined to the region south of it.

An interesting theme for idle speculation (rendered even more interesting by the fact that from the outset one knows that an answer is unattainable) is to imagine what was the bird population of our area before man began to influence his surroundings significantly. Before Neolithic man began making inroads with stone, axe, and fire to practise primitive agriculture, much of our area must have been dense woodland on the drier ground, while the valleys would have been mazes of marsh and carr. Dense woodland is inhabited by comparatively few specialist species so that the forests themselves were probably no more heavily populated than are their remnants today. But vast stretches of woodland must have had equally vast areas of the most favoured habitat for a great number of bird species—more open scrub and woodland edge vegetation. The marshes, with pools and reedbeds, would undoubtedly have held a huge population of waterfowl, both breeding birds and winter visitors, and there is quite recent evidence of this in nineteenth-century accounts from Otmoor, north-east of Oxford, one of the last remnants of such sites. The Otmoor waterfowl were sufficiently numerous to enable the duck decoy at Boarstall, now run as a research project by BBONT, to be run commercially.

Apart from the gradual changes in habitat brought about by clearance of woodland and drainage of marshes, two other factors, historically much more recent, must have played a significant part in either enhancing or diminishing the conditions favourable for certain species. The first, dating from the Roman occupation onwards, was the construction of permanent stone or brick dwellings, ultimately increasing sites for all our three swallow species, directly for swallows and house martins and indirectly enabling the sand martin to exploit the banks of sand- and clay-pits excavated for building materials. One can safely assume that 2,000 years ago when these species were limited by the availability of such natural nesting sites as caves for swallows, cliffs with eave-like overhangs for house martins, and workable strata in river banks for sand martins, all three would have been comparative rarities. Swifts, barn owls and house sparrows come into the same category, although one can imagine sparrows exploiting the first Neolithic farmers' corn before the 'house' epithet became applicable, for then as now house sparrows, betraying their weaverbird ancestry, could have built their shaggy-domed nests in trees and bushes.

The second factor must surely have been the use of gunpowder to kill flying birds. It is perhaps significant that some of the earliest guns were known either as 'muskets' which originally meant male sparrowhawk, or 'fowling pieces', because before their advent the killing of birds in flight by arrows was a chancy business with the odds strongly in favour of the birds. A direct result was more killing of game birds and wildfowl for sport, leading to the rearing and preservation of game, in our area pheasants and partridges, with emphasis on the exclusion of human or avian competitors from the sacred preserves. The results were twofold: the sites were left undisturbed and therefore became ideal breeding grounds for other small birds, while on the other hand the price paid in the destruction of some of our larger and nobler avifauna, particularly hook-beaked species such as hawks and owls, has been high. On the other hand, the smaller numbers of these, and of carrion crows, jays and magpies (all commonly seen on keepers' gallows in former days) undoubtedly favoured the breeding success of small song-birds.

The earliest form of farming—pastoral—had already begun to alter our local

1. Sparrowhawk brooding young

landscapes long before agriculture speeded up the process. It is now considered that what was once accepted as 'natural' downland on our chalk and limestone hills—the short lawn-like turf, treeless except for dwarf scrub of thorn or juniper—is just as artificial as hedged or walled ploughland. Centuries of grazing by sheep, assisted much later in the story by rabbits, ensured that there would be no regeneration of woodland trees—thus producing the ideal habitat for wheatears, whinchats and stone curlews.

The coming of the plough culminated in the creation of 'typical' rural scenery of hedged fields, a landscape probably at its zenith about a century ago when the hedgerow planting of trees by landowners of the previous two centuries came to maturity. This must have brought about a significant change in bird populations, because before arable land became available it is difficult to imagine any natural habitat suitable for a large population of rooks, while stubbles must have enabled many seed-eaters such as finches and buntings to overwinter more successfully than their ancestors had been able to do. The great mileage of hedgerows, many of them eventually overgrown, must also have provided breeding and feeding sites for former woodland-edge birds deprived of their natural habitats by the ever increasing clearance of woodland.

The advent of the breech-loader and cartridges, coupled with game preservation

2. Woodcock brooding eggs

and the collecting mania of the naturalists of the old school, is almost certainly the major reason why it is no longer possible to see groups of three or four kites circling over the river at Folly Bridge, Oxford, or to find marsh harriers as the commonest hawks in the marshy areas around Newbury and Reading. Nor will birdwatchers at Blenheim see a raven nesting on top of the pillar in the Park. All these sights were possible little over a century ago, and it is on record that the last nesting pair of ravens at Blenheim were shot in 1847 by the current 'His Grace'.

But just as significant as the replacement of the muzzle-loader by the modern quick-fire weapon has been the substitution of the tractor for the less powerful teams of horses or oxen to speed the plough. This has resulted in the cultivation of the very summits of the rolling downland. Just thirty years ago I first became familiar with the Berkshire Downs, now partly engulfed in the new Oxfordshire, and at one favourite site—a flint-strewn stretch of almost bare chalk studded with rabbit warrens and bounded by open scrub—I was delighted to find stone curlew, wheatear, woodlark and nightjar breeding. Within a few years, thanks to the tractor, fertilizers and subsidies, it was considered worthwhile to bring this last remnant of unspoilt downland into cultivation, and barley replaced the viper's bugloss, candytuft and rock-rose, and of course the typical birds of the former habitat disappeared. Almost adjoining this site was a little knoll in a valley famed

3. Curlew with newly hatched chick

4. Barn owl

5. Tawny owl with earthworm at nest hole

for its crowning glory of pasque flowers—I once estimated around 2,000 clumps in full bloom—and also raddled with rabbit burrows in which wheatears nested. At this period rabbits were so plentiful that they kept the hillock as effectively grazed as the former sheep had done, thus rendering the site suitable for both pasque flowers and wheatears. With the outbreak of myxomatosis in 1954 the grass grew apace and effectively smothered both the plants and the nesting holes, and the former glory departed.

With Dutch elm disease destroying the landscape created by far-seeing landowners of former centuries (altruistic, even if one eye was on the subsequent economic return in the form of timber for their descendants) and the ever-increasing uprooting of hedges to form fields more suitable for modern mechanized agriculture, coupled with drainage schemes to convert hitherto unmanageable low-lying areas into arable land, one would assume that there must be a general decline both in total bird population and in the number of species.

Other factors which within the last few decades must have reduced both the numbers and the variety of species of birds within the three counties are: the replacement of deciduous woodland or heath by coniferous plantations, the virtual disappearance of the coppice as a provider of small timber (a habitat which particularly when interspersed with standard oaks probably held a greater variety of birdlife—to say nothing of flora—than any other), and the disappearance of the old open-type of sewage disposal plant, once so attractive to waders on passage, such as the one at Sandford-on-Thames, where greenshanks and little stints could be seen among the onions and sprouts. But in the long term probably the most inhibiting factor affecting bird life will prove to be the increasing use of chemicals as a normal agricultural procedure. The greatest menace, the use of persistent insecticides of the DDT group, so disastrous in the late 1950s and early '60s, has been diminished by legislation here at home, but the same chemicals may still take their toll on migration, and particularly in tropical winter quarters. Even apparently harmless procedures such as the production of weedless crops by the application of herbicides may be indirectly detrimental, as was demonstrated by the investigation into the threatened extinction of our native grey partridge—the attendant insects on the weeds were found to be essential constituents of the diet of the chicks in their first few weeks of life. With the widespread practice of straw-burning in the wake of harvesting, old-fashioned stubbles, often formerly available throughout the winter, have ceased to exist. We are also witnessing the beginning of what will almost certainly be a new era in land tillage—direct drilling into land prepared only by the application of weedkiller—which dispenses, after thousands of years of service, with the plough. If this form of tillage does indeed become general practice one can foresee a drop in the rook population and less inducement for black-headed gulls to winter inland.

From this gloomy overall picture we might well come to the conclusion that loss of habitat must have greatly contributed to the diminution of our local bird population both in total numbers and in variety of species. But not all the losses of formerly regularly breeding species can be attributed to this factor. After an absence of many years I have now returned to a woodland area (Wychwood) with which I first became acquainted as a boy over seventy years ago. Then redstarts nested in the wall of our house, in the high garden wall, in several hollow oaks in the surrounding park, on the ledge inside the eaves of a sawmill, in the quarry and in the drystone supporting wall of a ha-ha, apart from those in the main forest itself. Apart from the quarry face, now overgrown, all the original habitats remain unchanged, yet in the ten years of my renewed acquaintance with the area no redstart has frequented these sites and only the occasional pair appears in the area at all. Likewise there has been no significant reduction in the amount of beechwood available for wood warblers, once common in the Chilterns yet now mainly recorded as a transient spring visitor, proclaiming its presence for a few days by its unmistakeable song and then passing on. Some twenty or thirty years ago the distinguished ornithologist, the late Reg Moreau, accompanying me on a visit to my local pairs of red-backed shrikes, said that the rule for their choice of habitat seemed to be 'the scruffier the better', for whether in the scrubby hedge bounding an airfield, in a disused chalk pit or on a gorsy and thorny common, the unvarying factor was the litter of 'civilization'. Such sites still exist and, thanks to the increased use of non-biodegradable plastic materials, the scruffiness still prevails, but no shrikes are attracted. The regular sites for wrynecks and cirl buntings, albeit never plentiful, have also ceased to be occupied except for a very few pairs of the bunting.

Another factor beyond our control which can affect bird populations is the weather. A recent example was the succession of droughts in the Sahel sub-desert area of Africa, where many of our summer visitors overwinter. This was at first thought to explain the sudden decline in the numbers of whitethroats returning to their breeding grounds, and probably this was correct to a certain extent. But then it was discovered that Continental whitethroats examined on passage contained significant amounts of toxic organochlorines. One of the peculiarities of these compounds is that, although practically insoluble in water, they are readily absorbed by fat or oil, so that lethal doses can accumulate out of circulation in the birds' fatty food-reserve tissues to be tapped with fatal effects in times of food shortage. It is possible that these poisons, wherever they are picked up, may make the difference between death and survival during near-famine conditions in winter quarters. I am convinced that the phenomenal bird deaths resulting from the prolonged cold winter of 1962–3 were aggravated by the presence of DDT, aldrin and dieldrin in the victims' subcutaneous fat, for at that time the use of these pesticides was widespread and uncontrolled.

It has been suggested that an almost imperceptible change in our climate, mainly a lowering of the mean temperature for the year, has been responsible for the disappearance or reduction of some species. This is particularly true of those of the south-eastern quarter of England (in which our counties are marginally included) which even in more favourable climatic conditions were on the northern fringes of their continental distribution. Yet within my lifetime several more southerly species (golden oriole, firecrest, Cetti's warbler, little ringed plover, collared dove) have established themselves in Britain, while at the same time, from the other direction, first tufted duck and much later redwing, fieldfare, Temminck's stint and wood sandpiper have come to stay as British breeding species. All that we can be certain of is that in the lifetime of a birdwatcher there will be ups and downs of both weather and the abundance or dearth of bird species, and no one as yet can correlate the two with any precision.

The first essential for bird life is available habitats. Hedges, copses, marshes and old-type sewage works have greatly diminished, rivers and streams have been dredged and had their banks cleared of vegetation, and stubbles and weedy crops are increasing rarities. But we have only to look at the annual reports of the various ornithological or natural history bodies within the three counties to realize that somewhere a great variety of birds is still to be seen and the list grows annually. Of course more intensive watching by an ever increasing body of competent observers, especially those who undertake regular surveys for wildfowl counts, farmland censuses and the keeping of nest records, is largely responsible for the coverage in our annual bird reports. Even the much-maligned 'ticker' or 'twitcher' may play an important part in ensuring that no rarity passes through his area unseen, for many enthusiasts in this branch of birdwatching are meticulously expert in identification.

Perhaps the greatest habitat gain is water, the vast areas of gravel-pit pools and reservoirs along the Thames and its tributaries. Although there is little left of what must once have been marsh or fen, it is probable that within geologically recent times there were no extensive areas of deep water comparable with those available today. So it is reasonable to assume that today we probably have many more wintering diving ducks and breeding great crested grebes than when only natural waters existed. Indeed even within my experience winter exploitation of such waters seems to be on the increase. Thus whereas some twenty years ago anyone in the Oxford area had to travel to the reservoirs at Staines, Middlesex, to see goosanders, now we can see winter assemblies of over a hundred birds at either a gravel pit or a reservoir within a few miles of the city. Results of years of intensive observation at the old-style sewage farms demonstrated that a great variety of waders, many of them once considered as extreme rarities so far inland, regularly came down both to rest and to feed during both migration periods. It is thus plausible to assume that a short-cut flight path, perhaps from our southern and south-western shores to the region of the Wash, has always been used by waders, terns and gulls on migration. Probably much of this passage takes place at a great height and only a few 'drop outs' come down as tokens of what is happening overhead. I was once fortunate enough to witness such a descent in Berkshire, at the now disused Wallingford sewage farm: one May, out of a clear sky which I had been scanning through binoculars, first a turnstone, then a party of ringed plovers came down, shortly followed by a spiralling mass of black terns, and though none of the terns could be seen overhead yet their numbers increased at every count. Although the almost sterile waters of reservoirs and the absence of suitable shallow muddy shores at most gravel pit pools obviously offer far from ideal feeding sites for transient waders, nevertheless such sites still do on occasion attract waders, terns and gulls in transit—on one day in 1978 no fewer than eleven species of wader stopped, presumably to rest, bathe and drink, on the seemingly inhospitable concrete banks of Farmoor reservoir south-west of Oxford.

But it is not just these transient visitors which are attracted to these artificial banks and waters, for both those which have been left to nature and those which have been planted for amenity (and here it should be noted with commendation that one local firm with branches in all three counties has its own nursery of trees and shrubs for such refurbishing) in due course become breeding habitats for many passerines, including warblers, reed buntings and even the occasional nightingale. Both reservoirs, with their lawn-like surrounds and gravel pits with bare open ground between the regenerating sallows, reeds and willowherb attract several passerine species such as wagtails, pipits and wheatears with the occasional stonechat or whinchat during migration periods and these areas may become the commonest breeding site for yellow wagtails.

The next largest recent change in available habitats has probably been the

6. Dipper

proliferation of conifer plantations on sites of felled deciduous woodland or on otherwise unproductive heath. The resulting landscape is often considered aesthetically undesirable and from the naturalist's viewpoint practically sterile. Certainly mature conifer plantations (unless of larch) can look somewhat dour, but in their early stages they are the next best thing to copses. Until the young trees get within touching distance of one another, particularly if, as is common practice, weeds and shrubs are allowed to flourish in between them, birds of open scrub such as most of the common warblers (including the less common grasshopper warbler), tree pipits, robins, dunnocks, wrens, finches, long-tailed tits and even the odd woodlark or nightjar find such surroundings acceptable. These habitats are of course ephemeral, but so long as quick-return crops such as conifers are the forester's main objective there will always be some plantations in this optimum state, and newly-felled coniferous areas if left to nature for a few years before replanting are far from sterile.

Two other changes are first the increasing popularity of ornamental trees and shrubs in gardens, providing nesting and roosting sites for many species and often winter sustenance in the form of berries, and second the ever-increasing practice of feeding birds in winter. Undoubtedly many first-year birds with a statistically low chance of survival during their first winter survive on this account alone. There is

7. Great spotted woodpecker

the added bonus that kind-hearted householders may become seriously interested in birdwatching. Many records of comparative newcomers to these 'feeding stations', such as those of siskins deep in suburbia, have encouraged their observers to greater interest. Nest-boxes have replaced many of the tree holes and crannies that used to be found in mature trees, but I doubt whether their effect is as beneficial as that of winter feeding. The accommodation may be highly suitable but all too often the territory contains too few insect-infested trees (a deficiency aggravated by the lavish use of garden chemicals) and investigation has shown that tits and other garden nest-box species have a far lower breeding success than woodland nesters.

So to sum up my original idle speculation, I would say that our area, with its still considerable remnants of woodland, heaths, downlands, agricultural land, private estates and above all abundant watery sites, in spite of losses of some species (and not forgetting additions such as collared dove, Cetti's warbler and firecrest) can probably produce as many bird species per annum as it ever did, and long may it continue to do so.

Some birdwatching sites

A great deal of birdwatchers' observation and interest is centred on watery sites—the abundant gravel pit pools and reservoirs and the last remnants of ancient marshes and Victorian sewage farms and, particularly in winter and early spring the flooded or waterlogged meadows in the river valleys. From their open nature and from the large size of the waders and waterfowl found there, such sites are less likely to contain undetected species whether breeding or transient than are woodland or downland habitats where small birds may be overlooked and where a good ear may be of more value than binoculars. It is also significant that many of these watery sites figure largely in the records of birds not specifically associated with such habitats from hobbies and great grey shrikes to warblers, wheatears and swifts, swallows and martins which seem to show up first at such places on arrival or passage. Many reservoirs have lawn-like banks and surroundings attractive to wagtails, pipits and wheatears, and both aquatic insects and those seeking the nectar or pollen on the early-flowering sallows at gravel pits or along riversides provide sustenance for insectivorous warblers and hirundines before such food has become generally abundant, but of course these sites are highly attractive to birdwatchers as well as to birds.

However the stray rarity may choose much smaller pools. Some years ago, in response to a telephone call from a puzzled farm worker who had been watching 'a funny sort of snipe' twirling round and round on a mere duckpond, I found a female red-necked phalarope which stayed for several days—and this with, from a very low altitude, a bird's eye view of both Dorchester and Farmoor reservoirs a few miles away. Similarly, the chain of smallish ponds in Wychwood Forest, formerly never productive of anything unusual, has in recent years provided me with not only my first records for the site of both osprey and bittern, but also with a repeat visit of each in the second year. Such potentially interesting pools cannot be listed in a brief survey, but the major aquatic sites are as follows:

Berkshire: the Kennet valley complex of gravel pits around Burghfield, Aldermaston and Theale (the two latter now mostly united in a vast area); the reed beds of

Thatcham; the gravel pits in the Reading/Sonning area; Radley gravel pits; the reserve on the former sewage farm of Ham Fields near old Windsor; the waters of Windsor Great Park and the borderline territory of Virginia Water.

Buckinghamshire: Wraysbury reservoir and gravel pits; Weston Turville reservoir; Newport Pagnell and Linford gravel pits; Foxcote reservoir; Chesham.

Oxfordshire: Port Meadow in Oxford itself; Farmoor reservoir; the complex of gravel pits around Dorchester; the network of gravel pits in the Stanton Harcourt–Standlake area; Clattercote reservoir (one of Aplin's haunts); the reservoirs of Grimsbury and Byfield (highly productive perhaps simply because they are highly watched); the chain of lakes at Blenheim Park (though because of a change in the water level they no longer attract so many waders, there are still large numbers of breeding, wintering and passage waterfowl, including gadwall); the water meadows between the Cherwell and the Oxford canal in the Somerton area (perhaps the county's most regular winter quarters for wild swans, formerly mainly Bewick's but of late years whoopers have become regular visitors).

At any one of these waters within our three counties there is always the chance of encountering the odd rarity or at least less common species from outright transatlantic foreigners such as ring-necked duck, pectoral sandpiper or lesser yellowlegs to European vagrants such as arctic or great skua, whiskered or white-winged black tern or even storm petrel, little auk, puffin, Manx shearwater and shag. Terns of all our native species occur on both spring and autumn passage from time to time, with common or arctic predominating, but numerically black terns on passage to or from the Continent are the commonest representatives of this group, and in some years huge influxes occur: on 15 September 1974 flocks appeared at waters throughout our whole area and many hundreds, if not thousands, of birds must have been present. But the most interesting tern development within the last few years has been the successful breeding of common terns in at least two of the three counties, each at gravel-pit sites.

Apart from the thousands of mallard, teal, wigeon, pochard and tufted duck frequenting these waters during winter, other species, such as goldeneye, shoveler and pintail and, more recently, goosander, occur regularly, often in considerable numbers, while smew, scaup and red-breasted merganser are regular but sparse visitors and common and velvet scoter, eider and long-tailed duck are less frequent. The newcomer to our list of local breeding ducks, the gadwall, seems to continue its increase, mainly at Windsor and Blenheim Park, with the latter probably its chief breeding centre. But the most unexpected duck to breed so far inland has been the shore-haunting shelduck which has bred at Windsor and still exhibits

8. Long-tailed tit with caterpillar at nest

breeding displays there, although success has not been confirmed recently.

From the increasing number of records of ruddy duck from North America, often in small parties, it seems probable that this will be yet one more species to join the abundant mandarins (from East Asia) of Virginia Water and Windsor as feral birds which have 'gone native', and the wood duck, also from North America, has already bred at Windsor. Genuinely wild native geese are comparative rarities, occasional large flocks of grey geese passing over are likely to be white-fronts on passage to or from Slimbridge, as indicated by checking arrival and departure dates there. The phenomenal increase of the feral Canada goose, especially in the Thames valley, coupled with the popularity of keeping wildfowl on ornamental waters has led these flocks to attract strays from such collections and one must not be surprised to find snow geese (white or blue), greylags, white-fronts, pink-feet barnacles or even bar-headed geese as hangers on in such company. To confuse matters further it seems that interspecific breeding is occurring already, for I have come across an apparent Canada/barnacle brood, and others of less obvious and more unlikely parentage.

In such a water-rich area gulls now abound in winter. Two factors which must have played some part in their recent increase are the concentration of rubbish at huge centralized dumps and the great increase in the area of open water available for roosting sites. Apart from black-heads, lesser black-backs and herring gulls in their thousands, together with common gulls on both Cotswolds and Chilterns, less common species for inland waters—little gull, kittiwake, glaucous and Mediterranean gulls may occur from time to time.

Great crested and little grebe are common at most suitable sites but the other three species, usually confined to offshore water in winter, may come in during certain weather conditions or on passage: early in the winter of 1979 red-necked, black-necked and Slavonian grebe were all recorded, the red-necked in exceptional numbers. Divers too, of all three species, may turn up sporadically.

Mineral extraction creates many suitable habitats from sandy cliffs for sand martins, and at least one stockdove colony, to shallow lagoons with shingly shoals and islets for little ringed plovers, but their impermanence results in their eventual desertion. However, there is as yet no lack of new replacement sites. An interesting development within the last few years has been that the mainly coastal-breeding ringed plover, one of our most familiar passage waders, is establishing itself as a regular breeder on at least three sites near Oxford.

Of passerine newcomers, firecrests, although recorded from all three counties, seem to have established themselves mainly in the Wendover area of Bucks, while

Cetti's warbler first appeared, and one hopes has come to stay, in the reed beds of the Kennet valley in the Newbury area. On the heathlands of all three counties the lingering remnants of declining species such as nightjar, stonechat and woodlark still breed, particularly in east Berkshire, but the stonechat is more widespread as a winter or spring passage visitor. Black redstarts did not keep up their early promise of extensive colonization, but pairs have bred successfully at Windsor, Maidenhead and Bracknell and some are recorded at likely sites annually, while single birds turn up on both passages, and often stay for some time. Cirl buntings have also decreased greatly since the hard winter of 1962–3 and the few known breeding sites still occupied are in the West Wycombe, Chinnor and Goring areas. Nightingales fluctuate in abundance and are still widespread in most seasons, though they have markedly declined in west Oxfordshire during the last decade, no breeding having been recorded for Wychwood Forest where formerly at least half a dozen pairs bred regularly. However the Maidenhead area and the woodlands of the Bucks/Oxon border around Bernwood Forest have shown no decline. Dippers breed with some regularity along a swift brook in north Oxfordshire and occasionally on the Windrush in the Witney area.

7 Reptiles and Amphibians

JAMES A. BATEMAN

These two groups of animals are frequently studied together and collectively referred to as herptiles.

The slow-worm *Anguis fragilis*, a common legless lizard, is generally distributed on lower ground in river valleys but it is also found on heath and downland. It is frequently seen in gardens, particularly where there is shelter under logs or sheets of corrugated iron. More than a dozen slow-worms can be exposed when such shelters are moved, but populations can fluctuate seasonally, probably from temperature and humidity changes which affect the supply of food such as slugs and worms. There are records from around the Oxford and Reading areas, but there is an indication that these reptiles may occur less frequently on the high ground of the Cotswolds and Chilterns.

The sand lizard *Lacerta agilis* has only been recorded from south and east Berkshire. The most recent record, from an undisclosed site in east Berkshire, was noted by the Middle Thames Natural History Society in their report (No. 23) for 1970. Other records in the area date from before the early 1960s.

Although the common lizard *Lacerta vivipara* is likely to be found on higher ground, especially south-facing slopes, there are only a few records from the southern edge of the Chilterns and none from the higher areas of the Cotswolds. Elsewhere, as the name suggests, it is more frequently found and there is a fair number of records from the Reading area and east Berkshire, the sandy areas of Oxfordshire, and the low-lying lands of Bucks. This scattered distribution based upon field records probably reflects the movements of recorders rather than a real scarcity of lizards.

The grass snake *Natrix natrix* is well distributed in the three counties, being found in hedgerows, open forest, heath, and common land. It is common in damp areas, especially lakes, ponds, and reservoirs, but has also been recorded in dry areas away from water. Because of its association with water, it will feed on frogs, toads, and newts and is itself preyed upon by herons. Sloughed skins are found occasionally and road casualties are not uncommon.

1. Young common lizard

2. Grass snake

As a poisonous species the adder *Vipera berus* suffers continual persecution, yet it does not appreciably diminish in numbers in those areas where its presence has been noted. It is common in forestry areas of east Berkshire and on heath and scrubland; Wychwood Forest particularly has a reputation for adders. They are recorded from south-facing slopes of the Chilterns and Cotswolds and are generally found in drier areas less frequented by grass snakes.

Although there have been records of the smooth snake *Coronella austriaca* close to the borders of Berkshire, there has only been one record in the county, on the Hampshire border south of Reading in 1963.

The progressive disappearance of ponds and the decline of many surviving ones inevitably influence the populations of many of our British amphibians, so that the general or local scarcity of some species must be attributable to these factors. According to records the common toad *Bufo bufo* is not as well distributed as might have been expected. It appears largely to be absent from the higher levels of the Cotswolds and Chilterns and even in the valleys it is by no means common, although year-to-year fluctuations may be related to annual spring migrations to the breeding grounds and the variable numbers of fatalities accompanying these. Common toads were only associated with two out of twenty-one ponds and pools in the Oxford area examined by T. R. Halliday. Carter (1973) lists a range of records for the Reading area and east Berkshire but these appear to have been fewer in the last two years than a decade ago. There seems some likelihood that the very rare natterjack toad *Bufo calamita* may still be present in Berkshire south of Reading. The last firm report was in the *Reading Naturalist* of 1963, since when there has been further confirmation by the Middle Thames Natural History Society in 1970.

There are no records for either the edible frog *Rana esculenta* or the marsh frog *Rana ridibunda* in the three counties, but an edible frog has been reported at the King George VI reservoir near Staines, just over the Bucks border. The *Provisional Atlas of the Amphibians and Reptiles of the British Isles*, by Henry Arnold (1973) shows a solid presence of the common frog *Rana temporaria* in south central England, but these records have not been substantiated in recent years. Certainly they still breed in some ponds; Halliday records them in two of his twenty-one ponds around Oxford, and Carter has recent records for it in the Reading area. The generally accepted population decline of the now not so common frog has resulted in most recorders adopting a code of strict confidentiality concerning the sites where it can still be found. Bucks records are predominantly from the east and south of the county.

Oddly, the *Provisional Atlas* suggests a scarcity of newts far greater than that

3. Copulating frogs

indicated for the common frog, and yet these tailed amphibians are likely to be widespread wherever there are pools and ponds. The great crested newt *Triturus cristatus* occurs sporadically throughout the area and has been recorded around Reading and in south-east Berkshire in recent years. It has been recorded at South Leigh, Blenheim, and Kidlington in central Oxfordshire, and Halliday recorded it in nine of twenty-one ponds around Oxford. Clearly the palmate newt *Triturus helveticus* is generally the least common of the three British newts and probably is slowly declining in numbers. According to Carter there seem to have been no records in the Reading area since the early 1960s and Halliday found it in only one of the twenty-one ponds examined in the Oxford area. The smooth newt *Triturus vulgaris* is likely to be found in most lakes and ponds although, once high ground is reached in the Cotswolds and Chilterns, records are likely to be fewer. It appears to be reasonably common in the valleys but the distribution depends entirely upon the presence or absence of suitably permanent pools of water. Halliday found it in nineteen of the twenty-one pools surveyed in the Oxford area.

8 Fishes

MARGARET E. VARLEY

The British freshwater fish fauna has relatively few species compared with the rest of Europe or with temperate North America. This is the result of the Pleistocene ice ages which must have brought about the disappearance of all except a very few fish species (such as char *Salvelinus alpinus*). When the ice retreated rivers could be recolonized from two sources: firstly, species which could move through coastal waters and estuaries (salmon, trout, minnow), and secondly, species which could move through river connections that existed until the rise in level of the North Sea and the English Channel cut Britain off from continental Europe. The Great Ouse and the Thames were probably connected with a large continental river, now represented by the Rhine, and part of our fauna probably derived from this source. The present fish faunas of these two British rivers include the majority of British species. They lack species associated with deep, cool lakes (char, whitefishes *Coregonus* spp) and adult sea trout are, at present, absent, but almost all the native cyprinid species are present.

From medieval times, fish faunas have been affected by human activity. On the negative side, pollution has rendered waters unsuitable for fishes: salmon were native to the Thames until the last century. On the positive side, fish species have been introduced both from other British waters and from abroad, either for food or to provide sport for anglers. This process continues and fish farms, usually producing rainbow trout, are being established; anglers frequently move fishes, especially into new still waters provided by new reservoirs or the flooding of gravel pits. As a result the area contains a considerable diversity of fishes and some waters contain unexpected species. Salmon fry *Salmo salar* from Scotland have been introduced into the Windrush as part of an attempt to restore a salmon run to the Thames. Adult salmon were caught by anglers in 1983.

The flowing waters of the area include all sizes from small streams to the large main channel of the Thames. Local geology is dominated by chalk or limestone and many of the tributaries of the Thames are chalk streams, fed by springs and characteristically having a good flow of water through the year. In these nutrient-rich rivers, there is a good growth of rooted aquatic plants and a rich and diverse invertebrate fauna. Areas with gravel beds usually occur, providing spawning grounds for brown trout *Salmo trutta*, bullheads *Cottus gobio*, and minnows *Phoxinus phoxinus*.

The Cherwell and Thame are very different because they have such high winter flows and, in a dry summer, very low summer flows. Their beds are clay or earth and usually there are more emergent than submerged plants; their fish faunas are more restricted than those of the chalk and limestone rivers or of the main Thames and Ouse.

There is a general relationship between the gradient and width of a river and the fish species present. Small turbulent streams typically support many brown trout, bullheads, and minnows. Further downstream, grayling *Thymallus thymallus* become more numerous than trout, and dace *Leuciscus leuciscus*, bleak *Alburnus alburnus*, and chub *Squalius cephalus* may become common. Still further downstream the fauna is often dominated by chub and barbel *Barbus barbus* and there are also many perch *Perca fluviatilis*, roach *Rutilus rutilus*, and pike *Esox lucius*. Where the gradient is small and the river is wide and deep the most common species is usually the bream *Abramis brama*, accompanied by tench *Tinca tinca*. The zonation of fish species down a 'typical' river can be explained in terms of their tolerance of environmental conditions and their requirements for feeding and for reproduction (Varley 1967), but in fact any river is a mosaic of habitats and there may be deep, muddy sections far upstream and shallow turbulent reaches downstream, each with a characteristic fish fauna.

The chalk-stream tributaries of the Thames are typically dominated by brown trout, bullhead, minnows and grayling, depending on their size; most of them are maintained as trout fisheries, and rainbow trout *Salmo gairdneri* are often 'planted' to provide more sport. The species does not normally breed in British rivers but self-propagating populations have been reported in the Chess and the Misbourne (both small streams in Bucks). Brook lampreys *Lampetra planeri* are often present in small chalk streams, as are stone loach *Nemacheilus barbatulus*. Eels *Anguilla anguilla* are likely to be present in all waters of the upper Thames area; they can move overland through damp grass.

The main Thames, from Lechlade downstream to Teddington, is subject to heavy angling pressure. The Thames Water Authority arranged for a survey of fish species to be carried out between Lechlade and Dorchester in the summer of 1977. Full results are not available and the method used (electric fishing) probably gave biased samples, with relatively few bottom-living species (Banks 1979) but nineteen species were caught and at each of the four principal sampling points, the most abundant were bleak, roach, chub and gudgeon *Gobio gobio* in descending

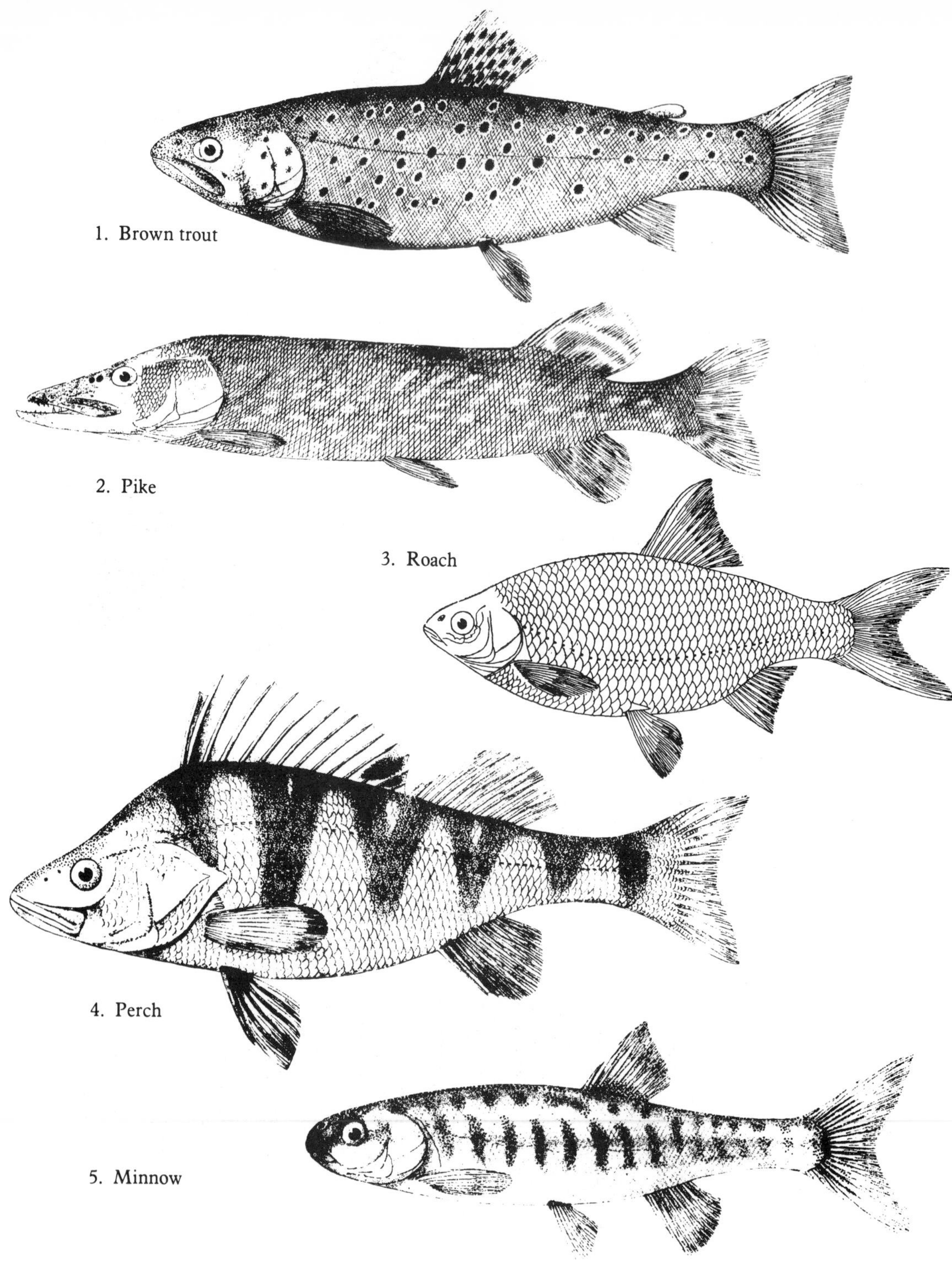
1. Brown trout
2. Pike
3. Roach
4. Perch
5. Minnow

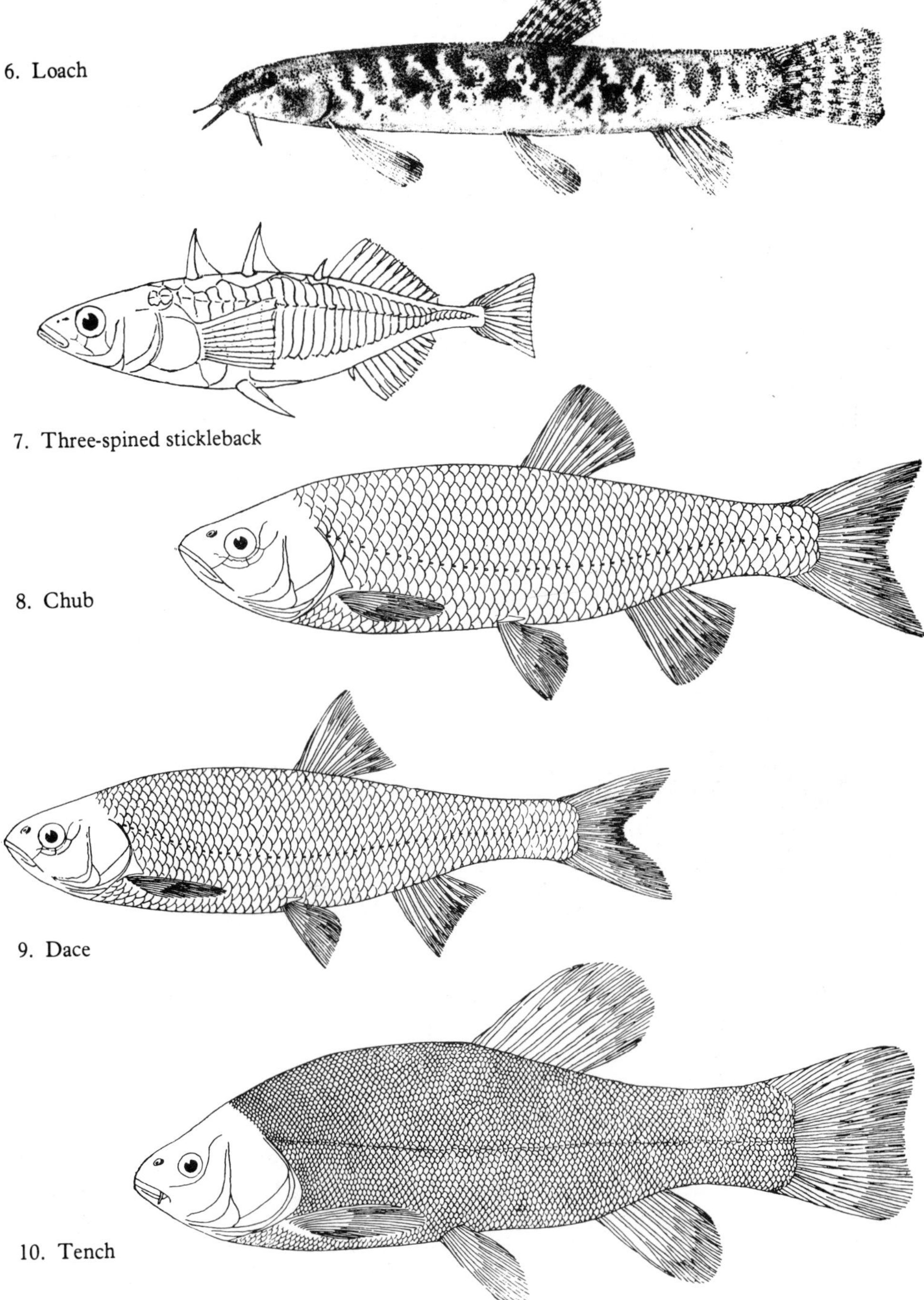

6. Loach

7. Three-spined stickleback

8. Chub

9. Dace

10. Tench

order of numbers. Chub and barbel can be observed to spawn in shallow water at Godstow, near Oxford, and this part of the Thames, between Lechlade and Oxford, belongs to the chub/barbel zone. Bream and tench are also present where the river is deep.

T. J. Pitcher carried out a detailed investigation of fishes in the Seacourt stream which is one of the channels of the Thames above Oxford. It leaves the main channel by a sluice, flows past Wytham, and rejoins the main river at Botley. During regular electric fishing operations between January 1967 and June 1969 nearly 23,000 fishes were caught, marked and released. Of these, nearly 9,000 were minnows and there were more than 1,500 each of gudgeon, bleak, roach, chub, and dace. Fifteen other species were recorded (making a total of twenty-one), all with fewer than 800 individuals: bullhead, perch, stone loach, barbel, pike, bream, ruffe *Gymnocephalus cernua*, grayling, eel, brook lamprey, three-spined stickleback *Gasterosteus aculeatus*, rudd *Scardinius erythophthalmus*, tench and brown trout. Pitcher was also working on the population dynamics of the minnows and found that their biomass in summer was about 10 grams/square metre, their growth was good compared with other waters and so was that of the other common species in the stream.

Below Oxford the Thames increases progressively in volume and width. During an investigation of the main river at Reading as part of the International Biological Programme, Williams (1967), using a seine net on fourteen occasions, caught more than 11,000 fishes. The two commonest, roach (nearly 5,000 individuals) and bleak (more than 4,000 individuals), made up more than 80 per cent of the total. In descending order of numbers of individuals caught, the remaining fourteen species were gudgeon, perch, dace, bream, ruffe, pike, three-spined stickleback, bullhead, minnow, chub, eel, barbel, brown trout, and tench. In contrast with the Seacourt stream, the Thames at Reading supports a population of slow-growing fishes, probably because they are overcrowded and limited in their food supply. Williams calculated that there were 2.5 bleak and one roach for each square metre of river bed. This part of the river is probably bream zone but is actually dominated by roach, possibly because the river bed is rather hard.

The parts of the Great Ouse river system in north Bucks are relatively small streams subject to flooding in winter. At Newport Pagnell, minnows are the commonest fish but trout are present further upstream in the Ouse and also in the upper reaches of the Ouzel. The lower part of this stream is recovering from pollution and at Walton (Milton Keynes) there are now three-spined sticklebacks, ten-spined sticklebacks *Pungitius pungitius*, bullhead, minnows, stone loach, and also a few gudgeon and spiny loach *Cobitis taenia*. This last small species is not present in the Thames or its tributaries but is found in many of the Great Ouse tributaries.

Canals provide a different habitat for fishes, similar in some ways to the bream zone of rivers but sometimes subject to deoxygenation, to disturbance of the bed and banks by boat traffic, and to pollution. In a recent survey based on electric fishing of sample sections Yoxon (1975) calculated that the Grand Union Canal, in the twenty-one kilometres within the Designated Area of Milton Keynes, contained about 140,000 fishes including roach (about 100,000), perch (about 15,000), gudgeon (about 12,000), ruffe (about 9,000), bream (about 2,000), pike (about 1,500), bullhead, dace, and rudd.

The still waters of the area are mainly artificial and include some reservoirs and many disused gravel pits. Farmoor reservoir, near Oxford, is managed as a very successful trout fishery by stocking with rainbow and brown trout. The water is pumped in from the Thames, so small individuals of the wild fish species must frequently be introduced and provide part of the food supply for the large trout. Another set of reservoirs are those near Tring, Hertfordshire, that maintain the level in the Grand Union Canal. These support good populations of bream and roach, and are considered good coarse fishing.

Many of the gravel pits are managed for recreational activities including both trout and coarse angling. Pits close to rivers receive water by seepage, and small fishes can enter with this water so the pits become colonized with the local fish species. Pits that are further away from rivers are frequently managed by angling clubs that introduce the fish species for which they wish to angle. Thus certain pits are notable fisheries for carp *Cyprinus carpio*. With permission from the Thames Water Authority, some clubs have cleared their gravel pits of species that arrived casually and have then introduced their desired species. Consequently it is not possible to predict what species will be present in a gravel pit unless its past history is known. Some of these waters are very productive and support excellent angling; others, usually those with steep sides, deep water, and few plants, have few fishes in them.

Yoxon (1975) investigated the numbers of fish in Mount Farm Lake, an old gravel pit of about 9 hectares recently extended to form a 'balancing lake' in the Bletchley area of Milton Keynes. It has several small inflows from an industrial estate and discharges over a weir into the Ouzel. By seine netting and the mark-recapture method, Yoxon estimated that it held roach (about 15,600), bream (about 3,000), gudgeon (about 800), crucian carp *Carassius carassius* (about 250), tench (about 200), pike (about 100) and small numbers of perch, rudd, and common carp.

The upper Thames area contains, in its numerous and varied water bodies, a very diverse fauna of native fishes, as well as introduced species, of which the most widely spread is the rainbow trout, to be found in 'stocked' fisheries and also in a growing number of fish farms. Other introductions are confined to one or a few artificial still waters (Wheeler and Maitland 1973). Rock bass *Ambloplites rupestris* (from North America) have been established for many years in a small gravel pit in north Oxford. Two European species which probably live in the area are the zander *Stizostedion lucioperca* and the giant catfish or wels *Siluris glanis*. Both may be present in one or more of the Claydon lakes (flooded gravel pits). Zander are now spreading through much of the lower Great Ouse system and might move upstream. Wels may still be present in Tring reservoirs, Herts, and in the Grand Union Canal. Zander and wels are both carnivores, preying on other fishes. It is to be hoped that these species will not be spread beyond their present restricted distribution since the native fishes already provide plenty of diversity and interest for anglers and naturalists.

9 Butterflies and Moths

B.R. BAKER

More than two-thirds of all the known British species of butterflies and larger moths have been recorded from the three Thames counties. If we broaden our comparison by considering all species of our Lepidoptera irrespective of size (almost 2,500 species) between one-half and two-thirds is represented. From this large number we have selected certain examples; some of them rare, some widespread but local, others very common, but all helping to illustrate the diversity within our region.

Some species occur throughout the three counties irrespective of habitat, be it woodland of various types, heathland, chalk down or grassy fields and reed beds in river valleys—these are the biologically successful species. Others, and here are included many of the butterflies, are far less catholic in their tastes. They may live within compact colonies confined to a few acres within a wood or be restricted to a single slope upon a wide chalk down—several will have only a single species of plant on which to breed, and should the plant for any reason disappear the butterfly or moth will vanish too.

Woodland

Oakwoods

The very local wood white butterfly *Leptidea sinapis* occurs in north Bucks and has also been recorded from the oakwoods north-east of Oxford. The eggs and caterpillars are to be found on various vetches and peas, often on those plants growing along the edges of rides, though the butterflies seem to pursue an unending, steady flight through heavily shaded woodland. In the oakwoods along the south Berkshire border and in the wide arc north-east of Oxford the pearl-bordered fritillary *Boloria euphrosyne* and the small pearl-bordered fritillary *B. selene* occur. They appear in late May and early June and live in compact colonies, although their food plant, common dog violet *Viola riviniana*, may be widespread through the woodland. In high summer their place is taken by the splendid silver-washed fritillary

1. White admiral

Argynnis paphia whose caterpillars also feed on dog violet. A dark form of the silver-washed fritillary female, variety *valezina*, occurs regularly in one or two south Berkshire oakwoods. The high brown fritillary *A. adippe* is on the wing at the same time as the silver-washed but is far more locally distributed in the three counties. By comparison, the white admiral *Ladoga camilla* occurs in many of our woodlands providing there is an abundance of honeysuckle *Lonicera periclymenum*. In such places it glides around in the forest canopy and frequently comes down to feed on the bramble blossoms, but rarely ventures far from the woodland edge. That much publicized butterfly the purple emperor *Apatura iris* also has a number of strongholds in each of the three counties from north Bucks down to south Berkshire. Typically it is associated with oak woodland having a good growth of goat willow *Salix caprea* in the understorey, but the woodland need not be extensive, or necessarily of oak, as has been proved at the Warburg Reserve at Bix in Oxon where the butterfly has been recorded on several occasions. Oak must be present, however, if one is looking for our other purple-coloured butterfly, the purple hairstreak *Quercusia quercus*. This is widespread in our region and is sometimes common but can easily escape notice unless a watch is kept on the higher branches of the oaks. The brown hairstreak *Thecla betulae* is very seldom

2. Purple emperor

seen as a butterfly, though the caterpillars occur in some quanitity where there are extensive blackthorn *Prunus spinosa* thickets. It has not been recorded from Berkshire for many years, but strong colonies exist in Oxfordshire and Bucks and others doubtless await discovery in the Chilterns. Whereas the brown hairstreak will lay its eggs on scrubby little blackthorns, the black hairstreak *Strymonidea pruni* favours high, well grown bushes. It is one of the butterfly specialities of our region and though very local occurs in a number of localities in Oxfordshire and Bucks.

The beautiful light crimson underwing moth *Catocala promissa* has been recorded from Bernwood, Bucks, and, perhaps with more regularity, from the south Berkshire oakwoods. Other typical oakwood moths to be found in these same localities include the orange moth *Angerona prunaria*, small brindled beauty *Apocheima hispidaria*, oak beauty *Biston strataria*, merveille-du-jour *Dichonia aprilina* and heart moth *Dicyla oo*, the last named now far rarer than in pre-war years. This also applies to the day-flying broad-bordered bee hawk *Hemaris fuciformis* although a revival of this species seems to have occurred in the exceptional summer of 1976. Rarely does a previously unrecorded species move into our well-worked oakwoods, but this happened in the early 1960s when the little rosy

3. Black hairstreak

marbled *Hapalotis venustula* was recorded in south Berkshire. By 1970 the moth was well established and numbers could be seen at dusk flying along the edges of rides where the foodplant, tormentil *Potentilla erecta*, was common. The rosy marbled has also extended its range into Bucks and has been reported from Medmenham.

Beechwoods

By comparison with the oakwoods the extensive beechwoods of the Chilterns offer a less varied population of Lepidoptera, but these woods are noteworthy for several specialities. The white-letter hairstreak butterfly *Strymonidea w-album* exists in a number of well-spaced colonies from Mapledurham and Goring Heath, Oxon, in the south to Wendover, Bucks, further north. These colonies are centred on wych elms *Ulmus glabra*, occasionally on English elms *U. procera*, and a single tree may support a colony for year after year. For example, an isolated wych elm in the centre of a beechwood near Goring Heath has been producing its white-letter hair-streaks for at least forty years. Following the loss of so many elms, the present status of this butterfly in the area is uncertain. For many years the lobster moth *Stauropus fagi* was reported more frequently from the south Oxfordshire beech-woods than from any other area in Britain. In those days the resting moths were found by diligently searching the beech trunks, but with the advent of high-powered light traps the lobster was found to be widespread in both oak and mixed deciduous woodland. Our beechwoods still have their lobsters but these woodlands are perhaps more highly regarded nowadays as the home of the very local plumed prominent *Ptilophora plumigera*. This November-flying species exists in several localities between Marlow, Bucks and Watlington, Oxfordshire and favours sheltered valleys with an abundance of field maple *Acer campestre*. In 1969 it was first recorded from the Warburg Reserve and occasional specimens have even been reported from the centre of Henley-on-Thames, Oxon. The maple prominent *Ptilodontella cucullina* is another very local species with its main centre of distribution in the Chiltern beechwoods. Occasional specimens have been reported from small coverts on the Berkshire Downs, from the vicinity of Didcot and even one from the unlikely locality of Moor Copse Reserve in a Berkshire river valley.

Apart from these specialities, regular inhabitants of the beechwoods include the pale tussock *Dasychira pudibunda*, the nut tree tussock *Colocasia coryli* and the green silver lines *Pseudoips fagana*. These species are not exclusive to beechwoods but are more often evident in such places, particularly after a late summer gale when their showy caterpillars, having been catapulted out of the canopy, are making their tortuous re-ascent of the smooth trunks. The lichens and algae on these trunks provide food for the caterpillars of footman moths, particularly the orange footman *Eilema sororcula*, though in other parts of southern England this species appears not to be confined to beechwoods.

Perhaps these Chiltern beechwoods should be accorded pride of place in any review of the Lepidoptera of the Thames counties, for in 1962 they were found to be the home of a little moth thought to have been unrecorded in Britain for almost a hundred years. In 1859 the Revd B. H. Burkes of Stonor, Oxon, took a specimen of the olive crescent *Trisateles emortualis* in these beechwoods, after which the moth was thought to have become extinct, though another specimen was taken in the same place by the Revd F. J. Perry in 1910. Since 1962 the olive crescent has occurred with regularity in three or four Bucks localities and in 1967 its caterpillars were found in one of these localities for the first time in Britain. When fully fed the caterpillars cocoon among the dead leaves on the woodland floor, thus passing the winter and spring months until a new generation of olive crescents hatch in June and July.

Pinewoods

Lepidoptera confined solely to pinewoods are few in number but include the grey pine carpet *Thera obeliscata*, the bordered white *Bupalus piniaria* and the pine beauty *Panolis flammea*—all of them more prevalent in Berkshire than in either of the other two counties. Nevertheless, although species-sterile when compared with our oakwoods and beechwoods, pinewoods possess their speciality in the form of the pine hawk-moth *Hyloicus pinastri.* This fine grey-and-black streaked moth, which can usually be found at rest on pine trunks by the careful observer, was not recorded in Berkshire until 1945 following a steady spread northwards through Hampshire. The pinewoods around Crowthorne, Burghfield, Padworth and Tadley, all Berkshire localities, are good pine hawk-moth country; Oxfordshire and Bucks with fewer suitable breeding areas have provided fewer records.

Heathland

On the dry sandy soils of south Berkshire a wide discontinuous arc of heathy country extends from Ascot across to Greenham Common near Newbury. Colonies of the little silver-studded blue butterfly *Plebejus argus* occur on many of these heaths, and the walker across the heather on a sunny July day can hardly fail to disturb the bright blue males and the brownish females. The grayling *Hipparchia semele* also occurs in this type of country and appears when the silver-studded blues are beginning to look worn.

The beautiful green caterpillar of the emperor moth *Saturnia pavonia* may occasionally be seen in full view on the heather in midsummer, but one is more likely to see the male moths dashing wildly over the heath in April and May as they seek out the females. Two other large day-flying moths occur on these Berkshire heaths, the fox moth *Macrothylacia rubi* and the oak eggar *Lasiocampa quercus*, though inexplicably the oak eggar is restricted to the heaths around Crowthorne. The true lover's knot *Lycophotia porphyrea* and the beautiful yellow underwing *Anarta myrtilli* are widespread, but the dark tussock *Dasychira fascelina* is rare and only likely to be encountered in east Berkshire.

On these heaths birch is a rapid colonizer and in places such as Padworth the bushes are regularly cut every few years. The stumps left in the ground are often colonized by the large red-belted clearwing *Synanthedon culiciformis*, whose caperpillars form tunnels between the bark and heart wood. Another clearwing caterpillar, the white-barred *Conopia spheciformis*, feeds in the uncut birches making a larger, more central tunnel which is only revealed when the trunk is cut down. Both these moths bear a superficial resemblance to wasps and can easily escape detection. The birch stumps become unsuitable for the clearwings after a year or two and decay sets in, initiated by ants and completed by fungi; the clearwings then have to find fresher stumps to colonize. At one time the waved black *Parascotia fuliginaria* was thought to be a great rarity and the only specimens known all came from warehouses in London's dockland. The moths inhabited dilapidated riverside warehouses whose damp timbers were covered with mats of fungi. Years later the moth's true home was found to be the Bagshot Sand areas of Surrey and Berkshire and the caterpillars were found feeding on fungi growing on fallen birch trunks. The waved black is still a Berkshire speciality and occurs not uncommonly from Ascot across to Aldermaston. The beautiful dotted chestnut *Dasycampa rubiginea* is something of an enigma. Like the waved black it is associated with the Bagshot Sand areas but to a far more limited extent. It occurs in east Berkshire and is attracted to ivy blossom in the autumn and, after hibernation, visits sallow catkins *Salix* spp in the spring. It is never common but occurs with regularity and has often been bred in captivity, yet its caterpillars still await discovery in the wild.

Chalk Downland

It is arguable that during the past twenty-five years our chalk downs have deteriorated to a greater degree than any other habitat type. Loss of the rabbit, desirable as it may have been, has allowed the slow spread of rank grasses and scrub while a more immediate change has resulted from ploughing ancient grassland and seeding it with a monoculture of cereals. However, pockets of high-grade chalk grassland are still to be found, much of it in BBONT reserves, and in such places a splendid variety of skipper butterflies, blues and browns may still be enjoyed. The silver-spotted skipper *Hesperia comma* occurs at Streatley, the Fairmile and Aston Upthorpe in Berks, also on the Chiltern escarpment above Watlington, Oxon. This very local butterfly appears in July and August, as does its much commoner relative the small skipper *Thymelicus sylvestris*; both species breed on grasses, the silver-spotted favouring sheep's fescue *Festuca ovina*. The chalkhill blue *Lysandra coridon* is to be found almost on Reading's doorstep and on the Berkshire Downs from Streatley to White Horse Hill; on the Chilterns it occurs from Watlington northwards to Tring, Herts. Its close relative the beautiful adonis blue *L. bellargus* is much rarer but still occurs in Berkshire and Oxfordshire, though prior to 1976 its numbers had dropped alarmingly low. In that long, hot summer the adonis blue reappeared in localities where it had not been recorded for almost forty years and the following year its recovery was still maintained. Both of these blues have only a single food plant, the horseshoe vetch *Hippocrepis comosa*, a specialization which is

4. Red admiral

hazardous in a changing landscape. Less restricted by choice of food plant are the dark green fritillary *Argynnis aglaja*, the Duke of Burgundy fritillary *Hamearis lucina* and the marbled white *Melanargia galathea*. All these occur on our downland with those colourful day-flying moths the six-spot burnet *Zygaena filipendulae* and the wood tiger *Parasemia plantaginis*.

If the downs are visited on a warm summer evening moths soon become evident when they begin their dusk flight, for they are not screened from view as they are in woodland. If a moth lamp is operated the various species can be identified, as happened for example on open downland west of Streatley in mid-July 1978, when over eighty species were recorded. The largest of these was the impressive privet hawk-moth *Sphinx ligustri*, which breeds regularly on these downs. Less diversity would have resulted had this recording taken place a mile or so westwards where cereals now replace the native chalk plants; yet paradoxically, a formerly rare moth, the Brighton wainscot *Oria musculosa*, would have been found in abundance. In the past twenty years this species has spread steadily northwards from the wheatfields of Salisbury Plain and is today well established in Berkshire and Oxfordshire with isolated records from the Chilterns at Fawley and Medmenham, Bucks.

5. Marbled white

Wetlands

The calcareous fen at Cothill, Berks, is noted for its variant colony of scarlet tigers *Callimorpha dominula*, but typical colonies of this colourful moth also exist along the Kennet banks between Woolhampton and Hungerford and in the Pang Valley from Moor Copse to Bradfield, all in Berks. An uncommon butterfly, the marsh fritillary *Eurodryas aurinea*, has also been recorded from Cothill and there are other colonies on the marshy fields of Otmoor, Oxon. In the Kennet Valley between Woolhampton and Kintbury, isolated but still extensive *Phragmites* reed beds are the home of wainscot moths whose caterpillars feed either on the leaves or within the stems or reed rhizomes. These wainscots include the obscure *Mythimna obsoleta*, the southern *M. straminea*, the silky *Chilodes maritimus*, the twin-spotted *Archanara geminipuncta* and the brown-veined *A. dissoluta*. The scarce burnished brass *Diachrysia chryson* is to be found close to the Kennet banks among dense growths of hemp agrimony *Eupatorium cannabinum*, preferring those plants shaded by trees, while that uncommon moth the butterbur *Hydraecia petasitis* has been recorded along several miles of river bank where luxuriant stands of its food

6. Scarlet tiger moth

plant *Petasites hybridus* occur. The isolated reed beds on both banks of the Thames between Oxford and Windsor are mere remnants of those existing when the Thames was free of the shackles that control it today, so the diversity of their Lepidoptera cannot compare with that found on the Kennet.

Man-made Habitats

Railway embankments and motorway cuttings may seem unlikely habitats for butterflies and moths but they can form important linkways allowing a species to expand its range through otherwise unsuitable country. For example the Essex skipper *Thymelicus lineola* has been found recently along grassy railway banks in east Berkshire and blue butterflies are beginning to appear on the grassy slopes of the M40 on its way through the Chiltern scarp. Gardens, large or small, can produce surprises and it is likely that even those in built-up areas could produce an impressive species list. Many of the 371 moths recorded from a garden at Caversham in the Borough of Reading will have flown far from their normal habitats, but others have benefited by their food plants finding favour with gardeners. For example the growing of species of *Cupressus* and sweet william *Dianthus barbatus* have helped the spread of former rarities such as Blair's pinion *Lithophane leautieri* and the varied coronet *Hadena compta*. Finally, there is always the chance of seeing a rare immigrant butterfly or moth, for these appear at unspecified times and places. In 1976, of the recorded 270 Camberwell Beauty butterflies *Vanessa antiopa* that visited Britain from Scandinavia three were seen in Berkshire, nine in Bucks and two in Oxfordshire; almost all were in gardens.

10 Other Terrestrial Invertebrates

C. O'TOOLE

The invertebrates, especially the insects, offer the naturalist a bewildering variety of species to ponder. In their roles as herbivores, pollinators, scavengers, and recyclers, they have an enormous influence on the visual impact of our countryside: witness the recent devastation by Dutch elm disease, a fungal condition transmitted by the elm bark beetle *Scolytus scolytus*.

The invertebrates form a major part of the biomass in many habitats and, in terms of species, easily exceed the combined numbers of the plants and vertebrates. The open woodlands of the Oxfordshire–Buckinghamshire border, for example, support about eighty species of bees and wasps and several hundred species of beetles and flies. Equally impressive lists have been compiled for the fauna of domestic and college gardens in Oxford. But such lists, consisting of scientific names with few, if any, vernacular equivalents, have no place here. The following is an account of the invertebrate species of special interest which may be encountered on country walks in the three counties. Some of the species mentioned are widespread and common, others are rarities; a few require a little persistence to find, but looking under bark, logs, and stones will soon repay the effort involved. Inevitably, most of them are insects, not only because they are numerically superior to the other groups, but also because they have been the most intensively recorded.

Many groups of invertebrates are difficult to identify and the resultant gaps in our local knowledge are indicated. On p. 150 there is a discussion of some changes detected in the invertebrate fauna that derive from changing habitats in our area. By comparison with that of other areas of similar size, the invertebrate fauna of the Thames counties was well recorded until the late 1930s. This was largely owing to the efforts of past members of the Hope Department of Entomology at the University Museum, Oxford, and a dedicated band of amateur naturalists associated with that institution. The results of their labours were summarized in the *Victoria County History of Berkshire* (1906) and the volume in the same series for Oxfordshire (1939). Bucks was and still is the most under-recorded of our three counties and only a few records were published in 1920. In addition to these faunal lists, occasional supplementary records have been published at intervals by the Ashmolean Natural History Society and in the *Reading Naturalist*, journal of the Reading and District Natural History Society. Hobby *et al* (1954) summarize interesting records for invertebrates since the publication of the *Victoria County Histories*.

Since the war there has been relatively little surveying of the invertebrates, though a few selected sites have been studied intensively. Thus for many years under Charles Elton ecologists at Oxford University have compiled records for Wytham Wood, Berks/Oxon, just to the west of Oxford. The insects associated with oak trees at Wytham were studied for 25 years by the late Professor George Varley and his students. Dr Denis Owen and his students at the Oxford Polytechnic are studying insect diversity at Bernwood Forest, Bucks with particular reference to the butterflies and hoverflies, and I have studied the bees and wasps of Bernwood and of several BBONT nature reserves.

Nevertheless, the *Victoria County Histories* remain the basis of our knowledge of the invertebrate fauna of the Thames counties. Much of their information will of course prove to be out of date, not least because of the large-scale changes in habitat since their publication. These changes result from the replacement of many old, broad-leaved woodlands with conifer plantations, and the gradual introduction of intensive agricultural practices. The latter onslaught has included not only the detrimental effects of pesticides, but also the loss of hedgerows, tracts of marginal land, ponds, the lowering of water tables and, in many places, a reduced floral diversity. The early faunal lists are valuable, therefore, as a record of the way things were before these changes took place; they form a base line for comparison with the results of present and future surveys.

Man's impact on the environment, however, is not entirely negative. Sand pits, quarries, railway and motorway cuttings and embankments are often important refuges for invertebrates. It is fortunate that some of the most productive habitats, both semi-natural and man-made, are now managed as BBONT reserves. Nevertheless, much work remains to be done before we have anything like a complete picture of the riches which undoubtedly await detection. This leaves us with the exciting prospect that nearly everything there is to know about our invertebrate fauna remains to be discovered.

Annelids and Molluscs

There are few published records of worms (Annelida) for the three counties, though we do have two noted rarities. The lumbricid earthworm *Eisenia rosea* var *macedonica,* found at Cothill, Berks/Oxon, (Macfadyen 1952), is otherwise known in Britain only from Wicken and Chippenham Fens, Cambs, and from localities in and around London. The rarity of Dutrochet's leech, *Trocheta subviridis*, however, may be apparent rather than real: its life-style makes it difficult to find. The species spends its entire life underground, where it feeds on earthworms and perhaps on other subterranean invertebrates. It has been found in an allotment at Cowley, Oxford (Taylor 1943) and in 1979 a specimen was brought to the University Museum from Denchworth Berks/Oxon, where it was found in blue clay. *T. subviridis* lives at a depth of about 30cm (one foot) in soils or clays where the water table is close to the surface. It should be sought, therefore, in land adjacent to the Thames and its tributaries.

Earthworms are also the victims of slugs of the genus *Testacella*. All the species are found in humus-rich soils and most local records are for gardens. As the generic name suggests, the species of *Testacella* have the rudiments of an external shell. This is best developed in Mauge's slug, *T. maugei*, which has been recorded from Faringdon, Berks/Oxon, but not since 1905. It is a south-western species and our area is at the edge of its range. The shelled slug *T. haliotidea* was recorded from Oxford, Blenheim Park and Bicester, all Oxon, but, like the shield slug *T. scutulum*, has not been found since 1939. The latter species was noted from Faringdon, Middleton Park, Oxon, and Bicester. The species of *Testacella* are difficult to find because they spend most of their time underground and this no doubt accounts for the sparsity of records. The rest of the Mollusca of the Thames counties are quite well known. Dr H. Bowen has compiled records for several sites and I am grateful to him for access to unpublished records. Details of the molluscs found in the Reading area are given in Bowen (1975).

All the slugs recorded in England have been found in the three counties. The most familiar species is the black slug *Arion ater*, which thrives in a variety of habitats, including acid soils. It is the common slug of gardens and is variable in colour. Black forms are mainly northern in distribution, while the brightly coloured red form is commonest in the south, especially in cultivated land.

Woodland species in our area include the hedgehog slug *Arion intermedius*, which is widespread, as are Bourguignat's slug *A. circumscriptus* and the dusky slug *A. subfuscus*. The great slug *Limax maximus* is common and the tree slug

L. marginatus is frequent under the bark of dead trees. The ash-black slug *L. cinereoniger* is to be found at Bagley Wood, just to the south of Oxford; it is an uncommon indicator of old woodlands.

Our most abundant species is the field slug *Deroceras reticulatum*, which is an important pest of crops. Its relative, the marsh slug *D. laevis*, is widespread and common in very wet places, especially damp woods, river banks and wet meadows. This species can survive submersion in water for long periods.

Land snails need a certain amount of lime in their diet in order to secrete a shell, and the greatest diversity of species is to be found in old woodland on chalk soils. About half the British species are less than 1cm in diameter, though most of them are, nevertheless, relatively easy to identify with a little practice. The most recent field guide is that of Kerney and Cameron (1979) and it is also useful to refer to the older, standard text of Ellis (1969) which gives common names for all species.

Woodlands provide snails with a variety of suitable habitats all affording protection from desiccation and extremes of temperature. Thus, while most species are active at night, when relative humidity is high, in the daytime woodland snails should be sought under bark, moss, leaf litter, stones and logs.

The largest British species is the Roman snail *Helix pomatia* (p. 123), so called because of the belief that it was introduced into Britain by the Romans. However, this uncommon southern species is known from archaeological sites of pre-Roman age. It lives in old woodland, downland and dry fields in limestone areas. *H. pomatia* avoids cultivated land and in our area has been found at Hambleden, Bucks, and in Oxon at Wychwood Forest, East End, North Leigh, Charlbury, and in the railway cutting at Stonesfield. For Bucks, there is also an old record from Great Marlow.

A related species, the common snail *Helix aspersa*, the largest British snail of domestic habitats, is frequent in both town and country gardens in the three counties. It lives in a wide range of habitats, including woods, hedgerows, rocks, old walls and dunes. *H. aspersa* is often eaten in the west country and is sold in the Bristol area as 'wall-fish'.

A noted rarity in our area is the plaited snail *Spermodea lamellata*. It is uncommon south of Staffordshire and is characteristic of old, native deciduous woodlands. It was recorded from Theale Lock, Berks, and Burnham Beeches, Bucks, in the early part of this century and the most recent record is from Aston Clinton, Bucks, in 1926. It should be sought in places like Windsor Forest, Berks, and the relatively undisturbed parts of Bernwood.

The mountain bulin *Ena montana* is a national rarity and its presence in the

1. Roman snail courtship *Helix pomatia*

decidedly unmountainous Thames counties is remarkable, for its preferred habitat in montane forest; it has been found at over 2,000m in the Alps. In our region it is known from nine localities, including Whitehill Wood, Oxon, and the BBONT reserves at Bix Bottom and Sydlings Copse, both Oxon. The commoner lesser bulin *E. obscura* is a widespread inhabitant of woodland litter.

The very local point snail *Acicula fusca* lives in moss and damp litter and is known from nine sites, the most recent records being for Ibstone, Bucks, and Bix Bottom. Another local species is the three-toothed snail *Azeca goodalli*, known from Wytham, Bagley Wood, Dancer's End, Bucks and Bix Bottom, where it lives in rather open woodland. It is also found in rocky areas such as Headington Quarry, Oxon.

Rolph's door snail *Macrogastra rolphii* is rather uncommon in our area, the three most recent records being from Wytham Wood and Silchester, Berks and Akeley, Bucks. It lives on the ground, in moss and litter in moist deciduous woods and also in hedgebanks. A related species, the door snail *Clausilia bidentata* (p. 124) is more widespread, being recorded from nineteen localities in the Thames counties including the BBONT reserves at Dancer's End, Bix Bottom and Hook Norton, Oxon. The species frequents moss in woods, rocks and old walls.

Some of the commoner woodland species in our area are that ubiquitous fungus

2. The door snail *Clausilia bidentata*

feeder, the rounded snail *Discus rotundatus*, the glossy snail *Oxychilus helveticus*, the glass snail *Aegopinella pura*, the smooth snail *A. nitidula*, the pellucid snail *Vitrina pellucida*, the hairy snail *Trichia hispida* and the strawberry snail *T. striolata*, which is often a pest of strawberries. The last two are unusual in that their shells are conspicuously hairy, though the hairs are lost in mature individuals of *T. striolata*. The seven common woodland species listed above, together with fourteen others, have all been recorded from Sydlings Copse, near Oxford, which makes it one of the better known BBONT reserves for snails.

Marshy areas provide suitable habitats for many snail species. The commonest is perhaps the slippery snail *Cochlicopa lubrica*. Its shells are invariably present in riverine flood refuse. The Kentish snail *Monacha cantiana* is confined to damp areas on calcareous soils. There are records from many localities, including Dancer's End, Bix Bottom, Aston Rowant, Oxon, and Cothill. It is often found among nettles and brambles, feeding on rotting vegetation.

Flood refuse around fens and marshes is the habitat of the very local marsh whorl snail *Vertigo antivertigo*. It was last found in 1926, at Burnham Beeches. Des Moulins's snail *V. moulinsiana* is another noted rarity in the three counties. It is often found on common reed *Phragmites australis* in calcareous fens and is recorded from Stratfield Saye, Cothill, Denford and Kintbury, all in Berks. Other whorl snails have invaded drier habitats. Thus, *V. pygmaea*, our commonest species, lives in well drained calcareous grassland and only rarely in marshes. It is widespread in the Thames counties and its BBONT sites include Bix, Cothill and Bullingdon Bog, Oxon. The wall whorl snail *V. pusilla*, widespread though local, lives among dry rocks, stone walls and occasionally in ground litter in open woodland. Recent records are from Wood Eaton, Oxon, and North Leigh.

Old walls support several interesting snails and a survey of the drystone walls of the Cotswolds would be very rewarding. Their crevices provide a daytime refuge from the desiccating effects of bright sunlight and it is mainly at night that the snails emerge to graze on mosses and lichens, though they may remain in sight on damp, overcast days. The walls are a man-made adjunct to natural habitats such as rock falls and dry, ivy-clad cliff faces. The rock snail *Pyramidula rupestris* is also a common inhabitant of old limestone walls, where it feeds on lichens. In the three counties it is known from North Leigh, Buscot, Berks, and Kencott, Oxon. The tree snail *Balea perversa* is rather perversely named, for it is rarely seen on trees, but is characteristic of dry, exposed rocks and old stone walls. It is known from Wood Eaton, Studley and Pixey Mead, all Oxon.

Friable soil in calcareous regions is the habitat of several species adapted to withstand the rigours of life in dry habitats. The round-mouthed snail *Pomatias elegans* is the most notable example in our region. This gregarious snail, related to the marine winkles, is largely subterranean in habits and feeds mainly on dead leaves. It is locally common and is recorded from the BBONT reserves at Dancer's End and at Warren Bank, Ipsden, Oxon.

Both the garden snail *Cepaea hortensis* and the grove snail *C. nemoralis* live in a wide variety of habitats and are common in our area. The grove snail is of special interest, as the subject of research by Professor A. J. Cain and the late Professor P. M. Sheppard when both were at Oxford University. It is very variable in ground colour, ranging from green (yellow when shell is empty), through pink to brown. Dark bands may be present or absent and are of variable number and width. Cain and Sheppard (1954) studied the frequencies of all the different colour forms in many populations of *C. nemoralis* in Oxfordshire and Berkshire. They found that the forms which predominated in any given habitat were those which were least conspicuous when seen against the general background. Thus green forms were of high frequency in rank, green herbage, while brown forms were dominant in beech litter. Examination of shell remains at the 'anvils' of song thrushes showed that the victims were of colour forms that were conspicuous against the local background. The thrushes thus acted as selective agents, modifying the frequency of colour forms by preying on those individuals that were most conspicuous in any given habitat. Because colour and band patterns are genetically controlled the thrushes also modified the frequency of genes in the snail populations they preyed on. Thus inconspicuously coloured snails had a better chance to survive and reproduce and the frequency of adaptively coloured individuals remains high in any population. Cain and Sheppard went on to demonstrate this experimentally. They also found that widely separated and genetically unrelated populations of snails tended to have very similar frequencies of colour forms if the local background colours were similar. This was potent proof of the selective advantage of being appropriately coloured and the strength of pressure exerted by the predatory thrushes. The work on *C. nemoralis* was one of the earliest and most impressive demonstrations of natural selection in action. Cain and Sheppard had put the Thames counties populations of this snail on the world map, for wherever evolutionary biology is taught or studied our local grove snails are examined with interest.

With a total of eighty-six species of land snails, the Thames counties have 74 per cent of the known British land molluscan fauna within their boundaries. While this is impressive, more work needs to be done as many species are still known from only one or a few localities.

Crustacea-Isopoda (Woodlice)

Woodlice are one of those small groups which tend to be neglected. The excellent field guide by Sutton (1972) should encourage naturalists to pay them more attention. Six species are common in the Thames counties, *Porcellio scaber*, *P. rathkei*, *Oniscus asellus*, *Philoscia muscorum* and *Armadillidium vulgare*. As the generic name implies, the last-named is armour-plated and resembles a tiny armadillo. All woodlice feed on decaying vegetation in a variety of damp habitats and are important in the breakdown of leaf litter and the return of nutrients to the soil. They are active at night and *Porcellio scaber* ascends trees at night, where it grazes on the epiphytic alga *Pleurococcus viridis*. *Armadillidium* is an important consumer of litter in *Brachypodium* grassland. Hobby *et al* (1954) observe that more species of woodlice are to be found in gardens than elsewhere. Thus while eight species may be found under a single stone in the Botanic Garden of Oxford University, only six species are regularly found in natural habitats and rarely all together.

Our most interesting woodlouse is the impressively-named *Platyarthrus hoffmannseggii*, a white blind species which lives exclusively as a scavenger in the nests of ants. It is widespread and common in colonies of the black ant *Lasius niger* and the yellow meadow ant *L. flavus* and is completely tolerated by the worker ants.

Myriapoda (Centipedes and Millipedes)

Centipedes and millipedes are another neglected group and are under-recorded in the three counties, partly because their cryptic habits make them difficult to find. They are, nevertheless, an important constituent of woodland, hedgerows and gardens.

The centipedes (Chilopoda) have one pair of legs on each body segment and are for the most part carnivorous. The commonest species is the large, brown *Lithobius forficatus*, which lives in woodland litter, under bark and stones and is often found in gardens. It feeds on snails, slugs and insects and preys on fly larvae in compost heaps. I have studied the feeding habits of *L. forficatus* in woodland. At night they climb trees and the examination of gut contents showed that they preyed on resting flies and moths, whose presence was betrayed by spines and wing scales. During the day activity is confined to leaf litter and crevices in the soil and dead logs, when fragments of soil mites and earthworm spicules predominate in the gut. The related *L. variegatus* is a regular inhabitant of leaf litter in our area and the relatively uncommon house centipede *Scutigera coleoptrata* is recorded from cellars in north Oxford. The burrowing centipede *Haplophilus subterraneus* is the long, thin, yellow centipede familiar to gardeners with damp soils. It lives under stones or in soil spaces and feeds on plant material as well as small invertebrates. Keys for the identification of British centipedes are provided by Eason (1964).

The millipedes (Diplopoda) have two pairs of legs on each body segment and are vegetarians, often feeding on damp, decaying plant material. There are no recent lists for the Thames counties. The commonest species in our area is the black millipede *Tachypodiulus niger*, which lives in leaf litter, under stones, bark and in old walls. It emerges at night to graze on algae and lichens and in autumn sometimes feeds on blackberries in daylight. The pill millipede *Glomerus marginata* is common almost everywhere and, unlike most millipedes, can withstand dry conditions. When disturbed it rolls up into a ball and, with its armour plating, is easily confused with the woodlouse *Armadillidium vulgare*. The resemblance is perhaps no coincidence, because both millipede and woodlouse have a similar life style: their greatest numbers are found in *Brachypodium* litter, on which they feed. The cylindrical shape of typical millipedes has been abandoned by *Polydesmus angustus*, which has a rather flattened body; it is common in all areas and feeds on roots.

British millipedes can be identified with the aid of Blower (1958).

Arachnida (Pseudoscorpions, Harvestmen and Spiders)

The pseudoscorpions (Cheliferidae) are poorly known because they are tiny and attract little attention. The resemblance to true scorpions resides in the pair of anterior pincers, which they brandish erect, scorpion-fashion. Unlike true scorpions, however, they have no tail or sting and are quite harmless. They are active predators and in gardens can be seen on fences and walls; in woodland, they live in leaf litter, in moss and under bark. One of the most abundant species is *Chelifer cancroides* with *Chthonius rayi* and *Obisium muscorum* almost as common, the latter inhabitating moss.

The harvestmen (Opiliones) are well known only in the Oxford region; Todd (1949) gave detailed information on their abundance and habits, including all the species on the British list, except for one which is strictly coastal. Most harvestmen feed on spiders, insects and even other harvestmen. They occasionally eat bird droppings. The commonest species in gardens and woodland is *Phalangium opilio*. Like most of its relatives, it is active at night, spending its days in leaf litter and under stones and bark. *Homalenotus quadridentatus* is an uncommon species found on Wytham Hill, associated with limestone grassland. The British species of harvestmen can be named with the keys in Sankey and Savory (1974).

Spiders (Araneae) are the best-known arachnids in the Thames counties and the local fauna is noted for several rarities. The most familiar spiders in houses are the large and sinister *Tegenaria domestica* and *T. atrica*. They make extensive sheet webs in sheds and cellars and in their nocturnal ramblings are frequently trapped by the slippery surfaces of baths and sinks. *T. atrica* is sometimes known as the cardinal spider because it is said to have terrified Cardinal Wolsey in Hampton Court. In eighteenth-century Devon it was used in spider races; it can sprint a distance 330 times its own body length in ten seconds, that is, 5.9 metres (20 feet). It was also eaten as a cure for endemic malaria.

In gardens, the large garden spider *Araneus diadematus* with a conspicuous cross on its back, is commonly seen especially in autumn, when it spins large orb webs. It is also found in hedgerows and its webs often obstruct narrow paths in woodlands. A related species, *A. quadratus*, often olive green in colour, has the distinction of being the heaviest British spider and often attains a body length of 15mm or more. It is widespread in the three counties and is numerous at the BBONT reserve at Hitch Copse Pit, near Tubney, Berks/Oxon, where it frequents the brambles fringing the old quarry workings. It often takes large insect prey, such as bumblebees (p. 129). The rarest spider in the Thames counties is *A. bituberculatus,* which in

3. A relative of the garden spider *Araneus quadratus* eating a bumblebee

Britain is known only from Burnham Beeches, where it lives among heather. Several species in our area live under stones, one of the commonest being *Dysdera crocata*. Its presence is often betrayed by the little silken cells in which the adults hide by day. The species is numerous at Dry Sandford Pit, Berks/Oxon, and preys on woodlice.

The jumping spiders (Salticidae) are noted for their prominent eyes, attractive markings and the complex semaphore signalling of courting males. The largest and one of the commonest in gardens and dry woodland is the zebra spider *Salticus scenicus* so called because of its eye-catching black and white stripes. It occasionally wanders over window panes and hunts small flies in dry, sunny situations such as walls and wooden fences. Another salticid, *Euophrys lanigera*, is associated with old buildings and is found mainly on roofs. It was first added to the British list by W. S. Bristowe and was later found to be living freely on and in the Natural History Museum at South Kensington. Years later, the arachnologist Dr J. A. L. Cooke was visited by a specimen while he peered down a microscope in what is now my own room in the University Museum, Oxford. The spider is still a daily visitor and lurks among the impedimenta which invariably clutter a taxonomist's desk. *E. lanigera* is now known to be more widely distributed in Britain, but in Oxfordshire is still only recorded from the University Museum.

Of the wolf spiders (Lycosidae), *Lycosa amentata* is the commonest and lives wherever sun and easy shelter can be found together. Thus, it favours dry litter in open woodland and gardens. Its relative, *L. monticola* is common on chalk downland. The females of Lycosidae have in common the habit of carrying silken egg sacs under their abdomens. *Pirata uliginosus*, a rare wolf spider associated with limestone grassland, is recorded from Wytham Wood.

The crab spiders (Thomisidae) are so called because of the crab-like stance they adopt while lurking in flowers in wait for their unsuspecting insect prey. The commonest species in our area is *Misumena vatia*. Individuals vary in colour, some being sulphurous yellow, others pure white. Whatever its colour, an individual *M. vatia* always matches the ground colour of the flower it frequents. The species is common at Wytham, Dry Sandford Pit, Shotover and Bernwood, where white forms seem to favour the white florets of the ox-eye daisy *Leucanthemum vulgare*. Yellow specimens are frequent on dandelions and ragworts. *M. vatia* can cope with large prey and often takes worker honeybees, paralysing them before they can mobilize their stings. An uncommon crab spider, *Oxyptila nigrita*, is recorded from Wytham, where it is associated with limestone grassland; it should be sought in the Cotswolds and Chilterns.

The spitting spider *Scytodes thoracica* is now commoner than originally thought. In the three counties it was first found in Merton College, Oxford, in 1866. It is normally associated with human habitations and catches its insect prey by rapidly engulfing it with a sticky, thread-like secretion. *Hyptiotes paradoxus* has recently been found in large numbers at Bagley Wood. Hitherto, it was recorded in Britain only from Box Hill, Surrey and the New Forest. *Dipaena inornata*, another rarity, is recorded from Yarnton, Oxon; it normally lives in fens, and Wicken Fen is its only other British site. Frilford Heath, Berks/Oxon, is the second British locality for the rare *Centromerus incilium*, a spider otherwise known in Britain from only a single female collected in Aberdeenshire.

The spiders of the Thames counties are sufficiently well known to indicate that there is a rich and varied fauna, but most records date from before the Second World War. Further work should be encouraged by the excellent keys in Locket and Millidge (1957–8, and Locket *et al* 1974). Bristowe (1971) gives an account of the natural history of British spiders. Special attention should be paid to Shotover, Brasenose Wood, Oxon, Bernwood, Rushbeds Wood, Bucks, and Frilford Heath.

Insects

The recorded distribution of most of our insects reflects the distribution and preoccupations of entomologists, for they, more than any other group of naturalists, are wont to return time and again to those localities which guarantee rich pickings. In recent years, however, this tendency has been offset to some extent by national recording schemes such as those for grasshoppers and crickets, dragonflies, hoverflies, social wasps and bumblebees. Nevertheless many groups still remain under-recorded and some of the records must be regarded as suspect because of more recent advances in our understanding of their classification. Chinery (1975) is a good guide to the identification of British insects. His bibliography lists all the specialist works cited below.

Mayflies (Ephemeroptera), Dragonflies (Odonata), Stoneflies (Plecoptera) and Caddisflies (Trichoptera)

These orders are grouped together here for convenience. All have aquatic larvae and are therefore to be found near water, though adult caddisflies are often attracted to light and the powerful dragonflies may be found at considerable distances from their waters of origin. For these reasons, only the presence of aquatic larvae should be taken as definitive evidence of breeding in any given locality.

There are few recent records of mayflies (Ephemeroptera), though thirteen species are recorded for the Thames counties and several are common. They are relatively easy to name with the aid of Kimmins (1950). *Ephemera vulgata* is widespread and its relative, *E. danica*, is found in the Reading area. Mayflies should be sought at dusk in the summer months, around the margins of rivers, canals and ponds, at which time large numbers may be seen in mating swarms.

The dragonflies and damselflies (Odonata) are the largest and most conspicuous of the insects associated with water. Both the aquatic larvae and the aerial adults are active predators. The adults are superbly adapted for catching insect prey on the wing. Their large eyes, sensitive to the slightest movement, occupy most of the head and the spiny, forwardly inclined legs hang in a permanent grasping posture. They are accomplished acrobats and can both hover and fly backwards. The true dragonflies (Anisoptera) are robust and hold their wings open when at rest, while the more delicate damselflies (Zygoptera) hold their wings closed, over the abdomen, when at rest.

In the three counties the largest common dragonflies are the brown aeshna *Aeshna grandis* and the southern aeshna *A. cyanea*. The common aeshna *A. juncea* is uncommon but is recorded from Bagley and the Reading area. The golden-ringed dragonfly *Cordulegaster boltonii* (p. 161) is known from localities near Reading and should be found elsewhere in the Thames valley. Brasenose Common, Oxon, is the only local site for the emperor dragonfly *Anax imperator* and it has not been seen there since 1941.

Our commonest species in summer and autumn is the common sympetrum *Sympetrum striolatum*. This is the yellowish dragonfly frequently seen hawking up and down woodland rides and footpaths. It is particularly common at Bernwood Forest, Dry Sandford Pit, Cothill and Snelsmore Common, Berks. The four-spotted libellula *Libellula quadrimaculata*, the most frequent of the thick-bodied species, is widespread throughout our area and breeds in large numbers at Cothill and Dry Sandford Pit. Our rarest species is the club-tail dragonfly *Gomphus vulgatissimus*, for which there is only one recent record. In the three counties it has always been associated with the Thames and there are old records for Eynsham and Godstow, both Oxon.

Of the damselflies, the brilliantly metallic banded agrion *Agrion splendens* and demoiselle agrion *A. virgo* are common near slow-moving canals and rivers. They are the largest British damselflies and their delicate, fluttering flight is a pleasant spectacle over quiet summer waters. The red damselfly *Pyrrhosoma nymphula* emerges in late April or early May and is our earliest species; it is common throughout the Thames counties. The little blue-banded species, however, are more conspicuous and are often seen in large numbers. The common ischnura *Ischnura elegans* is common around weedy ponds, lakes and slow rivers. Two other blue and black-banded species are found in the same habitats, namely the common coenagrion *Coenagrion puella* and the variable coenagrion *C. pulchellum*.

With twenty-two species recorded in the three counties, we have 50 per cent of the total British dragonfly fauna. Because of the widespread destruction of ponds, however, the status of many of the species needs checking. A good account of the biology of dragonflies is given in Corbet, Longfield and Moore (1960) and adults and larvae can be identified with the excellent keys and figures in Hammond (1977).

The stoneflies (Plecoptera) are perhaps the most neglected insect order in our area. There are no recent published records. The adults are poor fliers and never wander far from water. They can be seen during the day, roosting on waterside vegetation. *Dinocras cephalotes* and *Perla bipunctata* are common in most areas and are the largest British species, with wing-spans of up to 50mm. Stoneflies are the models of many of the flies made by fishermen; they can be named with Kimmins (1950a).

Caddisflies (Trichoptera) are very closely related to the butterflies and moths (Lepidoptera). Their aquatic larvae are noted for the protective cases they build around themselves. Despite the many suitable habitats in the Thames counties, there are no recent published records of caddisflies. *Phrygaena grandis* is common along the Cherwell and smaller tributaries of the Thames, as are *Limnephilus lunatus* and *L. vittatus*. The caddisflies are worthy of more attention and can be identified with the keys in Mosely (1939), though this work is somewhat unreliable and is largely out of date.

Lacewings (Neuroptera)

The Neuroptera contain a number of distinct groups, the principal ones being the alderflies and snakeflies (Megaloptera) and the Lacewings proper (Planipennia). Alderflies have aquatic larvae and the slow-flying adults are found in waterside vegetation and hedgerows near streams. There are only two British species and *Sialis lutaria*, the commoner, is widespread in our area.

The snakeflies are entirely terrestrial. The females lay eggs in crevices in and under bark. Both the larvae and adults are carnivorous. There are four British species and two, *Raphidia notata* and *R. maculicollis*, are recorded from the three counties. Neither is common. The former has been recorded from Stanton St John, Oxon, and the Reading area and the latter from Bagley and Tubney Woods; in 1978 it was found several times at Shotover.

Of the lacewings, the green *Chrysopa carnea* is common everywhere. Adults often enter buildings to hibernate over winter, during which time they develop a pinkish hue. The females lay eggs at the end of mucus threads, which dry to form thin stalks. The Neuroptera can be named with the aid of Fraser (1959).

Cockroaches (Dictyoptera)

Three species of cockroach are indigenous to Britain. The large, household species such as the misnamed 'black beetle' *Blatta orientalis*, are not native, but have tropical origins and are now cosmopolitan by virtue of human commerce. Two of the native species are recorded from the Thames counties, in dry heathy areas. The dusky cockroach *Ectobius lapponicus* reputedly once occurred at Bagley Wood, Sunninghill, Berks, and in the Reading area. The tawny cockroach *E. pallidus* has been recorded from Berkshire but not recently. Both sexes of the latter species and the males of the former will fly, but only in the hottest weather.

Crickets and Grasshoppers (Orthoptera)

In these days of intensive agriculture, our crickets and grasshoppers are no longer so common as they used to be. They are really only numerous in old pastures, undisturbed deciduous woodland and in man-made habitats such as sandpits and quarries. There are no recent records for the mole cricket *Gryllotalpa gryllotalpa*, which was once found at Besselsleigh, Berks/Oxon. It lives in damp soil, preferably in water-meadows and flood plains. The species was never common and with so much of our pasture land now improved, it must be considered as one of our rarest insects. The house cricket *Acheta domestica* is also now rare, its decline no doubt being due to the lack of large, open hearths in today's housing. The only locality known to me is the Bell Inn at Charlbury, Oxon.

Three species of bush cricket (Tettigoniidae) are common in our area. The oak bush cricket *Meconema thalassinum* is, as its name implies, associated with oak, but is also found in beechwoods. This is the only British species which spends nearly its entire life in trees and is to be found in most deciduous woods in the three counties. Its diet consists largely of caterpillars, aphids and other small insects. The dark bush cricket *Pholidoptera griseoaptera* lives in bramble brakes, nettles, the margins of woods and hedgerows. It is flightless, but is, nevertheless, well distributed. Recent records include Shotover and the BBONT reserves at Cothill and Dry Sandford. The speckled bush cricket *Leptophyes punctatissima* is common and widespread and in our area is known from Shotover and Bagley Wood. Our least common species is the great green bush cricket *Tettigonia viridissima* (p. 135), though in recent years there has been a local improvement in its fortunes. Until recently Faringdon was its main stronghold, but it is now known from Dry Sandford Pit, Hitch Copse Pit, Warren Bank, and Buttlers Hangings, Bucks, all BBONT reserves. It has also been recorded from Wytham, Tubney and Streatley, all Berks. The species is largely carnivorous and stalks around in coarse, marginal vegetation such as hedgerows or the edges of fields. Its song is very distinctive and resembles the sound of a push-bike free-wheeling downhill; in hot weather it may continue all through the night.

Four species of grasshopper (Acrididae) are reasonably common in the Thames counties. Lush grassland, woodland clearings and overgrown verges are the favourite habitats of the common green grasshopper *Omocestus viridulus*, which is widely distributed. The common field grasshopper *Chorthippus brunneus* prefers drier habitats and lives in railway cuttings, dry banks, quarries and well-drained chalk grassland. The related meadow grasshopper *C. parallelus* tolerates a wide

4. Great green grasshopper *Tettigonia viridissima*

5. Woodland grasshopper *Omocestus rufipes*

variety of grassland habitats and will live quite happily in damp heathland and marshy areas; it is common everywhere. Dry heathland and patches of exposed soil in calcareous grassland are favoured by the mottled grasshopper *Myrmeleotettix maculatus*, the only common grasshopper with a distinct club at the end of each antenna.

The adults of all the British cockroaches, crickets and grasshoppers can be found in the summer months and can be named using Ragge (1965).

True Bugs (Hemiptera)

True bugs possess piercing and sucking mouthparts and, according to species, feed on sap or the body fluids of other insects and animals; a few are at home with either diet. Although the impressive list of species recorded for the three counties in the *Victoria County Histories* indicates that just over 50 per cent of the British fauna has been found, the status of the majority is still unknown and there has been little subsequent collecting of this group.

Apart from the aphids the most familiar bug in gardens is the pied shieldbug *Sehirus bicolor*. It feeds on white deadnettle *Lamium album* and is common everywhere. In lush woodland and waterside vegetation, the large two-spined shieldbug *Picromerus bidens* (p. 137) is frequent. It is an active predator of caterpillars and the larvae of leaf beetles (Chrysomelidae). There are records for Tubney, Yarnton, Oxon, and Dry Sandford Pit. The gorse shieldbug *Piezodorus lituratus* is common wherever gorse and broom are found; it sometimes invades gardens, where it feeds on lupins. The vast majority of green bugs noticed by the casual observer are the so-called capsid bugs (Miridae) and almost any patch of vegetation will yield several species. *Monalocoris filicis* is common wherever bracken grows and hawthorn, hazel and oak are foodplants of the ubiquitous *Campyloneura virgula*.

Of the bugs parasitic on larger animals, the martin bug *Oeciacus hirundinis* is found wherever house martins nest. After the birds leave on their southward migration in autumn, the flattened bugs, which are closely related to the bed bug *Cimex lectularius*, often enter houses and occasionally feed on human blood.

All the above bugs and their many relatives can be named with the aid of Southwood and Leston (1959).

The familiar cuckoo-spit seen on lush vegetation from spring onwards is the work of immature frog-hoppers or spittle-bugs (Cercopidae). They secrete a frothy substance over themselves as a protection from both predators and desiccation while they feed on the sap of plants. Our commonest species, found everywhere, is *Philaenus spumarius*, though, being a dull brown colour, is not so well known as the

6. The two-spined shieldbug *Picromerus bidens*

much larger and conspicuously marked *Cercopis vulnerata*. This handsome black and red species, the largest British cercopid, is common in all deciduous woodlands in the three counties. There is no complete or adequate literature available for the identification of frog-hoppers and their allies.

Scorpionflies (Mecoptera)

The scorpionflies are so called because of the scorpion-like fashion in which the males hold the tips of their abdomens. In appearance they are unique in that the head is produced downwards into a beak which bears the biting jaws. The wings have complex veins and are mottled with black and brown. Scorpionflies belong to an ancient and primitive group which are believed to have given rise to the ancestors of the caddisflies, butterflies and moths, flies, beetles, wasps and bees. Three of the four British species are found in the Thames counties. *Panorpa communis* is the commonest and, like the other two species, is a denizen of hedgerows, where it scavenges on dead insects and occasionally feeds on bird droppings. It often basks in patches of sunlight in dense bramble clumps and in autumn eats over-ripe blackberries. The rare *P. cognata* is known from Cothill, Besselsleigh and Henley-on-Thames. *P. germanica*, also uncommon, is recorded from Tubney, Bagley Wood, Boars Hill, Berks/Oxon and Bullingdon Bog. Scorpionflies can be named with Fraser (1959).

Two-winged Flies (Diptera)

Nearly 2,000 species of true, two-winged flies have been recorded from the Thames counties. Flies have invaded all habitats and are one of the most successful insect groups. For both rambler and gardener, the most familiar and conspicuous flies are the hoverflies (Syrphidae). From spring to autumn, there can be no patch of sunlit flowers without these colourful insects. Their bright colours and, in some cases, dense fur, lead many people to mistake them for wasps or bees. Indeed this mistake is exactly what is required of potential predators, for the resemblance to stinging insects is no coincidence. It exploits the ability of insectivorous birds to learn by their mistakes; the callow fledgling, stung by a warningly-coloured wasp or bee, will learn to associate such colours with a painful experience and will avoid a repetition. The commonest wasp-coloured hoverfly is *Syrphus ribesii.* It is ubiquitous in the three counties and can be seen feeding or basking at a wide range of flowers. The larvae of this and many other hoverflies are useful predators of aphids. This is particularly true of the orange-bodied *Episyrphus balteatus*, which reached swarm proportions in the hot summer of 1976, when aphids underwent a population explosion.

The drone-fly *Eristalis tenax* is a very good mimic of honeybees and is common everywhere. The larvae live in stagnant water rich in decaying organic matter and are called rat-tailed maggots because of their long, thin, telescopic breathing tubes. Another common species is *E. arbustorum*, which mimics solitary bees of the genera *Colletes* and *Andrena. Volucella bombylans* (p. 139) is found in several different colour forms, each of which is a near-perfect mimic of one of the common species of bumblebee. The resemblance is not only in colour but also in movement and is so effective that it can fool experienced entomologists. The females lay their eggs in the nests of bumblebees, where the larvae develop, living as scavengers on waste matter. *V. bombylans* is common everywhere. *V. inanis* is much rarer and has been recorded only at Shotover, Oxon. The larvae live in the nests of hornets. One of our national rarities, *Chilosia chrysocoma*, is found at Cothill and Dry Sandford Pit. It is covered with dense, foxy red fur and is a more than passable mimic of the common mining bee of spring, *Andrena rufa*.

Of the 250 or so species of hoverfly found in Britain, more than 140 are known from the Thames counties. They can be named from Stubbs and Falk (1983).

A protective resemblance to wasps is not confined to the hoverflies. The soldier-flies (Stratiomyidae) contain species which are conspicuously marked with black and yellow bands. *Oxycera pulcella* is the commonest and is known from Bullingdon Bog, Sydlings Copse and Cothill. The rare *Stratiomys chamaeleon* was

7. Hoverfly *Volucella bombylans*

formerly numerous at Bullingdon Bog, but is now apparently absent from this BBONT reserve; it has recently been found at Dry Sandford Pit.

Wasp-like markings are also found in the Conopidae, an interesting family of flies whose larvae are internal parasites of adult wasps and bees. The females are armed with a stiletto-like egg-laying tube (ovipositor) with which they inject an egg into the body cavity of the host. Female conopids can often be seen 'shadowing' a host species and pouncing on it for a fraction of a second, during which the egg is laid. *Conops quadrifasciatus*, a bumblebee parasite, is frequent throughout the three counties and mating pairs can often be seen in flight and on flowers. The rare *Myopa buccata* is recorded from the BBONT reserve at Hook Norton, where it is a parasite of the equally rare mining bee, *Andrena bucephala* (see below). Conopids can be named with the aid of Smith (1969).

The bee-flies (Bombyliidae) are not only bee-like in appearance, but are, like some of the conopids, parasites of solitary mining bees, though it is the larval bees, not the adults, which succumb to the fly larvae. Adult bee-flies resemble the common gingery bumblebee, *Bombus pascuorum*, though their rapid, darting flight and their ability to hover and fly backwards is most unbee-like. Three species are found in our area. *Bombylius major* is common in early spring and frequents open woodland and earth banks which are the nest sites of its bee hosts. It hovers low over the ground and scatters its eggs: these soon hatch into minute, worm-like larvae, which migrate into the bees' nests. Both sexes of the adult bee-fly visit primroses and cowslips. Their hosts are mining bees of the genus *Andrena*. The largest and least common of the bee-flies in the three counties is *B. discolor*. It too parasitizes *Andrena* and flies in spring with *B. major* at Dry Sandford Pit. The smallest species, *B. minor*, appears later in the year and is associated with another genus of solitary bees, *Colletes*.

The robber flies (Asilidae) boast two species which resemble stinging insects and both are rare in the Thames counties. The bee-like *Laphria marginata* was once found at Stanton St John and Tubney. *Asilus crabroniformis*, Britain's largest fly, used to occur at Shotover, Boars Hill and Tubney, but has not been seen there since the war. It is strikingly marked with black and yellow and should be sought on the sandy heaths of Berkshire. Robberflies are voracious predators and use their piercing mouthparts to feed on the body fluids of other insects. They are rapid fliers and are very sensitive to movement; *Dysmachus trigonus* is the common grey species with the tantalizing habit of alighting on the ground just ahead of the walker and then flying off again almost immediately.

Piercing mouthparts are also put to good effect by the horseflies (Tabanidae) and all too often the victim is a human. The commonest man-biter in the vicinity of cattle and deer is *Haematopota pluvialis*. This is the persistent grey horsefly which is difficult to knock off one's clothing and equally difficult to kill. The large *Tabanus sudeticus* is widespread in the area but is never very common. The bee-flies, robberflies and horseflies can be named with Oldroyd (1969).

The common yellow dungfly *Scatophaga stercoraria* also has piercing mouthparts and is an active predator of other flies visiting dung. The species visits cow-pats not only to catch prey, but also to mate and lay eggs, for the larvae are dung-feeders.

Members of the parasitic family Tachinidae form a high proportion of the bristly flies to be seen on country walks. The commonest in high summer is the handsome, red-bodied *Eriothrix rufomaculatum*, whose adults are extremely numerous on ragwort flowers. The parasitic relations of the larvae are unknown, but they probably attack caterpillars. *Servillia ursina* is less common. It resembles a brown bumblebee and flies in early spring, in open areas in old, deciduous woodland. There are records for Windsor Forest, Wytham and Bernwood. The hosts are caterpillars of noctuid moths.

The important task of disposing of animal corpses is in part carried out by the blowflies (Calliphoridae). The bluebottles *Calliphora* spp. are common everywhere, as is the greenbottle *Lucilia caesar*. A related species, *L. bufonivora*, lays its eggs in the nostrils of toads and the larvae migrate throughout the body, feeding just beneath the skin. The species is locally common where toads occur. The grey fleshfly *Sarcophaga carnaria* is another common recycler of corpses. This is the large grey fly with shot-silk tessellations which is always to be found basking on flowers and warm stones.

The golden clusterfly *Pollenia rudis*, ubiquitous in the three counties, often attracts attention by its habit of entering houses in large numbers to hibernate. The flies are clothed with a dense covering of short golden hairs and often annoy householders when they awake from their winter slumbers on warm days. Their larvae are internal parasites of earthworms. The very striking *Mesembrina meridiana* often sunbathes in large numbers on tree trunks, fence posts and warm stones. It is a large, blue-black, spinose fly, with bright orange flashes at the bases of its wings. A member of the same family (Muscidae) as the housefly, *Musca domestica*, *Mesembrina* is unusual in that the females retain their eggs in a uterus and when they hatch, larvae are laid singly in dung.

The tachinids and calliphorids can be named with the keys in van Emden (1954), but this is a difficult work to use and a microscope is essential. The same applies to Fonseca (1968), which can be used to name the Muscidae. Good general accounts of the natural history of flies are to be found in Oldroyd (1964), Colyer and Hammond (1968) and Stubbs and Chandler (1978).

Wasps, Ants and Bees (Hymenoptera)

The Hymenoptera of the three counties have been well studied by successive generations of Oxford entomologists and there are full lists for all the groups. Nearly 200 species of sawflies Symphyta have been recorded and many are common in our area. Sawflies are the most primitive of living Hymenoptera; they lack the 'wasp-waist' that characterises the rest of the order. Female sawflies lay their eggs in incisions made in plant tissues by means of a specially modified, saw-like ovipositor. The larvae are caterpillar-like and feed on or in plant tissues. Most species are fairly plant-specific. Adult sawflies feed at flowers and a few are also carnivorous and prey on small flower-visiting insects. The common black sawflies of spring are *Dolerus aeneus*, *D. coracinus*, *D. niger* and *D. nigratus*. All are found in lush vegetation and their larvae are grass-feeders. Three of our most interesting species are found at Bernwood, *Cephus cultratus*, *C. pygmeus* and *Calameuta filiformis* (Cephidae). All have grass-feeding larvae, which on occasion attack cereal crops. They are, however, uncommon. Because they have a hint of a 'wasp-waist,' it is believed that the rest of the Hymenoptera may have had their origins among cephid sawflies. One of the rarest British sawflies is recorded from Cothill: *Aprosthema melanura* was hitherto known only from two specimens taken in the New Forest.

As a rule, sawflies are poor fliers. However, there are exceptions. The large and powerful *Cimbex femoratus* (Cimbicidae) is found in birch woods and the females make a loud whirring noise as they fly between birch trees, where they lay their eggs in young shoots and leaf stems. Two other cimbicids, *Trichiosomus lucorum* and *T. tibiale*, frequent in the three counties, are associated with hawthorn. The large wood wasps or horntails (Siricidae) are also strong-flying sawflies. The commonest is *Urocerus gigas*, which is often mistaken for a hornet. The long, horny 'tail' is a tough ovipositor, with which the females lay eggs in dead or dying conifers. *U. gigas* is common in the three counties wherever conifer plantations are well established. The British sawflies can be named with the keys in Benson (1951, 1952 and 1958).

Of the ichneumon wasps (Ichneumonidae), our largest species is *Rhyssa persuasoria*, a parasite of the wood wasp *Urocerus gigas*. The female can detect the movements of a wood-wasp larva in a piece of timber and, with her long ovipositor, bores down through the wood and injects an egg into the host. *R. persuasoria* is frequent at Wytham, Tubney, Bernwood and Sydlings Copse. The ichneumons are a vast group and are extremely difficult to identify. Many of the published records for the three counties must be regarded as suspect because of subsequent advances in taxonomy. However, in recent years nearly 400 species have been recorded from Bernwood Forest and my wife has recorded more than 200 species from our garden at North Hinksey, Oxford.

One of the most frequently seen species is the pale reddish-brown *Ophion luteus* which is often attracted to light in houses. Like most ichneumons, its larvae are internal parasites of caterpillars, in this case, those of noctuid moths. Another common species, frequent in gardens, is *Pimpla instigator*. With its jet-black body and orange legs, this is one of our handsomest ichneumons. The females lay their eggs in the pupae of moths. While most ichneumons are fairly host-specific, a few have an astonishing range of hosts. Thus the common *Hemiteles areator* has been bred not only from Lepidoptera, Diptera and Coleoptera, but also from other ichneumons.

The Braconidae are a related family of parasitic wasps, with many species. Depending on the size of the host, up to 150 larvae may develop at the expense of a single host larva. One of the commonest and most useful species is *Apanteles glomeratus*, a parasite of the cabbage white butterfly *Pieris brassicae*. Perhaps as many as 150 larvae burst out of the skin of the dead host and spin white cocoons, which are sometimes mistaken for caterpillar 'eggs'. Another species, *A. melittaearum*, parasitizes the marsh fritillary butterfly *Melitaea cinxia* and is recorded from the BBONT reserve at Otmoor. One of the commonest braconids in the three counties is *Alysia manducator*, whose larvae are internal parasites of blowfly larvae. The females are often seen running over animal corpses in search of their hosts.

The parasitic Hymenoptera also include the chalcid wasps (Chalcididae and related families) and the proctotrupid wasps (Proctotrupidae and related families). Although many are extremely common, they are all small to minute and are very difficult to name without access to a good, reliably named reference collection.

A few of the Cynipidae are also parasites, but the majority of the species are gall wasps. That is, the larvae develop in plant tissues which react to their presence by producing a tumour or gall that is characteristic in shape for each species of wasp. The wasp larvae feed within the gall and the gall may well be the plant's way of isolating the larvae and minimizing the damage they cause. The easiest galls to find are those which develop on oak trees. *Andricus kollari* is responsible for the familiar marble galls. It is common everywhere in oak woods and the small, circular holes in the galls are the exits chewed out by the emerging adult wasps. The artichoke galls on oak are caused by *A. fecundator*. These galls really do look like miniature globe artichokes. The spangle galls on the underside of oak leaves are the work of the asexual generation of the wasp *Neuroterus quercusbaccarum* which is common throughout the Thames counties. The wasps which emerge from these galls in April are entirely female. They reproduce without mating and their unfertilized eggs are laid in oak catkins and young leaves. This produces a quite different kind of gall, the so-called 'currant gall', which is soft, spherical and sappy. These galls contain both male and female wasps which mate on emergence. The females lay eggs at the sides of the veins underneath oak leaves, which, by the time they fall in October, bear the spangle galls of the next asexual generation. A similar alternation of generations is found in another ubiquitous gall wasp of oak woods, *Biorhiza pallida*. The developing sexual generation stimulates the familiar 'oak apple' gall. The asexual generation produces small, potato-like galls on the roots of oak trees.

The familiar robin's pincushion galls found on the stems of wild roses are the work of the cynipid *Diplolepis rosae*, a common gall wasp of waysides and hedgerows. An excellent account of the biology and identification of galls is given in Darlington (1968).

The rest of the Hymenoptera dealt with here belong to the Aculeata, or stinging insects, the ants, wasps and bees. The ants of the three counties are well known and about 50 per cent of the forty-two native species have been found in the area, though some are rare and others have declined since records were started. A most notable decline is that of the red wood ant *Formica rufa*. Formerly common at Frilford and Tubney, its only known locality near Oxford is now two colonies at Bernwood, but it is still to be found among pines on some of the Berkshire heaths. *Formica cunicularia* is known from Wytham and *F. fusca* is common in most localities.

The black ant of gardens, *Lasius niger*, is common everywhere and the yellow meadow ant *L. flavus* is still frequent in old pasture land. This subterranean, mound-making species is well represented in the Oxfordshire Chilterns at Chinnor Hill, Aston Rowant and Warren Bank. The much less common glossy black ant, *L. fuliginosus*, is known from Wytham Hill, Dry Sandford Pit and Tubney Woods. It is also found on the Berkshire heaths and should be sought on shaded, dry earth banks. Tubney Woods was once a locality favoured by several heathland Hymenoptera, notably the uncommon ant *Tetramorium caespitum*. This species is still found in dry habitats in Berkshire, but is now apparently absent from Tubney, no doubt due to afforestation. The rare ants *Stenamma westwoodi* and *Myrmecina graminicola* are still found at Wytham, but there are no other recent records from the Thames counties. Of the red ants, *Myrmica rufa* and *M. ruginodis* are common everywhere and well drained calcareous grassland supports *M. sabuleti* in all three counties. British ants can be named with Bolton and Collingwood (1975).

The majority of the solitary wasps and bees require light, well-drained soils in which to nest. Except for Shotover, Tubney, Frilford Heath, a few sandpits and the Berkshire heaths, there are few such habitats in the three counties. Nevertheless, these groups are well represented, though some species have declined since the 1930s.

Of the spider-hunting wasps (Pompilidae), *Pompilus cinereus* and *Priocnemis exaltatus* are ubiquitous in sandy area. *Priocnemis hyalinata* is recorded from grassy rides at Bernwood. At Shotover and Dry Sandford Pit the beautifully marked *Ceropales maculata* is frequent. This species has abandoned the habit of catching and paralysing spiders for itself; instead, the female lies in wait for a spider being dragged to the nest by another female pompilid and, in an instant, leaps on the prey and injects an egg into the spider's respiratory opening. The *Ceropales* larva then develops at the expense of that of the other pompilid wasp.

Three solitary vespid wasps are common in the Thames counties, *Odynerus spinipes*, *Ancistrocerus parietinus* and *A. parietum*. The first nests in earth banks or the mortar of old walls and builds an earthen turret at the nest entrance. Both species of *Ancistrocerus* nest in existing cavities such as beetle-borings in dead wood and all three prey on caterpillars. A fourth solitary vespid, *Gymnomerus laevipes*, preys on the larvae of leaf beetles (Chrysomelidae). It inhabits old deciduous woodland in our area and is known from Wytham, Shotover and Bernwood. The rarest solitary vespid in our area is *Microdynerus exilis*, known from only a few British localities, among them Silwood Park near Ascot, Berks, and the BBONT reserve at Hitch Copse Pit.

As picnickers are only too well aware, the social vespids are common in the area and often seem to achieve plague proportions. The common wasp *Paravespula vulgaris* and the German wasp *P. germanica* are common everywhere and both the tree wasp *Dolichovespula sylvestris* and the Norwegian wasp *D. norvegica* are widespread. The red wasp *Vespula rufa* is frequent, especially near pinewoods. The hornet *Vespa crabro* seems to be making a come-back after an apparent absence for some years. In 1978, 1979, and 1980, it was recorded from Blenheim, Wychwood Forest and Wytham Wood. It is much maligned, for it is much less aggressive than the other social vespids; it nests in hollow trees.

Our commonest solitary hunting wasp in the Sphecidae is *Mellinus arvensis*, which preys on flies and nests in large numbers in overhung banks in sandy areas. Other fly-hunting wasps which are widespread and common in the area are *Crabro cribrarius* and *Ectemnius cavifrons*. Both nest in old beetle-borings in dead wood. The largest hunting wasp recorded from the three counties is *Ammophila sabulosa*, which may attain a body length of 25mm. It preys on caterpillars and was once common at Tubney, Dry Sandford Pit and even in the grounds of the University Museum in Oxford. The only recent records are from the Berkshire heaths. Two sphecids are very rare in the three counties; *Cerceris arenaria*, which preys on weevils and *C. rybyensis*, which captures tiny, solitary bees. Both are found at Dry Sandford and Hitch Copse pits and the latter also at Shotover.

The genus *Andrena* contains many of our solitary mining bees, the most familiar of which is the attractive, foxy-red *A. fulva*, which nests in lawns in spring. *A. haemorrhoa* (p. 146) and *A. jacobi* are also common. Three of our nationally rare species are found in the Thames counties, namely *A. marginata*, *A. hattoffiana* and *A. bucephala*. The first two forage exclusively on field scabious *Knautia arvensis* and have recently been found at Dry Sandford Pit. There are old records for both species from Hermitage, Berks.

A. bucephala is known from the BBONT reserve at Hook Norton and a wood near Reading. It is unusual in that there are invariably many females associated

8. Mining bee *Andrena haemorrhea*

with a single nest entrance. Hitherto, it has been thought that each female had its own nest or group of cells within the entrance, but recent work on the Hook Norton population suggests that the species may be primitively social.

Our rarest mining bee is *Dasypoda altercator*. It was recently found at Dry Sandford Pit and is normally associated with coastal habitats in the south and west and the sandy heaths of Dorset, Hampshire and Surrey. The population at Dry Sandford is further inland than any previously recorded. Another uncommon species is *Eucera longicornis*, known from Hook Norton, Rushbeds Wood, Bucks, and Bernwood. A related species, *E. tuberculata*, has recently been added to the British list and should be sought in the calcareous grasslands of the Chilterns. The males of both species pollinate bee orchids *Ophrys apifera*.

The primitively social bees in the three counties include *Lasioglossum calceatum* and *L. albipes*. *Halictus rubicundus* is also common everywhere and all three species belong to the family Halictidae, which is noted for a wide range of social behaviour.

One family of solitary bees, the Megachilidae, specializes in nesting in ready-made cavities. Our commonest species is the red mason bee *Osmia rufa*, which nests in old beetle tunnels in wood, crevices in mortar, keyholes and, once, in Oxford, in the spout of an old kettle. The females seal their cells and the entrances to their nest with mud. *O. aurulenta* and *O. bicolor* nest exclusively in old snail shells and line their cells with pieces of chewed leaf. Neither are common in our area and the only recent record for both species is from Blewbury Down, Berks. The females of the rose leaf-cutter bee *Megachile centuncularis* nest in similar situations to those of *Osmia rufa*, but use pieces of cut leaf rather than mud with which to fashion their cells. This species is very common in gardens throughout the area. The females of *Anthidium manicatum*, which are common in gardens, collect the cottony down that clothes the leaves of plants such as lamb's ears *Stachys lanata*. They too nest in ready-made cavities and Gilbert White described their behaviour in *The Natural History of Selborne*.

Seven species of bumblebee are commonly found in the three counties and all may be found in a single garden at any one time. They are: *Bombus lucorum*, *B. terrestris*, *B. lapidarius*, *B. pratorum*, *B. hortorum*, *B. pascuorum* and *B. ruderarius*. Another species, *B. ruderatus*, was formerly common but is now rare in the area. *B. cullumanus* is an extreme rarity and in Britain has only ever been recorded from the Chilterns, near Goring, Oxon, and Sussex. It is now apparently extinct. The uncommon *B. sylvarum* has been found at Waterperry, Oxon, and Dry Sandford Pit.

The nests of bumblebees are often invaded by cuckoo bees which have no worker caste of their own but, instead, lay their eggs to be reared by workers of the host species. The three common species of cuckoo bee in our area are *Psithyrus vestalis*, *P. bohemicus* and *P. campestris*, which parasitize, respectively, *Bombus terrestris*, *B. lucorum* and *B. pascuorum*. *Psithyrus rupestris*, which used to be frequent in the area is now rare; its host is *Bombus lapidarius*, which it closely resembles.

There is no single, reliable, or easily available work which can be used to identify the British aculeate Hymenoptera, though several handbooks in the Royal Entomological Society of London's series are in preparation.

Beetles (Coleoptera)

More than 2,000 species of beetle have been found in the three counties, that is, 60 per cent of the total British fauna. This is in large part due to the very intensive collecting in the early part of this century by J. J. Walker and entomologists on the staff of the Hope Department of Entomology at Oxford.

Some of our commonest, though little seen beetles are the ground beetles (Carabidae). They are largely carnivorous and for the most part nocturnal, spending the daylight hours under stones, bark, logs and leaf litter. *Pterostichus madidus* is common everywhere and is found on a wide range of soil types, as are *Abax parallelopipedus* and *Agonum dorsale*. The large and beautiful *Carabus violaceus* and *C. nemoralis* are widespread in the district and inhabit woodland, though they sometimes occur in gardens. The bronzy *Calasoma inquisitor* has been taken in Bagley Wood.

The Rovebeetles (Staphylinidae) are ubiquitous and many species are difficult to identify. The most conspicuous are the large devil's coach horse *Staphylinas olens* and the metallic-hued *Philonthus decorus*, both of which are common everywhere.

Several of the Thames counties beetles are adapted for feeding on slugs and snails. One, a ground beetle, *Cychrus caraboides*, has a narrowed and elongated head. This is thrust into the entrance of the snail shell and the beetle follows the snail until it can retreat no further. *C. caraboides* is local, lives in deciduous woodland and when handled makes a chirping noise by rubbing the ends of its wing cases against the tip of the abdomen.

The glow-worm *Lampyris noctiluca* injects digestive juices into slugs and snails with its hollow jaws. It is uncommon and confined to calcareous areas, but is recorded from Wytham, Bernwood Forest, Dry Sandford Pit and Chinnor Hill in the Oxfordshire Chilterns. Our third snail predator is *Phosphuga atrata*, a member of the carrion beetle family, the Silphidae. It is common in all types of woodland and is often found under stones in fields.

The carrion or burying beetles are important recyclers of animal corpses. The black and orange-marked *Necrophorus investigator* and *N. vespilloides* are common everywhere, especially in open woodland. The large black *N. humator*, is less common, but is known from Tubney, Shotover and Headington. Another black species, *Necrodes littoralis*, has become increasingly common over the last fifty years. It is normally a coastal beetle but is now numerous at Wytham, Shotover, Bernwood and Tubney.

Several species of beetle are characteristic of old, deciduous woodland. *Scaphidium quadrimaculatum*, a small fungus feeder, is recorded from Wytham, Bernwood and Windsor Forest. The same localities support the beautiful, metallic green *Agrilus viridis*, whose larvae feed on young oak twigs. This is one of the few members of the colourful tropical family Buprestidae found in temperate climates. The lovely green longhorn beetle, *Agapanthia villosoviridescens* is found at Shotover, Bernwood and Windsor Forest. This last locality is one of the most famous collecting sites in Britain for beetles; of the old woodland in the three counties, it is the only one which has all three British species of stag beetle (Lucanidae). The small stag beetle *Sinodendron cylindricum* is also found at Wytham, Bernwood and Tubney; the larvae live in dead oak and hawthorn. The lesser stag beetle *Dorcus parallelopipedus* is not uncommon in the same localities.

9. Longhorn beetle *Strangalia quadrifasciata*

The great stag beetle *Lucanus cervus* is known from Shillingford Berks/Oxon as well as Windsor Forest and may well also be present in Rushbeds Wood, Bucks. It is a popular myth among entomologists that the great stag beetle has never been found north of the Thames, but there are, in fact, some nineteenth-century records for the Richmond area of Yorkshire. If we take these six species of woodland beetles as indicators of old forest habitats, then apart from Windsor Forest, Bernwood scores highest, with five out of the six being recorded there, the only absentee being *L. cervus*.

Most ladybirds (Coccinellidae) are voracious and useful predators of aphids, both as adults and larvae. The six common species are the two-spot *Adalia bipunctata*, the seven-spot *Coccinella septempunctata*, the ten and eleven-spot *A.* 10-*punctata* and *C.* 11-*punctata*, the fourteen-spot *Calvia* 14-*punctata* and the twenty-two-spot *Thea* 22-*punctata*. The eyed ladybird *Anatis ocellata* was formerly an uncommon species of pinewoods, but is now more frequent as conifer plantations increase in number. It is recorded from Bernwood, Shotover and Wytham. *Harmonia quadripunctata* is rare and the only two recent records are from Bernwood and the arboretum at Nuneham Courteney, Oxon.

The rarest beetle of the Thames counties is the leaf beetle *Gynandrophthalma affinis*. The first British record was from Wychwood Forest in 1899 and it is still only known from that locality, where it was last seen in 1951. Other chrysomelids in the Thames counties include *Chrysolina populi*, which feeds on willows and the brilliant, metallic green *C. menthastri*, which feeds on mint.

There are many species of weevil (Curculionidae) in the three counties. One of the most numerous is the green *Phyllobius viridearis*, common on oak and hazel. *P. pyri* is a pest of pears and *Sitona bilineata* can be a serious problem for growers of broad beans and peas. The jaws of weevils are borne at the end of an elongated, snout-like structure called the rostrum. This is unusually long and thin in *Curculio nucum*, which develops inside hazel nuts. Two rare species, *Rhynchites harwoodi* and *R. pauxillus* are recorded from Oxfordshire. The former lives on sallows at Cothill and the latter has been swept from birch and hawthorn at Bernwood.

Several interesting beetles live in dry grassland and sandy wastes. These include the green tiger beetle *Cicindela campestris*, which is an active predator of other insects and flies readily in hot weather. *Amara aenea* a metallic green ground beetle, is active during the day and is often seen running about paths and lawns with a smaller relative, *Notiophilus biguttatus*. The bloody nose beetle *Timarcha tenebricosa*, is found in calcareous grassland containing bedstraw. This is the largest member of the leaf beetle family (Chrysomelidae) and is known from Shotover, Chinnor Hill and Aston Rowant. Its name derives from the habit of secreting a distasteful red liquid when handled roughly.

Many beetles are found at flowers, which not only provide food in the form of pollen, but are also a convenient meeting place for the sexes. The common red soldier beetle *Rhagonycha fulva* is abundant everywhere and in high summer, every ragwort and hogweed inflorescence has several mating pairs. In lush meadows, buttercups are the refuelling and mating stations for the metallic green *Oedemera nobilis*, whose males have greatly thickened hind legs. The tiny black beetles so numerous at hawthorn and hogweed are *Meligethes aeneus*. They are often a pest of cruciferous crops such as cabbages and oilseed rape. Two of our more attractive longhorn beetles (Cerambycidae), *Strangalia quadrimaculata* and *Clytus arietus* are fond of feeding and mating at flowers. Both species are conspicuously marked with black and yellow; indeed the latter species is often called the 'wasp beetle'. Both are found at Wytham, Bernwood, Shotover and Windsor Forest, where they can be seen on ox-eye daisies and hogweed.

A good general account of the natural history of beetles is given by Evans (1977) and the only single work which attempts to aid the identification of all British beetles is still that by Joy (1932).

Change and stability in the invertebrate fauna of the Thames counties

The records and collections of insects in the Hope Entomological Collections in the University Museum, Oxford, show that many insect species which were common between the wars are now extinct or rare in the Thames counties. Some of the decline can be attributed to intensive agriculture and the loss of many deciduous woodlands to conifer plantations. This is particularly true for the solitary bees, which have had to contend with a reduced floral diversity and fewer areas of marginal land in which to nest. Four species which were clearly once common and are now apparently extinct in the area are *Andrena timmerana*, *A. rosae*, *A. humilis* and *A. pilipes*. It is gratifying, therefore, that so many rare insects still survive, many of them on BBONT reserves. A few of the former rarities are, indeed, apparently gaining strength, namely the bee *Eucera longicornis* and the hornet *Vespa crabro*.

The relationship between floral diversity and insect diversity is exemplified by gardens, where, the contrived diversity of flowering plants can support up to fifty species of wild bee. Today, outside gardens, such riches are only to be found in a few special sites such as Bernwood, Dry Sandford and Hitch Copse Pits. This was not always the case. The Cherwell valley was, by all accounts, every bit as rich in wild bees as our suburban gardens.

Human activities are not always to blame for some of the detectable changes in the three counties. Thus the national tragedy of Dutch elm disease has, ironically, improved the fortunes of two rather uncommon beetles. *Thanasimus formicarius* preys on insects beneath the bark of dead elms and in 1979 suddenly appeared at several localities around Oxford. *Endomychus coccineus* lives in the same microhabitat and feeds on fungi and this species, too, has been found more frequently in the last year. By contrast no explanation can be offered for the steady inland colonization of the normally coastal carrion beetle, *Necrodes littoralis*.

The remains of invertebrates in archaeological sites provide further examples of inexplicable change (Lambrick and Robinson 1979). Thus the snail *Vertigo angustior* was found in three Iron Age sites in Oxford but today is known only from Eire and East Anglia. The rare weevil, *Apion urticarium*, occurs no further north than Leicestershire and no nearer to Oxford than Streatley, yet is found in Roman remains at three Oxfordshire sites and one in Gloucestershire. The foodplant is the stinging nettle, which is hardly rare anywhere, so the present-day scarcity of *A. urticarium* is a mystery.

There is, by contrast, surprising evidence of stability in the ant fauna. In the face of deforestation and the dramatic changes in land use which have occurred in the last four thousand years, it is remarkable that nine species of ant, recovered from archaeological remains at Farmoor, Berks/Oxon, by Mark Robinson and identified by me, should have persisted from Iron Age and Roman times until the present day. All have been found within five miles of the site in this century, though four are now uncommon, namely *Stenamma westwoodi*, *Myrmecina graminicola*, *Formica cunicularia* and *Lasius fuliginosus*.

11 Freshwater Invertebrates

URSULA BOWEN

In 1954 three Oxford University zoologists (B. M. Hobby, H. N. Southern and M. H. Williamson) writing about the fauna of the Oxford region commented on the lack of information about the distribution of freshwater invertebrates and the considerable scope for freshwater ecology. A quarter of a century later our knowledge of the distribution of freshwater invertebrates is still patchy, but we now have the results of several ecological surveys of rivers and artificial habitats such as gravel pits and reservoirs. Streams, ponds and lakes, however, still remain neglected. Species identification is one of the major problems hampering freshwater surveys, but for the purposes of biological surveillance, aimed at detecting and measuring long-term changes in freshwater ecosystems, identification to a convenient taxonomic level is acceptable. The identification of the macroinvertebrates of a freshwater community to the level of family or below is sufficient to indicate changes in the ecosystem; the major taxonomic categories of order, class and phylum are not sufficiently sensitive. Another factor contributing to the lack of records is that freshwater invertebrates have excited little interest from amateurs, but perhaps this less demanding approach towards identification will encourage them to participate.

The three counties possess a wide variety of freshwater ecosystems—springs, streams, rivers, canals, ponds, lakes, gravel pits and reservoirs. Village and field ponds are declining in numbers, but garden ponds, gravel pits and reservoirs are increasing, so that the total surface area of fresh water in the three counties has risen considerably since the beginning of the century. Loss of habitat does not appear to be a problem, but the quality of these freshwater ecosystems is threatened by pollution, the lowering of the water table and the reduced flow of water in rivers and streams; the last two result from the extraction of water for domestic and industrial use.

A Nature Conservation Review (Ratcliffe 1977) lists only one key freshwater site in the three counties—the ponds in Wychwood Forest, Oxon, which are a grade 2 site. However there are two grade 1 sites bordering the three counties—Tring

Reservoirs, Hertfordshire, and some worked-out gravel pits at the Cotswold Water Park on the borders of Wiltshire and Gloucestershire. These sites are marl lakes, the rarest type of standing water in Britain. Marl lakes occur only in areas of highly calcareous soluble limestone and chalk, or in glacial deposits derived from these rocks. The three habitats mentioned here are all man-made; natural standing water bodies are absent from the permeable chalk and Jurassic limestone of southern England, but as gravel extraction proceeds in the Thames valley a series of marl lakes are being created which, with suitable management, will develop the diverse flora and fauna characteristic of these water bodies. Marl lakes have a high alkalinity (>100ppm of calcium carbonate) but as the phosphorus is often present in insoluble form the production of phytoplankton is very low. There is an abundant growth of macrophytes and the water is extremely clear, permitting high rates of photosynthesis and resulting in the precipitation of calcium carbonate together with phosphorus as a deposit (marl). This encrusts the substrate and often the leaves of the macrophytes. The phenomenon can easily be seen in many of the Cotswold springs and streams where the mosses, liverworts and other macrophytes crumble when rubbed between the fingers.

In Wychwood Forest there are eight small artificial marl ponds all interconnected and fed by limestone streams arising from springs. They have been created by damming up the streams. The upper four ponds together with the springs and streams which feed them lie within the Wychwood NNR. They support a very diverse invertebrate fauna which is particularly rich in Corixidae (water boatmen) and in molluscs. Surrounded by woodland, they are protected from sources of pollution such as run-off of fertilizers and pesticides from the surrounding agricultural land. Species of freshwater invertebrates characteristic of oligotrophic, eutrophic and marl ponds and lakes are listed in *A Nature Conservation Review.*

The River Pollution Survey of England and Wales (Department of the Environment 1970) classifies rivers and canals by chemical criteria and biological assessment; it provides data on the two main causes of pollution—discharges of sewage and industrial effluent—but does not survey levels of pesticides and artificial fertilizers. The Thames with its tributaries is the major river system draining the three counties; a small area of north-east Bucks is drained by the Ouse and the Ouzel. The classification of the Thames and its tributaries by chemical criteria indicates that approximately 84 per cent of its length is Class 1 (defined as unpolluted and recovered from pollution), 13 per cent is Class 2 (doubtful quality and needing improvement), 2.5 per cent is Class 3 (poor quality), and 0.5 per cent is Class 4 (grossly polluted). Most of the lengths of river in classes 2, 3 and 4 lie within a 25km radius of Bracknell. The Thames Water Authority is taking steps to improve the situation so that only 3km of river classified as Class 3 or 4 will remain. The Thames is much less polluted now than it was 100 years ago. In 1981 the National Water Council published a survey providing up-to-date information on methods of biological assessment and pollution levels in rivers and canals in the Thames catchment area.

Using a biological assessment of river quality, approximately 44 per cent of the Thames and its tributaries is graded as Class A, 49 per cent as Class B, 6 per cent as Class C and less than 1 per cent as Class D. The degree of correlation between chemical and biological assessment is not so high as expected and the Water Authorities are considering a revision of the biological assessment. The Classes A–D are defined according to their invertebrate fauna and species of fish.

Class A: Rivers with a widely diverse invertebrate fauna including an appreciable proportion of Plecoptera (stonefly nymphs) and/or Ephemeroptera (mayfly nymphs), Trichoptera (caddisfly larvae) and Amphipoda (freshwater shrimps), salmon, trout and grayling fisheries, when purely ecological factors favour these fish, otherwise good mixed coarse fisheries including a variety of species.

Class B: Rivers in which the Plecoptera and Ephemeroptera populations may be restricted. Trichoptera and Amphipoda usually present in reasonable numbers and the invertebrate population as a whole quite varied. Good mixed coarse fisheries. Trout may be present but will be rarely dominant.

Class C: Rivers in which the variety of macroscopic invertebrate organisms is restricted and the population is dominated by the isopod *Asellus aquaticus*, the waterlouse, waterskater or hogskater. Although some Amphipoda may be present, Trichoptera and Ephemeroptera are relatively rare. Moderate to poor fisheries. Fish population restricted mainly to roach and gudgeon.

Class D: Macroscopic invertebrate fauna absent or severely restricted to the pollution-tolerant organisms Oligochaetes (worms) and *Chironomus thummi* (bloodworms). Rivers known to be incapable of supporting fish life.

Much more research has been done on the distribution of invertebrates in the Thames and its tributaries compared with the amount of work carried out on ponds and lakes. One of the reasons for this is the concern of the Nature Conservancy Council about the effects of management carried out by the water authorities along the rivers in the Council's South Region, including the Thames and its tributaries. Surveys of invertebrates and macrophytes in many of the tributaries have been sponsored by the NCC since 1976, culminating in a report which provides a system of river classification and a systematic plan for data collection. This will facilitate the evaluation of rivers for nature conservation and the formulation of a conservation policy for the rivers in the South Region (Goriup and Karpowicz 1976 and 1979; Hattey 1977).

Although the area of freshwater habitats is increasing in the three counties, there is very little information on the stages and rate of ecological succession in the new habitats—(flooded gravel pits, reservoirs and garden ponds)—so that it is impossible to give an accurate assessment of their conservation value in replacing and supplementing natural standing water bodies. The numbers of wintering and breeding wildfowl feeding in flooded gravel pits and reservoirs gives an indication of the richness of the invertebrate community but does not provide information on the actual species present and their abundance.

The Game Conservancy–Amey Roadstone Wildfowl Project which is being carried out by Michael Street at Great Linford gravel pits in North Bucks, is contributing to our knowledge of the colonization and succession of invertebrate species in these new ecosystems—most of the pits were excavated in the last twelve years. The main aim of the project is to determine the factors which affect the mortality of mallard ducklings and to devise suitable management practices for new gravel pits which will increase the survival rate of the ducklings. The major cause of duckling losses proves to be the lack of invertebrate foods which are essential for rapid growth in the first twelve days after hatching. The productivity of new gravel pits in terms of insect emergence is low because of the oligotrophic status of these immature ecosystems. The nutrient content of the water is low, and there has been insufficient time for the accumulation of the organic material which is necessary for the production of aquatic insect larvae. The ducklings are unable to collect sufficient invertebrates, especially emerging adult insects, and they turn to eating seeds which do not satisfy their high protein requirements during this rapid growth period. Diptera, mainly Chironomid (midge) adults, larvae and pupae, are the main invertebrate food, but adult Coleoptera (beetles) and freshwater molluscs make up a significant proportion of the diet. Mallard ducklings over twelve days old eat less invertebrate food and more seeds; the main invertebrates taken by the older ducklings are molluscs and sub-aquatic larvae of Trichoptera, Hemiptera and Ephemeroptera.

In May, June and July of 1975 and 1976 emergence traps were used to monitor insects emerging from the water, and the waterside vegetation was sampled using a sweep net. Ephemeroptera were found in very small numbers throughout the period, the most abundant species being *Caenis moesta*. The most frequent species

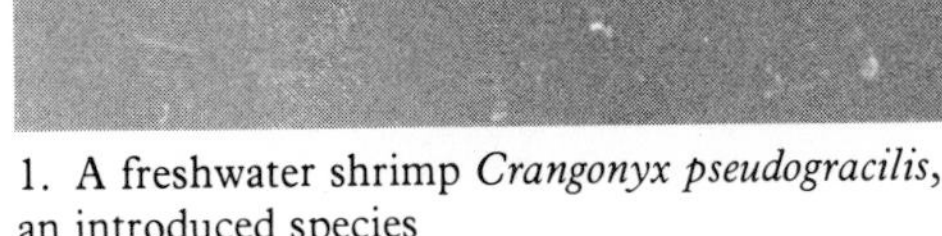

1. A freshwater shrimp *Crangonyx pseudogracilis*, an introduced species

2. A caddis fly larva in a case constructed of plant material

of Trichoptera were *Mystacides longicornis* and *Allotrichia pallicornis.* Members of three families of Diptera (two-winged flies) were caught, the most numerous being the Chironomidae (midges); *Probezzia venusta* was the dominant species of the Ceratopogonidae and the Culicidae (gnats) were represented by *Chaoborus flavicans.* To improve the diversity of the freshwater invertebrates at Great Linford pit, methods of increasing the nutrients and organic matter are being investigated.

The results of the Game Conservancy Wildfowl Project can be used to advance the plant and animal succession in newly flooded gravel pits so that they quickly develop rich freshwater communities. If there is not enough money to support this type of management, the same climax can be achieved by a policy of non-intervention or laissez-faire but it will take much longer. Whichever type of management is planned it is essential that the gravel extraction companies should be required by the planning authority to regrade the side of the pit to form gently sloping banks with a scalloped edge which will encourage the establishment of a high diversity of plants and animals, particularly the freshwater invertebrates.

At Milton Keynes the construction of six balancing lakes was started in the early

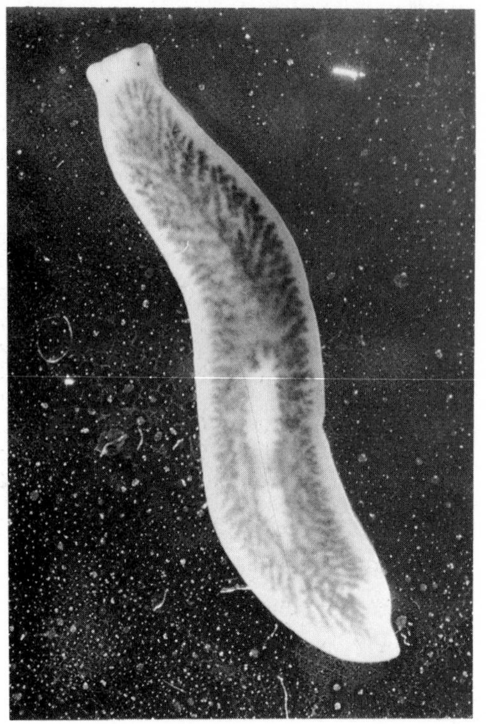

3. A free-living flatworm *Dendrocoelum lacteum*

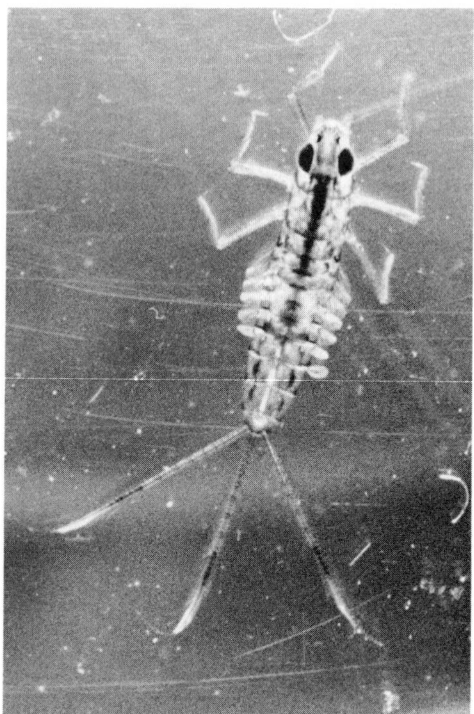

4. An ephemeropteran nymph *Cloëon dipterum*

1970s. The function of these lakes is to dispose of the surface water run-off resulting from the building of this new city. The Milton Keynes Development Corporation has appointed an ecologist to supervise the ecological management of these artificial habitats. The general ecological strategy for Willen Lake (68ha) is to speed up the rate of ecological succession by introducing organic matter and selected species of plants, freshwater invertebrates and fish. The purpose of this is to control the natural establishment of undesirable species such as biting midges, to prepare the lake for angling earlier than might otherwise be possible, to improve the landscape for recreational activities such as sailing and to help control the water quality. In addition these ecosystems will make a valuable contribution to the conservation of freshwater species and communities. Regular monitoring of these newly established ecosystems is being carried out to record the rate and stages of the succession; this information will also be of use in designing future lakes. Detailed information about the freshwater invertebrates has been published in a series of reports (Kelcey *et al*).

Today many village and field ponds have no practical use. Many have silted up or

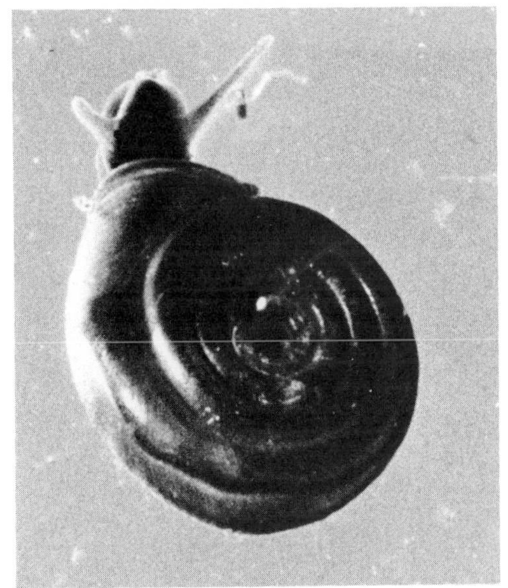

5. Water snail *Planorbis contortus*

6. A water bug *Ilyocoris cimicoides*

have been filled in; others are polluted by farm effluent, which at first causes eutrophication so that the plant and animal community rapidly increases and then dies as the bacteria responsible for decomposition of the organic material use up all the available oxygen. Fertilizers, insecticides and herbicides used on surrounding fields are carried by rainwater into ponds, where their concentration can build up because there is no outlet. Spraying, particularly aerial spraying, of insecticides and herbicides, can result in direct contamination of bodies of freshwater. A build-up of artificial fertilizers in a pond can cause eutrophication; a build-up of insecticides and herbicides could deplete the plant and animal community. The decline in village and field ponds can be offset by the creation of garden ponds. Practical instructions for the construction of ponds, with lists of native species of plants and invertebrates suitable for stocking them, can be found in the BBONT booklet *How to Make a Small Pond.* (Bowen 1977).

Ponds and lakes are continuously filling up with sediment so that they are in a state of constant and dynamic change; the stages of this ecological succession from open water to the final stage of woodland are called a hydrosere. One of the conservation problems which faces BBONT is the management of ponds, such as the one at BBONT's Henry Stephen/C. S. Lewis Educational Reserve, which is at a temporary stage in the succession. A newly formed lake or pond is at first oligotrophic (lacking in nutrients). In the course of time it will become enriched with nutrients and sediments (eutrophicated) as water drains into it from the

7. Hawker dragonfly *Cordulegaster boltonii*

surrounding land. This process of natural eutrophication proceeds faster in the three counties with their 'soft', easily eroded rocks of limestone and chalk than it does in hard-rock areas such as the Lake District. As the succession proceeds towards the climax (final stage) the species diversity increases. The pond at the Henry Stephen/C. S. Lewis Reserve is noted for its high diversity of invertebrate species (a list of species is available from BBONT). Within the next decade, the sediment which has accumulated on the bottom will need pumping out in order to maintain a body of standing water. However, this will destroy large number of freshwater invertebrates and the rarer species such as the water scorpion *Nepa cinerea* and the water stick insect *Ranatra linearis* might not recolonize.

Some species of freshwater invertebrates occurring in the three counties are of particular interest on account of their rarity or pattern of distribution. The triclad *Crenobia alpina* occurs in freshwater springs and the upper reaches of these streams. It is abundant in the spring-fed streams of Wychwood Forest, but absent in the streams connecting the ponds. The distribution of *Crenobia alpina* is strongly influenced by temperature—the upper limiting level is between 12°–14°. During the last glaciation this species was much more widely distributed, but as the climate warmed up it was eliminated from many streams and in Wychwood Forest is now restricted to the spring-fed streams, in a position downstream where the temperature does not rise above 12.5°C in summer. At this point its range overlaps with that of another triclad, *Polycelis felina,* which replaces *Crenobia alpina* in the lower reaches of these streams. A detailed survey of the distribution of invertebrates in four of the Wychwood Forest streams with particular reference to the triclads and of the environmental factors influencing their distribution was carried out in 1978, and is available from the Department of Biology, Oxford Polytechnic. Reports of preliminary surveys of the invertebrates in the Wychwood Forest ponds with particular reference to the Corixidae and measurements of the physico-chemical factors which influence their distribution are available (Department of Biology, Oxford Polytechnic). The crayfish *Austropotamobius pallipes* is still abundant in the unpolluted freshwater habitats of Wychwood Forest, and in the River Thame at Thame is still in sufficient numbers for boys to catch them to supply to local restaurants (R. S. R. Fitter, personal comm.). Elsewhere in the three counties, however, it is not so common as it was thirty years ago. This species requires high levels of oxygen and calcium and is particularly sensitive to pollution.

Of the seventy-one species of freshwater mollusc on the British list, fifty-eight have been recorded in the three counties. The high calcium concentration of the water in the region is the chief factor responsible for this high diversity of species. Two are of particular interest. *Planorbis acronicus* occurs only in the River Thames and some of its tributaries. *Valvata macrostoma* is recorded from only seven counties—Berkshire, Hampshire, Lincolnshire, Norfolk, Oxfordshire, Suffolk and Sussex; it inhabits nutrient rich rivers and draining ditches. In Oxfordshire there is only one record, taken from flood debris on Pixey Mead in 1974–5 (H. J. M. Bowen); there are two records from Berkshire, where it has been found in the Pang and the Loddon, (Goriup and Karpowicz 1976).

Of the insects, eleven species of Ephemeroptera, one species of Trichoptera and two species of Odonata are regarded as rarities in the Thames Water Authority Region. Two species of these insects are of interest here. The caddisfly *Leptocerus lusitanicus*, whose only breeding locality in the three counties is at the junction of the Isis and the Thame, and the dragonfly *Gomphus vulgatissimus*, which in Britain breeds only in Hampshire, Sussex, Berkshire, Bucks and Oxfordshire. This species breeds along the Thames from Lechlade to Marlow (see Fig. 11.1). At Pangbourne in 1979 approximately 100 exuviae were obtained in one day. Although this species is very local, it occurs in good numbers in Bucks, Berkshire and Oxfordshire, and there is no need for concern about its conservation (G. Vick).

12 Conservation Achievements and Problems

RICHARD FITTER

The beginning of organized wildlife conservation in the three counties dates back to 1902. In that year the Ashmolean Natural History Society of Oxfordshire, the oldest extant natural history society of Great Britain—it was founded in 1828—acquired part of Cothill Fen in Berks, a few miles south-west of Oxford. They called it the Ruskin Reserve in honour of John Ruskin, whose analysis of the ills of Victorian civilization has an increasingly modern ring. This four-and-a-half-acre calcareous fen, a highly endangered habitat even at the beginning of the century, was handed over to the National Trust, which later leased it to the Nature Conservancy. BBONT secured a lease in 1964 of the adjacent Parsonage Moor, where Professor E. B. Ford's world famous genetic experiments on the scarlet tiger moth *Panaxia dominula* were conducted.

The second historic step was the provisional list of proposed nature reserves in Britain drawn up in August 1915 by the Hon. Charles Rothschild on behalf of his infant Society for the Promotion of Nature Reserves (which in 1981 became the Royal Society for Nature Conservation) founded only three years before. Rothschild, who had been spurred to action by the wartime ploughing campaign, divided his sites into areas of primary and secondary importance. He listed six sites in Berkshire, seven in Bucks, and two in Oxon, all of primary importance, but only one (the Ruskin Reserve) starred as being of especial interest. This list was the direct ancestor, via the lists drawn up by the Nature Reserves Investigation Committee (also an SPNR enterprise) during World War II and by the Wild Life Special Conservation Committee (under Julian Huxley's chairmanship) immediately after it, of the present schedules of national nature reserves and sites of special scientific interest operated by the Nature Conservancy Council.

It is of some interest therefore to examine the fourteen Rothschild sites in the three counties, and see how they have fared in the past sixty-seven years.

Only two—the Ruskin Reserve and Wychwood Forest, Oxon—have actually become national nature reserves, and two more—Cadsdene, near Little Kimble (now known as Grangelands), Bucks, and Hartslock, Oxon—have become at least

1. Ruskin Reserve, Cothill, Berks/Oxon

2. Wychwood Forest National Nature Reserve, Oxon, oak woodland

in part BBONT reserves. Of the remainder, Bradenham Woods, Bucks, Coombe Hill, near Wendover, Bucks, and Heath Pool, near Crowthorne, Berks, belong to the National Trust, and Dorney Wood, near Burnham Beeches, Bucks, to the Corporation of the City of London, while Greenham Common, Berks, was largely destroyed by the construction of an airfield during World War II. The remaining areas, whose fate is undecided, are Brimpton Common, Cherbury Camp, and Compton Downs all in Berks, and Brickhill Heath, Bucks.

The links between the Rothschild list and that latter-day Domesday Book of natural history sites, the 1977 *Nature Conservation Review,* edited by Derek Ratcliffe for the Nature Conservancy Council, are also of some interest. Ratcliffe lists eight Grade 1 sites and six Grade 2 sites in the three counties, exactly the same number as Rothschild, but only six sites actually overlap in any degree. Ratcliffe's Grade 1 Cothill Fen, Parsonage Moor, Bradenham Woods and Wychwood Forest, together with his Grade 2 Burnham Beeches and Coombe Hill all correspond more or less with Rothschild selections. However, the NCR Grade 1 sites, Windsor Forest and Aston Upthorpe Downs, Berks, and Waterperry Wood, Aston Rowant, Pixey and Yarnton Meads with Port Meadow, Oxon, are new sites, mostly deriving from the wartime NRIC lists. The present status of the fourteen *NCR* sites is also of some interest. Six of them (Wychwood Forest and Ponds, Waterperry Wood, Aston Rowant Woods and Grassland, and Cothill Fen) are already at least in part national or forest nature reserves under the NCC, and four (Bradenham Woods, Windsor Hill in Bucks, Aston Upthorpe Down and Parsonage Moor) are at least in part reserves of BBONT. Of the rest, two (Coombe Hill and Ivinghoe Beacon, Bucks) belong to the National Trust (which also owns Bradenham Woods and part of Cothill Fen), and one each to the Crown Estates Commissioners (Windsor Forest), the City of London Corporation (Burnham Beeches), the Freemen of Oxford (Port Meadow) and Bucks County Council (Pitstone Hill). Apart from the need to strengthen the safeguards on the parts of these sites which are only partially owned or controlled by NCC and BBONT, the main need at present is to ensure the future of the ancient hay meadows of Pixey and Yarnton Meads; the third of these meadows, Oxey Mead, was largely destroyed by the Oxford western by-pass.

It took another world war to resuscitate Rothschild's effort. In 1942 his SPNR, which had slumbered happily for most of the inter-war years, set up a Nature Reserves Investigation Committee, which through county sub-committees was able to draw up a much fuller conspectus of potential nature reserves than Rothschild working alone had been able to do. The top selections in these lists subsequently formed the basis of the proposed national nature reserves listed in the

Report of the Wild Life Conservation Special Committee in 1947. This committee, in effect a sub-committee of the Hobhouse Committee on National Parks, sat under the chairmanship of Julian Huxley, with the present writer as its secretary; its report was the blueprint for the Nature Conservancy, set up by Act of Parliament in 1949.

The three regional sub-committees of the NRIC which covered our three counties recommended sixty-nine natural history (as distinct from geological) sites. Berks's sub-committee was chaired by Professor H. L. Hawkins, later to be a foundation member of BBONT Council, and recommended twenty-six sites. Bucks, joined with Herts under the chairmanship of Lord Brocket, and with Lady Barlow, later a BBONT Vice-President, as a member, suggested fifteen sites in the county. Oxon was the most prodigal, its sub-committee proposing thirty sites. Of this total of sixty-nine, BBONT now has all or part of nine among its present reserves, and is negotiating for another. Three of the remainder (Cothill Fen, Windsor Forest and Wychwood Forest) are either national or forest nature reserves; four more (woods north of Finchampstead, Berks, Coombe Hill and Ivinghoe Beacon, Bucks, and Watlington Hill, Oxon), belong to the National Trust, and five are in other public or semi-public corporate ownership. These last are Bagley Wood, Snelsmore Common, Thatcham Reed-beds and White Horse Hill in Berks, and Burnham Beeches with Dorney Wood, Bucks. It is interesting to note how many of the Rothschild areas failed to reappear in the NRIC lists. This may have been because the NRIC sub-committees did not know about them. (The one I personally served on, for the London Area, was not supplied with any such information.) Cothill Fen and Wychwood Forest have maintained their status through all the listings, and are now national nature reserves. Dorney Wood, Bucks, and Greenham Common, Berks, also featured in both the Rothschild and NRIC lists. However, several areas listed by Rothschild were not listed by the NRIC sub-committees, through some at least maintain their natural history interest to the present day. These were Brimpton Common, Compton Downs, Heath Pool and Cherbury Camp in Berks; and Bradenham Woods, Brickhill Heath, Cadsdene, Coombe Hill and Naphill Common in Bucks. But Rothschild, who lived at Tring Park, might well have had a more detailed local knowledge of Chiltern sites than did his successors thirty years later.

When the main NRIC reported in December 1945 it accepted only four of the regional committees' recommendations for national nature reserves: Windsor Forest, its only top category site in our region; Weston Turville Reservoir, which would presumably not have been chosen but for its association with the more important group at Wilstone and Tring just over the Herts border; Wychwood Forest, and Burnham Beeches. Cothill Fen was presumably omitted because of its small size. However, two conservation areas were recommended, a category which did not survive into the eventual legislation of 1949: the Chiltern Escarpment, which covered at least seven of the sub-committees' suggestions, and Moulsford Downs. In addition the NRIC's Geological Sub-committee recommended twenty-one geological sites in the three counties, not, incidentally, including the geological site of special scientific interest (SSSI) that now features among BBONT's reserves, Dry Sandford Pit in north Berks.

As the Wild Life Conservation Special Committee based its own official list of recommended national nature reserves largely on the NRIC list, it is not surprising to find that its proposed NNRs for the three counties included Wychwood Forest, Burnham Beeches and Windsor Forest, together with Aston Rowant Woods, Oxon (part of which lies in the modern Aston Rowant NNR) and Pulpit Hill and Lodge Wood, Bucks (part of which is now a BBONT reserve), but minus Weston Turville Reservoir, which had rightly been rejected as not really of NNR status. The WLCSC also recommended two geological monuments in our area, a Stonesfield slate mine in Oxon, and sarsens and blocks of puddingstone by the village green at The Lee, in the Bucks Chilterns. This, however, was another proposed category that did not survive the rigours of Civil Service mastication of the Committee's report. The WLCSC did not recommend any conservation areas for wildlife, but listed the conservation areas recommended by its parent body, the National Parks Committee, which were the ancestors of the present Areas of Outstanding Natural Beauty. These included, in our area, the Cotswolds (a small part of which lies in Oxon), the Berkshire Downs and the Chilterns. No actual national park was recommended for our region, nor is there any real prospect of one being declared even today. Our countryside is just too cultivated. The NPC would have liked to make the Marlborough and Berkshire Downs a national park, but found that too much of them had been ploughed up during the war to justify this designation.

During the 1950s the new Nature Conservancy made all the running in wildlife conservation in our three counties. It set up three national nature reserves (Aston Rowant, Cothill Fen and Wychwood Forest), two in Oxon and one in Bucks and two forest nature reserves (Beacon Hill, adjacent to Aston Rowant, and Waterperry), both in Oxon. (Forest nature reserves are established by agreement with the Forestry Commission.) At this time the voluntary movement made comparatively little impact, though the Royal Society for the Protection of Birds was bequeathed Church Wood, Hedgerley, Bucks, which it made into one of its sanctuaries, and the

Middle Thames Natural History Society arranged with the local authority to preserve part of Ham Fields sewage farm, near Windsor in a state suitable for migrant waders.

The foundation of the Berks, Bucks and Oxon Naturalists' Trust (BBONT) at the end of the decade brought a striking change. The initiative was taken by the Ashmolean Natural History Society and its Hon. Secretary, Miss Winifred Overend, following a conference convened by the South-Eastern Union of Scientific Societies in London in April 1958, with the object of promoting the formation of naturalists' trusts in its region. A preliminary meeting at the University Museum in Oxford on 28 February 1959, was attended by representatives of seven biological departments of Oxford and Reading Universities, seven natural history societies in Berks and Oxon, and Reading Museum. This group appointed a Planning Committee to prepare for a public meeting in Oxford in the autumn at which the proposed naturalists' trust would be formally launched. Dr E. F. Warburg of the Oxford Botany School was Chairman and Miss Overend Hon. Secretary of this committee, whose other members were: B. R. Baker, R. S. R. Fitter, L. R. Lewis and G. E. S. Turner. At its inaugural meeting a suggestion from the Middle Thames Natural History Society that Bucks should also be included in the proposed trust was approved, and at subsequent meetings Bucks was represented by Lady Barlow, Mrs Susan Cowdy and Mrs J. Grimmitt.

BBONT's inaugural meeting was held in the City of Oxford School Hall on 14 November 1959, with Air Marshal Sir Robert Saundby, a well known amateur entomologist, in the chair, and BBONT became the tenth county naturalists' trust. The first were Norfolk (1926), Yorkshire (1946) and Lincolnshire (1948). The Provisional Executive Committee consisted of most of the members of the Planning Committee, plus Dr Bruce Campbell, W. D. Campbell, T. Cottrell-Dormer, Mrs M. S. Fitter (Hon Editor), H. J. Harrison, Professor H. L. Hawkins, FRS, G. Guthrie Moir and H. C. Norton. The new committee's first act was to invite Sir Robert Saundby to be its chairman. At the same time R. S. R. Fitter became Hon Secretary and F. A. Glass Hon Treasurer, and three Hon County Secretaries were appointed: B. R. Baker (Berks), Mrs Cowdy (Bucks) and G. W. Humphreys (Oxon). The draft constitution prepared by this body was approved at a further public meeting at the University Museum in Oxford on 12 November 1960, at which Sir Robert Saundby was elected President, and three Vice-Presidents were appointed: Lady Barlow (Bucks), Dr Warburg (Oxon) and the Marquess of Willingdon (Berks). Additional names among the members of the first Council were John Cripps (Oxon), A. C. Fraser (Bucks), A. W. Hurst (Bucks),

3. Chinnor Hill Nature Reserve, Oxon

Professor G. C. Varley (Oxon) and Miss L. M. Watts (Berks). The first stage was completed when BBONT was incorporated as a company limited by guarantee on 9 January 1961. This enabled it to own land, which an unincorporated body such as a natural history society cannot do.

The first two annual reports of the new body showed it getting off to a rather slow start, boasting 377 fully paid up members by 31 December 1961. It had leased two small nature reserves, the Conigre Pond at Chinnor, Oxon, and Furzy Field Dell at The Lee, both of which, for various reasons, became unsuitable as reserves after a few years. The Trust had also started to deal with threats to sites: the erection of a radio tower on the Chiltern escarpment, the destruction of much of North Oxon by large-scale ironstone mining, the felling of trees in a heronry in Bucks. It tried to buy the crocus field at Inkpen, Berks; fenced in part of one of the two remaining pasque flower sites on the Berkshire Downs; wardened the site of the military orchid in Bucks; launched a local conservation corps in Bucks; and protested at an article in a national women's magazine that urged its readers to take a trowel and a polythene bag down to the Thames meadows near Oxford and dig up fritillary bulbs for their gardens. In other words it made a beginning on the multifarious activities in which it has sought to preserve and conserve the wildlife of the three counties ever since. Not for another three years, however, did it actually own a reserve, when Mr and Mrs E. H. T. Hambly presented Long Grove Wood, a small beechwood at Seer Green, Bucks, to the Trust.

If we turn from these two early reports to the latest one available at the time of writing, 1982-83, we naturally find great changes. Instead of all the officers being honorary, there are now salaried officers in a central office in Oxford: two conservation officers, an administrative officer and field officer and three other staff members. The total number of reserves is now eighty-five with a total area of nearly 1000 ha., with ten new ones in the previous twelve months. The capital reserve of the Trust stood at £307,592. Membership has risen to over 7,000. A network of ten regional committees has been established. Numerous meetings and fund-raising events are chronicled. The Education Committee maintains an active programme.

There are only two main threats to wildlife in any geographical region: direct killing or destruction by man, and habitat destruction, usually by man but also occasionally by natural causes, such as floods or landslides, which are themselves likely to be stimulated by human activity. Wildlife conservation in an area such as the three counties of Berks, Bucks and Oxon has therefore to grapple with these two main problems.

Direct killing of animals is no great threat in our area, except in so far as collectors still harry certain rare butterflies, notably the black hairstreak *Strymonidia pruni* and the purple emperor *Apatura iris,* which still have no national protection. BBONT has tried to remedy this by wardening the principal habitat of these butterflies during the season when predatory entomologists are in the habit of visiting it. Although various mammals are still killed regularly in our area, some, such as rats and rabbits, are pests, and others, such as the fox are not rare. The badger, which is protected, is probably still harried locally, but there is no evidence that this is seriously affecting its status in the three counties. Birds are adequately protected by existing legislation; in our area we have no really rare breeding birds—since the marsh warbler appears to have ceased to breed regularly—and there is no reason to suppose that any illicit killing that does take place may be endangering any species. Indeed one bird, the sparrowhawk, not protected until quite recently, is showing signs of recovering from a low point that was attributed to shooting by keepers. Some keepers no doubt still occasionally kill the occasional protected predator on the quiet, but gamekeeping appears no longer to be a serious threat to the status of any species. The recent increase in the hobby may also be due to a more enlightened attitude by keepers, as well as to a diminution of the threat from egg collectors, for whom a clutch of hobby's eggs used to be a special lure.

Curiously enough rare plants, in which our region is rich, are more threatened by direct destruction than are rare animals. Some thirty-five of the 321 species listed in the *British Red Data Book* for vascular plants occur with us. The most threatened of these are the five rare orchids; the monkey *Orchis simia,* military *O. militaris,* lizard *Himantoglossum hircinum,* ghost *Epipogium aphyllum* and red helleborine *Cephalanthera rubra.* Although most of these are on protected sites, some of which are wardened by BBONT during the flowering season, specimens have in recent years been picked, dug up and, more seriously, trampled or lain on by careless photographers. The fritillary *Fritillaria meleagris* is particularly subject to direct destruction; in many districts fritillaries are picked on a traditional day and used often to be sold in the local markets. This still happens, for instance, in the Ford district of the Vale of Aylesbury, on Frawcup Sunday in early May—frawcup being the plant's local name. In the days when fritillaries were abundant in many local meadows this did not matter, and was a pleasant local custom. Nowadays, when most of the meadows have been ploughed up, and fritillaries struggle to survive in only a handful of them, persistence in the local custom may all too soon exterminate the plant. The only remedy for this is to back up the protection afforded by the Wildlife and the Countryside Act 1981 by wardening, either on a field purchased as a reserve, or with the goodwill of the farmer.

Rare species, whether they have been made rare by direct destruction or by loss of habitat, can also be preserved directly by reintroduction. This was done with the most conspicuous success by the late Dr Roger Clarke, Oxon County Secretary of BBONT in its early days, who raised purple emperor butterflies at his home on the edge of Otmoor, and released them in a neighbouring Bucks woodland which has been well known for many years as a classic locality for this species. A refinement of this technique is the fertilization of the flower-spikes of rare orchids, to make sure that seed is produced. It has been suggested that one reason why some orchids become rare is that the insects which fertilize them have also become rare, and BBONT arranges for the regular fertilization of military and monkey orchids in its reserves to guard against this possibility.

Habitat destruction is, however, the main threat to wildlife in our three counties as almost everywhere else. As already indicated, there are no natural habitats left; all the remaining wildlife habitat is at least semi-natural. But modern agricultural practices are rapidly destroying the fine wildlife habitats that were created by medieval agriculture and forestry; housing, industrial development and road building finish off all too much of what farmland has been allowed to survive. The most threatened habitats in our area are neutral grasslands, which are ploughed up; calcareous grasslands, which are ploughed or turn to scrub; hedgerows, which are

4. Fly orchid

5. Monkey orchid

6. Military orchid

7. Lizard orchid

8. Pasque flower

grubbed out; heathlands, which are ploughed, built on or allowed to be overrun with bracken; wetlands, including fens, which are drained and cultivated; and deciduous woodlands, which are all too often replanted with conifers. Some wildlife, of course, can survive after all these processes have taken place, but the animals and plants of these grossly artificial habitats tend to be the common and adaptable ones, such as blackbirds, field voles *Microtus agrestis,* sycamores *Acer pseudoplatanus* and charlock *Sinapis arvensis.*

How can habitat destruction be dealt with? The only safe way is to acquire the land as a nature reserve, and this the NCC, BBONT, RSPB and other bodies attempt to do whenever possible. Twenty-six of BBONT's reserves are its own freehold. Alternatively the land can be leased, or an agreement made with the owner that the NCC or BBONT will be consulted over any changes in management. This is less expensive, but also less safe, because a change of ownership may mean that the reserve will be lost, and all the resources put into its management wasted. The county planning mechanism is another means of tackling the problem. It is important that as many wildlife conservation sites as possible are registered in county structure plans, so that when the planners are proposing major developments, they know what to avoid, although this would be of little avail if, for instance, the Central Government were to decide after all to build the Third

London Airport in North Bucks, or to allow more opencast iron-mining in North Oxon or coal-mining in the Cotswolds.

Much of the damage done to wildlife by the newer farming techniques can be alleviated if the goodwill of the farming community can be gained. There may be only marginal advantages in grubbing out certain hedges, felling certain copses, or draining certain damp corners of fields, but mony a mickle maks a muckle. If the farmer is a country-lover rather than an agri-business man, he may be persuaded to hold his hand, and even to plant more shelter-belts or clumps of trees about his farm. It is the main aim of the Farming and Wildlife Advisory Groups, which BBONT has recently helped to set up in the three counties, to create the atmosphere in which farmers are prepared to listen to wildlife conservationists and their suggestions for procuring a greater diversity of wildlife on their farms. Similar consultative mechanisms are needed for the various other authorities, such as the Water and Canal Authorities, whose clearing of river-bank vegetation can be very destructive. Since only a very small part of the important wildlife area of the three counties is ever likely to become an official nature reserve there is no substitute for gaining the goodwill and understanding of farmers, landowners and public authorities. The price of conservation, as of liberty, is eternal vigilance.

A benevolent public opinion is a fundamental need for wildlife conservation, and naturalists' trusts and other voluntary conservation organizations therefore take great care with their educational activities, which are described by Ursula Bowen below.

Once a reserve has been created or acquired the problems of management arise. At one time a fence to keep people out was thought to be all that was needed. Indeed this is still the public image of a nature reserve, and the reason why local people sometimes oppose the creation of one in their district. The classic story against the fence-and-leave-it theory was provided by the Badgeworth Marsh reserve in neighbouring Gloucestershire. This small marshy pond was acquired as one of the only two known sites in Britain of a rare buttercup, adderstongue spearwort *Ranunculus ophioglossifolius*, and was duly fenced off. After a few years, somebody noticed that the buttercup had become extinct within the fence, but was thriving in the field outside it, in the little pools created by the footsteps of the cattle that came to drink in the pond but could not get through the fence.

So every time a reserve is acquired, it must be managed, if only by a deliberate decision not to manage it. Neglect of a nature reserve is rarely benign. Both NCC and BBONT therefore aim to prepare management plans for all their reserves, laying down, usually for a period of five years, what needs to be done.

9. Hartslock Nature Reserve, Oxon, from across the Thames

The main problems arise with grasslands. Grassland is a more than usually artificial habitat in the British Isles, and can only be prevented from turning first to scrub and later to woodland by fire, mowing or grazing. For several hundred years chalk grassland over most of southern England was maintained by grazing, usually by sheep. But from the early 1920s onwards sheep grazing became increasingly uneconomic, and grassland was maintained, in so far as it was not either ploughed or allowed to go to scrub, by rabbits. The myxomatosis epidemic in 1954–5 brought a further increase in the rate of scrubbing up, as it reduced rabbit pressure for several years. This was more or less the point at which BBONT came in, and checking scrub growth to maintain its chalk grassland reserves has always been one of the main problems. Both national and local conservation corps are used to cut scrub, but even when the stumps are chemically treated, this is at best a palliative. Fire is difficult to use on small areas. Mowing may also be difficult on steep banks. So BBONT's only effective tool has been grazing, starting with the Chinnor Hill reserve in the late 1960s, and the Trust now owns its own flock of sheep for grazing its downland reserves. However, remarkably little is known about the effects of grazing on the secondary chalk grasslands which predominate in the Chilterns, where most grassland was ploughed during one of the two world wars, so it is not possible to predict how they will react to being grazed.

10. Conservation work, pond clearance, Dry Sandford Nature Reserve, Berks/Oxon

11. Conservation work, scrub clearance, Dry Sandford Nature Reserve, Berks/Oxon

A Note on Environmental Education

URSULA BOWEN

BBONT began to consider its educational role in 1966 when the first Education Committee was established. At first it covered too wide a field to be effective, but in 1968 the Committee decided to make a start by providing nature trails for the general public and by setting up in-service courses for teachers in primary, middle and secondary schools.

Environmental conservation is not a subject which can be taught in primary and secondary schools. It is an attitude which children gain from learning about their environment through practical experience. If you take children out to explore and investigate their environment at first hand, they will find it interesting and develop a love for it; they will want to care for it and grow up to become conservationists. The way to foster this attitude is to encourage teachers to integrate field work into the school curriculum. Many teachers lacked the expertise and confidence to tackle environmental education, but when given the knowledge and experience they had the opportunity to influence large numbers of children in their classes.

With three counties to consider, the Education Committee decided to limit its programme still further. Bucks Education Authority was making good provision for environmental education and by the 1970s had appointed a County Adviser in Environmental Studies, established five field studies centres and converted a good proportion of school grounds into wildlife areas with ponds. Berkshire seemed unreceptive, but Oxfordshire was beginning to encourage its teachers to introduce more field work into the school curriculum and so the Committee decided to direct its attention towards mounting in-service courses for teachers in Oxford city and county, and set about getting the courses officially recognized.

The following pattern has been successful in attracting large numbers of teachers and in stimulating them to undertake field work with their classes of children. The course occupies either a full day or two evenings after school. It is split into two sessions. The first is indoors and includes two lectures on ecology and conservation. These talks aim both to provide teachers with enough background knowledge of ecology to enable them to devise projects, interpret results and answer children's questions; and to help them to understand the long-term benefits of taking children out of doors to do field work. Teachers are then introduced to a range of projects and techniques such as pond-dipping, sweep-netting, investigating water flea populations and variation in leaf-shape so that they have plenty of activities to interest their children.

The second session is held out of doors on the particular nature reserve or site the teachers wish to use. They are given the opportunity to carry out projects and techniques to gain confidence and to experience the problems which their children may encounter. They also walk the nature trail; this is a vital component of the course particularly for inexperienced teachers, many of whom use it as a means of starting field work. During all these activities teachers are introduced to the conservation code for the nature reserve or site they are using and to the booking system.

The advantages of providing in-service courses are numerous. We can encourage enormous numbers of children to enjoy their environment with the most economic use of resources. If fifty teachers attend a course, each responsible for a class of thirty children, we have reached 1,500 children. Only the teachers are able to integrate field work into the school curriculum by preparing the children beforehand so that they gain the maximum experience from the visit which is reinforced by follow-up work in the classroom afterwards. In this way the site visit has a much greater impact on the children; children and teachers are motivated and the visits are likely to become a regular school activity encouraged by advisers and advisory teachers.

Field work should start and continue in the school grounds and the surrounding environment, but these usually need supplementing. The Bucks and Oxfordshire local education authorities have set up some field studies centres, but there is still a shortage of field work sites and the Trust has made a contribution by establishing educational nature reserves (ENR). In 1967 the Trust encouraged the Oxfordshire County Council to buy the Slade ENR at Bloxham and in the same year started negotiations with the Central Electricity Generating Board to establish a field centre in the grounds of Didcot Power Station, Berks/Oxon, which resulted in the opening of the Sutton Courtenay Field Studies Centre in 1969. BBONT advises on the management of these sites, supplies nature trail guides for schools and organizes in-service courses for teachers. In 1968 the Trust established the Henry Stephen/C. S. Lewis ENR at Risinghurst, near Headington, Oxon, now used by 2,000–3,000 children and adults every year. Chinnor Hill, Hook Norton and

Warburg (Bix Bottom) are three more BBONT reserves used by schools for field work.

The terminology for sites used primarily for educational purposes needs clarification. A field studies centre has permanent buildings, is well equipped with apparatus for field work, may have residential accommodation and often has a warden; it has access to habitats but the land is not usually owned by the centre. An educational nature reserve is an area used primarily for educational purposes; the conservation of species and ecosystems is important but takes second place, and children are free to wander and discover plants and animals for themselves at first hand; limited collection of specimens must be allowed so that children can take them back to school for further study.

Children learn best by first-hand practical experience. If the experience is rich they are likely to learn more, take a deeper interest in the environment and develop a responsible attitude towards conservation. Nobody who has observed children exploring a rich environment can doubt the value of educational nature reserves. At the Henry Stephen/C. S. Lewis ENR. I have had many opportunities to share the excitement of children as they watched a large pike basking in the sun, listened to the sound of rustling leaf litter as they walked through the wood, or marvelled at the large rounded 'dogger' stones. On one occasion, only a difference in size distinguished the children from a primary school and students from Oxford Polytechnic as they leaned over the edge of the pond watching hundreds of toads mating and spawning—the spectacle evoked the same degree of excitement from both children and students.

The BBONT Education Committee has also provided educational literature to back up its field study programme for schools, including suggestions for projects, making ponds, and nature trails at the Warburg, Chinnor Hill and other BBONT reserves, as well as trail guides for the National Trust and the Central Electricity Generating Board. Experience has shown that on-site education is much more effective in promoting an interest in conservation than lectures or films, and the effectiveness of nature trails is considerably increased if they are supplemented by a display at an information centre, such as the one at the Warburg Reserve.

The latest enterprise of the BBONT Education Committee is the promotion of Watch, the club for junior members of county naturalists' trusts, administered by the Royal Society for Nature Conservation. The club's activities bridge the gap between formal education in school and out-of-school activities.

The older generation passed their childhood at a time when access to the countryside was much easier and the collection of butterflies and flowers was not discouraged. Today large numbers of children are denied these experiences which have stimulated us to become conservationists and yet we shall expect them to support the conservation movement when they grow up. The Trust must take some responsibility for enriching their educational experience.

13 The Warburg Reserve, Bix Bottom A Case History

V. N. PAUL

In the autumn of 1962 BBONT was told that a clear-felling licence had been granted for 300 acres of woodland in the Bix Bottom valley, about five miles north-west of Henley-on-Thames, Oxon. This area was known to have a very rich flora, and the knowledge that the Forestry Commission intended to replant with conifers determined those members of the Trust who knew the area to try to prevent this from happening. The owners were informed of the value, from a natural history point of view, of the valley. Both they and the estate managers were interested in conservation and on 14 June 1963 a party of ten was conducted round the vulnerable area. The orchids were at their best and a completely albino white helleborine *Cephalanthera damasonium* attracted attention. Every member of the party was sensitive to the richness and beauty of the flowers and from that evening all were most co-operative in trying to help in the conservation of the area. In April 1964 the Trust was given permission to put stakes round the best sites for orchids and the woodmen were asked to avoid dragging trees over this ground.

Gradually it became apparent that the Forestry Commission was unable to finance the replanting of the 300 acres. It was suggested that the Trust might rent the valley for a year and examine the work involved in turning it into a nature reserve. On 27 May 1966 the Sites Committee of the Trust went round the site and agreed that it was a challenge which the Trust should take. A most successful public appeal raised £23,000; the reserve was eventually purchased in November 1967. Dr E. F. Warburg who had been BBONT's Oxfordshire Vice-President and co-author of the famous 'CTW' *Flora of the British Isles* died soon after the site meeting. It seemed appropriate to name this reserve, so rich in its flora, after him.

As a setting for a BBONT reserve Bix Bottom is ideal in many ways. It lies near the junction of the three counties, for the Thames separates Oxfordshire from Berkshire at Henley, and the Bucks county boundary skirts Stonor Park two miles north-east of the reserve. Two narrow roads lead to the valley—one from Bix village and the A423(T) and the other from the B480 at Middle Assendon. Footpaths and estate tracks lead from Nettlebed, Park Corner and Maidensgrove.

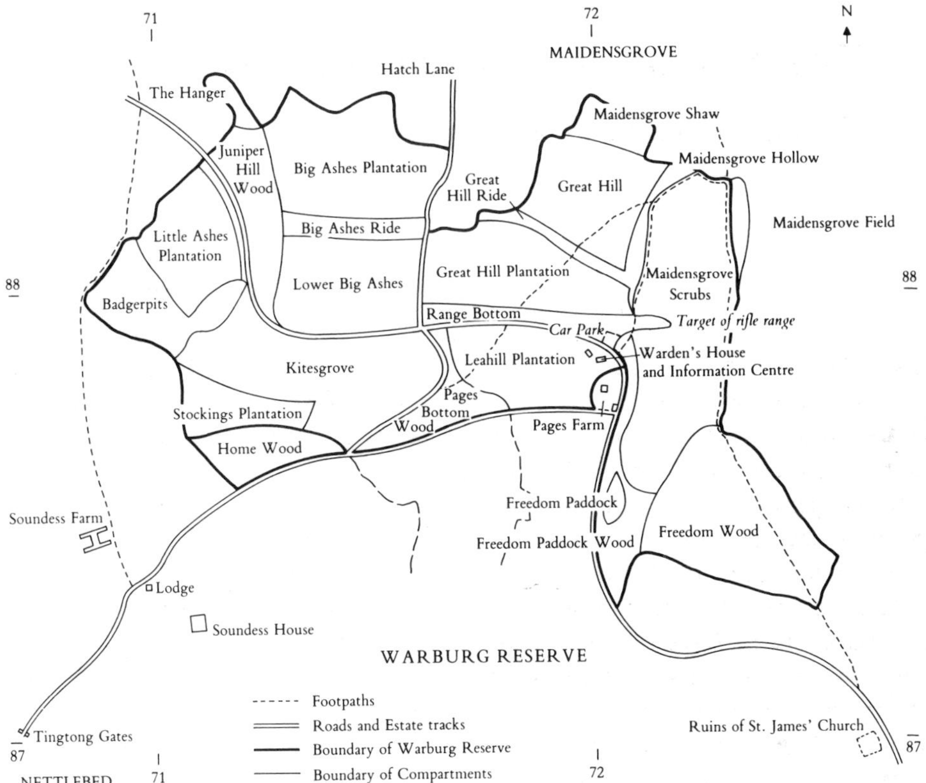

Warburg Reserve

The Stonor letters and papers of 1480 refer to two churches, Bixegebeon and Byxebrond, in Bix Bottom, which might indicate that the area was then more heavily populated than it is at present. The ruins of one of these churches still stand by the side of the road which leads to the reserve. In the reserve itself, near the car park, there is an old well which, so legend tells us, contains the jewels of Nell Gwynne. History does not relate whether this has ever been investigated. The well is 354ft deep and was, at one time, a major source of water for the surrounding district. The track from Nettlebed, which passes through the delightfully named Ting-Tong gates, leads to Soundess House and farm where Nell Gwynne lived.

The woodland known as Maidensgrove Scrubs is of particular interest. The residents of Maidensgrove could cut timber from this area under common rights which may date back to the fifteenth century, and continual coppicing until the end of the nineteenth century has given the wood a characteristic appearance. Very few

1. Warburg Reserve, Bix Bottom, Oxon, looking west along the disused rifle range

such beech woods remain in England today. Another feature of the reserve is the Volunteer Rifle Range which was used until March 1968. This is marked on a map dated 1877, which shows it to be 300 yards longer than the present range.

The reserve is divided into twenty-three compartments, many of which have banks of flints to mark their boundaries. These were built to retain the soil on the flat upper reaches of the valley. Past usage of the compartments has been variable and this gives a diversity of habitat which greatly adds to the ecological interest. The Trust has retained most of the old names of the compartments a map of which is shown on page 181.

The area of the reserve is 253 acres or 102.7 hectares. Maidensgrove Scrubs, Pages Bottom Wood, Kitesgrove Wood and Freedom Wood, comprising almost 40 per cent of the reserve, have had a continuous woodland history since 1768. The shallowness of the soil made agriculture difficult, although Badgerpits, Juniper Hill Wood and Maidensgrove Shaw were so used until about 1800. After this larches *Larix decidua* were planted as a crop. Parts of the woodland are now dominated by beech, others by birch or ash; there are mixtures of oak and sycamore, of larch and oak with scatterings of hornbeam *Carpinus betulus*, whitebeam *Sorbus aria*, yew, and wild cherry *Prunus avium*. Three open grassy glades add valuable habitats.

To facilitate accurate recordings and to enable long-term experiments to be carried out, the whole reserve was marked at 100-metre national grid points with inconspicuous metal pegs driven into the ground. One such experiment is the replanting of Freedom Wood. The Trust felt that this wood, the felling of which had led them to buy the reserve, should be replanted. Schoolchildren in the three counties raised £1,400 by selling leaves at one old penny each from tree cards to pay for this. Six species of deciduous tree were planted, scattered in one-acre plots at different levels on the steep slope so that their development could be compared. Oak, wild cherry, small-leaved lime *Tilia cordata,* hornbeam, beech and wych elm *Ulmus glabra* were planted with Scots pine as nurse trees. Ash and birch have come in of their own accord and a few yews had been left from the original wood. A 30ft band of beech trees was left on two sides from the original felling. This patchwork of trees should provide a great deal of information about the success of individual species on this shallow-soiled hillside and the association of plants and animals with each species. In the early stages schoolchildren again helped by weeding out the brambles and other plants which threatened to choke the young trees.

The management committee of the reserve was first chaired by the late Colonel Peter Fleming who had known the valley for most of his life. In the management plan it was stated that the object was 'to restore and maintain a woodland community characteristic of the Chilterns for the preservation of its distinctive fauna and flora'. In the first ten years, however, we have found that the area cannot be considered 'characteristic of the Chilterns'. Its richness is probably due to the heterogeneous character of the compartments and the varied nature of the soil. This is capped with clay and flints in the highest parts of Maidensgrove Scrubs, passing through Upper Chalk down to Middle Chalk in the valley bottom. Top soil in the valley has been leached of its chalk in many places, giving a fairly deep rich layer supporting nettles and bracken. Our plan will therefore be revised so that it is the local pecularities which are perpetuated. The wooded compartments of the reserve need little or no interference to remain in a satisfactory condition for several decades. A scattering of conifers provides shelter and nest sites as well as feed for both birds and small mammals and plays host to many fungi. The irregularly aged mixed species give diversity. Three other categories of plant communities will be maintained: coppice and tall scrub, short scrub and grass and short grass rides. These will be managed to give maximum diversity by rotational cutting.

The desirable status of all wildlife in the reserve is kept under review. Some plants and animals threaten other species. If they are not required, e.g. sycamore, then they are termed 'proscribed' and need to be suppressed. Then there are some which we would like to retain but their success threatens others. These fall under the heading 'restricted'. A plant such as hawthorn *Crataegus monogyna*, which is a host to many insects and provides food and nesting sites for birds, will colonise a grassy area if left unchecked. At the other extreme are the rare or at risk species which are 'protected' and require special conservation treatment. The other two groups are the 'stable' species which need little attention and the 'tolerated' ones which include species not necessarily required but not threatening others. Management is an interesting, complex and controversial subject. The management plan is in ten-year cycles but at the same time it is sometimes necessary to change these plans in the light of acquired knowledge.

Education was not uppermost in our minds when BBONT first bought the Warburg Reserve, but the reserve has proved to be a most valuable asset in this field. Scientific study for theses at degree and A level standard is encouraged; young children enjoy the colour, sounds and shapes, often producing interesting poems and illustrations after their visits. To avoid damage and disturbance to wildlife, parties are guided by the warden or by an authorised member of the Trust.

To appreciate the richness of the flora of these 102 hectares, one must compare it with the neighbouring 2km square which is being recorded for the new Flora of Oxfordshire. In the 400 hectares round Nettlebed, which is among the richest in Oxfordshire, 450 plants have been found. The area includes the wetland habitat around and in the ponds on Nettlebed Common. The reserve is a dry valley, yet we have already recorded 425 species of flowering plants and ferns. Some of these are casuals, coming in when the warden's house and information centre were built in 1974. There were six plants of the rare henbane *Hyoscyamus niger* and one of thorn-apple *Datura stramonium.* Care was taken not to bring in soil from outside, but some may have dropped from the wheels of the bulldozer which levelled the site. On the other hand, when the soil was disturbed, seeds which had lain dormant from the time when Pages Farm was a homestead may account for the henbane. Snowdrops *Galanthus nivalis* and star of Bethlehem *Ornithogalum umbellatum*, which grow in the wood opposite Pages Farm, are remnants from the old garden. Cornfield weeds such as the two little fluellens *Kickxia* are found, and weld *Reseda luteola* grows in the tractor tracks. Other plants are brought in by the corn which is fed to the pheasants. There had been a shoot on the estate for many years before it was sold and one of the conditions of sale was that this should be retained for

2. Green hellebore

twenty-five years. Some may consider it incongruous that a nature reserve and a shoot should be in the same area, but had it not been for the shoot other interests might have destroyed this lovely valley. It was better to buy the reserve with this restriction than not to have it at all.

Of the many interesting plants found in the reserve the green hellebore *Helleborus viridis* holds a particular niche. It was this plant which made me visit Bix Bottom in the 1930s. It still grows under the hedge at the side of the unmade road which passes through the reserve, and also at the bottom of Maidensgrove Scrubs. Here it marks the beginning of a spectacular band of herb paris *Paris quadrifolia*. Thousands of the four-leaved stems of this plant, ranging from tiny seedlings to mature plants, occupy a strip of wood which stretches from Freedom Paddock to the rifle range. Eighteen species of orchid have been recorded in the reserve area since 1950, but three of these have not been found in the last ten years and one, green-flowered helleborine *Epipactis phyllanthes*, was found, on one occasion only, by V. S. Summerhayes. Musk orchid *Herminium monorchis* grew in Freedom Paddock until it was ploughed in 1955. When Richard Walker published his *Flora of Oxfordshire* in 1883, under military orchid *Orchis militaris* he wrote: 'Beech woods between Fawley Court and Bixgibwen'—will this be a future record in the Warburg Reserve? In 1926 a single plant of the lizard orchid *Himantoglossum*

3. Birdsnest orchid

4. Herb Paris

hircinum was found at the bottom of the track which leads up to Freedom Wood from the ruins of St. James's Church.

After the replanting of Freedom Wood columbine *Aquilegia vulgaris*, which had grown in the wood, flourished. Wild candytuft *Iberis amara* also took advantage of the disturbed chalk soil, forming a white carpet between the rows of trees; typical of the Chilterns, it is very rare in most other parts of the British Isles. Fly orchids *Ophrys insectifera* are tolerant both of deep shade and open spaces; the two butterfly orchids *Plantanthera chlorantha* and *P. bifolia* grow together in Leahill plantation and separately in several other places; bee orchids *Ophrys apifera* and the variety *trollii* known as the wasp orchid occur in the short grass and in open spaces in the woods. Many other plants could be mentioned: Solomon's seal *Polygonatum multiflorum*, tutsan *Hypericum androsaemum*, pale St. John's wort *H. montanum*, lady's mantle *Alchemilla vestita*, nettle-leaved bellflower *Campanula trachelium*, orpine *Sedium telephium*. Two grasses should be mentioned: *Bromus benekenii* found by C. E. Hubbard when he visited the reserve in 1971 and wood barley *Hordelymus europaeus*, a Chiltern speciality which has persisted for many years in Freedom Wood.

Eleven ferns have been recorded in the reserve. The adder's tongue *Ophioglossum vulgatum* is often plentiful in Well Field plantation and occurs in several other places. Both the soft shield-fern *Polystichum setiferum* and the hard shield-fern *P. aculeatum* are found in Little Ashes Plantation and Juniper Hill Wood. Fungi were being studied by the late Dr F. B. Hora helped by a BBONT member Mrs H. P. Hack. This group of plants is particularly helped by the diversity of woodland structure. We are lucky also to have Dr E. Vernon Watson to help us in naming the mosses and liverworts.

Our knowledge of the fauna is in its infancy. Since Nigel Phillips, the warden, has lived in the warden's house which was built in 1974–5, we are gradually building up our records. Fallow deer are frequently seen and the smaller muntjac or barking deer is often heard giving its hoarse bark. Badgers breed and wasps' nests, routed out by them, are found in the woods round the sets. Foxes frequently pass through the reserve and have been known to breed in an old badger set. Brown hares are common and rabbits appear to be recovering from myxomatosis. A shallow nest of young rabbits was once found by a fallen tree trunk in Freedom Paddock Wood but when disturbed they were removed to a freshly dug underground burrow nearby. Grey squirrels, an introduced species from North America, do so much damage both to trees and birds' nests that they have to be controlled. A family of hedgehogs are sometimes seen in the evening making use of

5. Greater butterfly orchid

6. Columbine

7. Ramsons

8. Common Solomon's seal

the paths cut in the grass by the information centre, and on one occasion a stoat, which is not uncommon, was photographed killing a rabbit. Weasels are seen occasionally and brown rats are common in Freedom Paddock Wood. A group of students from Royal Holloway College, are recording the small mammals. They use release traps and their finds include common and pygmy shrews, bank vole, wood mouse and yellow-necked mouse. The house mouse is sometimes seen around the warden's house. One of the most appealing of our small mammals is the dormouse, which was common in the south of England at the beginning of this century, but is now much rarer. In March 1977 a group of teenagers clearing scrub in Maidensgrove Scrubs heard a squeak coming from the leaves on the ground, and found they had inadvertently disturbed a hibernating dormouse. They carried it to the information centre in a lunch container and it was released the following May, together with another one discovered in a bird nestbox.

Birds are perhaps the most popular subject for study. Each year we listen for the redstart; the season would seem incomplete without its characteristic song. In 1974 it built its nest in the old cartshed at Pages Farm where it could be watched and photographed from a hide. In 1978 a licence was obtained to build a hide in a neighbouring tree to one in which a sparrowhawk had built. A series of photographs and films, which form a valuable record, were taken by the warden.

9. Badger

The young of the great spotted woodpecker attract attention by the noise they make waiting for the adults to return with food. Reports of an exotic bird are often brought into the information centre when visitors see the beautiful green woodpecker for the first time.

Each year several long-tailed tits build their delightful bottle-shaped nests in bushes, and on one occasion quite high in the branches of a tree. Plate 8 shows a beak full of spider's web which the tit uses to bind together the lichens and mosses of which the nest is built. Many birds build their nests on the ground. One of the earliest is the woodcock. If the nest is found the sitting bird will remain tight to her eggs, camouflaged by her pattern of chestnut, brown, grey and black feathers. The young leave the nest almost immediately after they are hatched. Another ground-nesting bird is the tree pipit which from the rifle range may be watched perched at the top of isolated trees and then descending to the ground with its beautiful song-flight. Commonest among the warblers is the willow warbler, best separated from the chiffchaff by its song. Grasshopper warblers were common both in Little Ashes and on the rifle range, where their whirring song could be heard late into the night, until 1968 when their numbers declined in the whole of the region. Wood warblers on the other hand are on the increase. Nest-boxes are used by great, blue and marsh

10. Field vole

tits. Willow and coal tits are common, nesting in holes in old tree stumps. A spotted flycatcher had adopted a ledge under the roof of the information centre to build its nest and in April 1970 a solitary pied flycatcher was sighted in the reserve on migration.

The small artificial pond on the rifle range attracts many birds. A benefactor sent the money for this in the dry summer of 1970. Nearby a sheet of corrugated iron often shelters slowworms, which are legless lizards, and on the ride above when the spring sunshine warms the earth a handsome black and white male adder is sometimes seen curled up on an old anthill. The duller brown and black female adder is generally found among the bushes below the range. Grass snakes are fairly common in the long grass of the open glades. On warm days the tiny common lizard runs over the fallen trunks of trees or on the wood which went into building the shooting butts. In this dry valley amphibians are rarely seen although both toads and frogs have been found.

The study of the vast class of insects is very incomplete. Lepidoptera (butterflies and moths) come second to birds in their popularity with visitors and early in the history of the reserve some evenings and nights were spent with the late Dr Roger Clarke, then BBONT Oxfordshire Secretary, and other BBONT members catching and releasing moths by attracting them to powerful lights. By the end of

1975, 161 butterflies and moths had been recorded but this number is being added to every year. Doubt was cast on the recording of purple emperor *Apatura iris* in flight, but the argument was resolved when the warden was able to photograph one which settled on the wall of his house. Colonies of the rare woodland grasshopper *Omocestus rufipes* have been found in at least two widely separated places in the reserve and two unusual diptera (two-winged flies) *Rhagio annulatus* and *Tetanocera thyllophora* were recorded by Alan Stubbs.

Spiders are less well known than insects, but two visits have been made by members of other Trusts who are interested in the Arachnida. One of the commonest spiders in the reserve is the hunting spider *Pisaura listeri*, which is easily recognized when it is carrying its cocoon of eggs because, unlike the wolf spiders, which carry the cocoon attached to the spinnerets at the rear of the body, *Pisaura* grasps it in her palpi and carries it under the front legs. Later she spins a silk net in which she places the cocoon, sitting on the grass or shrub near the eggs apparently guarding them. If disturbed however, she will quickly drop to the ground. On the walls and window-ledges of the information centre the small jumping spider, so aptly called the zebra spider *Salticus scenicus* can be seen on a sunny day. A pale yellow crab spider *Misumena calycina* camouflaged against the yellow flower on which it was sitting caught an orange-tip butterfly *Anthocharis cardamines* just outside the information centre. This spider is capable of changing its colour slowly to suit that of its surroundings. One of the most exciting finds was the British equivalent of the trap-door spider *Atypus affinis*, located under the flints on one of the fire-breaks. This spider digs a burrow which it lines with silk. The lining is continued for two or three inches above the ground as a long thimble-like tube, and acts as a trap for insects. The male spider, when visiting the female, drums on the tube and judges from the female's reaction whether or not he is welcome. He enters the tube by tearing it open. The two live together for several weeks, but in the end the female may eat the male.

In 1969 a list of the molluscs was made. Thirty-four species were found, some of them little larger than a pin's head.

A list of the flowering plants and ferns and another of the animals found in the Warburg Reserve was compiled in 1975, and copies may be obtained at the information centre.

The reserve is crossed by several public footpaths and there is a nature trail marked by arrows. An illustrated guide helps the visitor to enjoy the walk.

Appendix: Museums with Natural History Collections

JAMES A. BATEMAN

Natural historians at all levels can use their local museum to advantage. Where there is a biological records centre they can use this as a source of information concerning the local status of species or of particular sites. In most instances biological record centres can supply data to the public inquirer but, since staff time and availability is usually under pressure, it is best to make an appointment in advance of a visit. It should be remembered that most records include species and sites which require confidentiality because of local or national rarity.

Apart from the resource of records, the reserve collections held by the museums included here can serve as a useful identification aid, usually superior to the information supplied in even the best field guides. There is often no substitute for a series of good comparative specimens.

The displays in public galleries will frequently provide an initial explanation of the species expected locally and since these are often exhibited in defined habitat groups there is an immediate interest for young field naturalists. Opening times are given but since these are liable to change it is as well to check before making a special visit.

Berkshire

Reading Museum and Art Gallery

The biological record has been built up from personal records acquired by members of staff and abstracted from local journals. The Keeper of Natural History is the vertebrate recorder for the Reading Naturalists Society and the Deputy Director is the insect recorder. Species and habitat records are cross-referenced.

There are reserve collections mainly of British insects within which is incorporated the local material. There are a few botanical specimens, but not all of these are of local material. (The important herbarium of the late J. E. Lousley was presented to Reading University). The galleries have displays some of which consist of systematic presentation of animal groups, but others refer to specific habitats and the wildlife these are likely to contain. The displays are old but they are gradually being restored and new labels printed.

Back issues of the *Reading Naturalist* are available for sale at the museum reception desk, but older issues not available there can be obtained from the office of the Keeper of Natural History. There are important lists of local fauna and flora in this publication.

Admission free, week-days 10.00 a.m. to 5.30 p.m. Saturdays 10.00 a.m. to 5.00 p.m. Telephone Reading 55911 Ext. 2242.

Newbury Museum

A part-time natural history assistant is gradually putting in order the various natural history records at the museum, so that these are more easily retrievable. The details of habitats on species cards in the filing systems are being up-dated, including appropriate information from older records and catalogues.

There are reserve collections of insects and geological material housed under showcases in one of the galleries. These are readily accessible, well preserved, and arranged systematically for easy reference. There are natural history and geological galleries. The wildlife displays are mainly based upon habitat groups but there are a few cases which deal with individual groups such as fishes. Various natural history charts display information about fauna and flora and wildlife conservation. These can also be purchased from the bookstall. The geology displays cover the Newbury district.

Apart from the sale of charts, there are also reports from the Newbury Environmental Study Group, some reports of other local surveys and a number of commercial publications dealing with the elementary study of natural history.

Admission free, April to September, daily 10.00 a.m. to 6.00 p.m. Sundays 2–6 p.m. October to March, daily 10.00 a.m. 4.00 p.m. Closed Sundays. Closed Wednesdays throughout year. Telephone Newbury 30511.

Buckinghamshire

County Museum, Aylesbury

A comprehensive and growing record is kept at the museum. Two sets of index cards relate respectively to numbered sites on a set of six-inch Ordnance Survey maps, and to species. Records are for both biological and geological material. The cards are being prepared so that eventually the information required can be abstracted by the use of an optical scanner. There is active co-operation between the museum and local societies in acquiring records.

The reserve collections are growing steadily and, in the biological field, contain some fluid-preserved specimens and some skeletal material. Vertebrate skins are kept only as mounted material for exhibitions. Among the insect collections is important material collected by Sir Eric Ansorge and also some from Captain Ellerton. Local material has been separated from the remainder having a British origin. All the geological collections are of local material and include the Lee Collection from Hartwell, one by Lea and Oakley and another by de Hunt. The contents are mainly fossils.

The natural history gallery consists of habitat groups arranged specifically for teaching purposes, but including entirely appropriate local species. The geology displays concentrate upon local rocks and minerals and the industries which have used them.

Among publications available for sale from the information desk is a list of Bucks nature trails and some off-prints from journals of local natural history societies.

Admission free, Monday to Friday 10.00 a.m. to 5.00 p.m. Saturday 10.00 a.m. to 12.30 p.m. and 1.30 p.m. to 5.00 p.m. Telephone Aylesbury 82158 and 88849.

Oxfordshire

County Museum, Woodstock

The unusual origins of this museum have resulted in the collection of records and the acquisition of reference collections being in the hands of the Natural History Officer of the Education Section, but there are no natural history galleries. It is hoped to make good this omission eventually but until this happens small specialist displays will be arranged from time to time in exhibition cases in the lecture room and temporary, circulating natural history exhibitions will serve the public of Oxfordshire.

The Oxfordshire Biological Recording Scheme began its ninth year of operation in 1984. Apart from the work of the Natural History Education Officer, there have been regular meetings of a volunteer study group at the museum to collate records and deal with collection material. It is now considered that 99 per cent of Oxfordshire mollusc records are on file and there are good records for butterflies, moths, and beetles. There are more limited records of microlepidoptera. A bird and mammal identification service is available. Records are card-indexed on special cards which combine locations on tetrad maps of Oxfordshire with written details of habitats and ecology. New records are distributed to national recording schemes on a regular basis and the progress of the scheme is circulated in an annual report. The possibility of computerizing records is being investigated. Information from the scheme is regularly sought by the Nature Conservancy Council, BBONT, local planning authorities, RSPB and BTO, as well as by private individuals.

The Natural History Education Officer arranges field excursions for children and adults, especially bird-watching in Blenheim Park and at Manor Farm Museum, Cogges, near Witney.

Natural history publications covering a wide range of subjects are available from the bookshops at the County Museum and Cogges Farm Museum. Enquiries for special items can be addressed to the Trading Manager at the County Museum (Woodstock 811456).

Admission free at the County Museum, May to September daily 10.00 a.m. to 5.00 p.m. (Saturday 10.00 a.m. to 6.00 p.m.), Sunday 2.00 p.m. to 6.00 p.m.; October to April Tuesday to Friday 10.00 a.m. to 4.00 p.m., Saturday 10.00 a.m. to 5.00 p.m. Sunday 2.00 p.m. to 5.00 p.m. There is a nature trail at Cogges Farm Museum, admission adults 50p, children, students, OAPs 50p 10.30 a.m. to 5.30 p.m. daily, Easter to September. Telephone enquiries about records and collections to Woodstock 811456.

University Museum Oxford

The scientific collections of zoological, entomological, geological, and mineralogical specimens of the University of Oxford are housed in this building.

Although it is principally a teaching and research institution, the museum is normally open to the public and visitors with enquiries concerning the reserve collections and libraries are welcomed by previous appointment.

The entomological collections have international coverage, but British material is easily accessible, as also is a fine antiquarian and modern departmental library. In the galleries a long run of cases deals with the systematic groups of insects and visitors would find this useful in a preliminary attempt to identify specimens, or understand more about this class of arthropods. More detailed comparative identification would be aided by use of the reserve reference collections. Other cases in the gallery illustrate the biology of insects and include sections which deal with household pests, pests of farm stock, forestry pests, medical entomology, insect physiology, and pollination. The entomological collections on display are currently being rearranged.

The zoological collections are also international in scope but include most of the British fauna other than insects. Almost all British bird species are on display in the public gallery, and comparative material is in reserve. Most of the British mammals are available in reserve, if not on display. There are smaller collections of British fish, reptiles, and amphibians. The British molluscs are virtually completely represented in the collections, but British crustaceans and other invertebrate groups are less well covered. A publication listing the zoological collections is available.

The geological collections cover most of the fossil forms likely to be found in the three counties, and a long and comprehensive public display dealing with fossils of Oxon includes interesting fossil reptiles of the Jurassic from the Oxford area, as well as mammals from the Oxon Pleistocene. Among collections of historical interest which include material from the area are those of Buckland and Arkell, together with a number from nineteenth-century amateur collectors from Oxfordshire. Visitors are welcomed by appointment and can consult the collections and library.

Owing to the poorness of the area as a mineral resource, there is little material of local interest in the mineralogical collections.

Entrance to the University Museum is between 12.00 p.m. and 5.00 p.m. Monday to Saturday free of charge. Telephone Oxford 57529.

GAZETTEER OF PRINCIPAL WILDLIFE SITES

Abbreviations

BBONT: Berkshire, Buckinghamshire and Oxfordshire Naturalists' Trust
Berks: Berkshire
Berks/Oxon: formerly Berkshire, now Oxfordshire
Bucks: Buckinghamshire
FNR: Forest Nature Reserve, maintained jointly by NCC and the Forestry Commission
Grade 1, Grade 2: sites so graded in the NCC's *Nature Conservation Review*, 1977
NCC: Nature Conservancy Council
NT: National Trust
Oxon: Oxfordshire
SSSI: Site of Special Scientific Interest, designated by NCC

Almshill Larches, Oxon: BBONT, by permit only: close to Stonor village: 10 acres of scrub on the chalk, with an interesting flora.

Ambarrow Hill, Berks: NT: ½m S of Crowthorne Station, SU 825629: 11 acres of pine-clad slopes.

Ardley Wood Quarry, Ardley, Oxon: BBONT, permit required: ¼m W of Ardley, SP 536274: a limestone quarry, which is both a geological SSSI and of botanical interest.

Ashdown, Aston Tirrold, Berks/Oxon: BBONT, one open day each year: a small reserve for one of the two remaining sites for the pasque flower S of the Thames.

Aston Clinton Ragpits, Bucks: BBONT, open to members: 1m N of Halton Camp, SP 887108: a disused 5-acre chalkpit, with good chalk flora and butterflies.

Aston Rowant NNR, with Beacon Hill FNR and Aston Hill (NT), Oxon: astride A40 and M40 between Stokenchurch and Lewknor, SU 7297: a mosaic of Grade 1 chalk grassland and scrub and Grade 2 beechwood, including Beacon and Bald Hills on the Chiltern escarpment, with a good chalk flora. Nature trail.

Aston Upthorpe Down, Berks/Oxon: BBONT, open to members: 2m S of Aston Upthorpe, SU 545834: Grade 1 chalk grassland and juniper scrub, with the larger of the two surviving colonies of the pasque flower S of the Thames and other good chalk flora and butterflies.

Bagley Wood, Berks/Oxon: St John's College, Oxford: ½m W of Kennington, SP 5102: an extensive mixed woodland, formerly extremely rich in flora, especially fungi, but now much reafforested with conifers.

Bald Hill, Oxon: *see* Aston Rowant NNR.

Baynes Reserve, Greenham, Berks: BBONT, permit required. 2m E of Greenham, SU 512652: 40 acres of ancient deciduous woodland, parts of Great Wood and Park Lodge Gully, with a rich flora, including snowdrop, wild daffodil and Solomon's seal. Bowdown Woods are close by.

Banbury Sewage Farm, Oxon: Thames Water Authority and BBONT, open to members: ¾m SE of Banbury, SP 470400: parts managed to protect migrant and wintering wildfowl, waders and other birds.

Beacon Hill, Oxon: *see* Aston Rowant NNR.

Bernwood Forest, Bucks and Oxon: Forestry Commission, NCC & BBONT: 3m NE of Stanton St. John, Oxon, SP 6009, 6110, 6210 & 6111: an ancient oakwood, now a state forest, which contains the Grade 1 Waterperry Wood FNR, noted for its wild service trees, another FNR in Shabbington Wood for the black hairstreak butterfly and a small BBONT property; has a good flora, nightingales, both fallow and muntjac deer and an especially rich butterfly and other insect fauna. Collecting is strictly controlled by the Forestry Commission.

Bernwood Meadows, Bucks: BBONT: on the W side of Bernwood Forest, SP 607109, public footpath: 18 acres of old-established grassland with a fine colony of green-winged orchids.

Bix Bottom, Oxon: *see* Warburg Reserve.

Black Park and Langley Park, Bucks: Bucks CC: 3m NE of Slough, TQ 0083: Black Park is a country park with coniferous and mixed woodland and an ornamental lake. The adjoining Langley Park has some acid grassland, an arboretum and a farm. Both have nature trails.

Blenheim Park, Oxon: Marlborough Estate: ¼m W of Woodstock, SP 4316: an outstanding site for ancient trees, including the finest stand of old oaks in Central England, deer, insects, lichens, the poisonous toadstool *Boletus satanas* and good waterfowl on the lake produced by damming the River Glyme.

Bloxham, The Slade, Oxon: Oxon CC: ¼m W of Bloxham, SP 425355: a small educational reserve with a relict alder swamp and marsh.

Boarstall Decoy, Bucks: NT & BBONT: 3m W of Brill, SP 623151, limited access: one of only 3-4 remaining working duck decoys, surrounded by a small oakwood on Oxford Clay.

Bowdown Woods, Greenham, Berks: BBONT, permit required: 1¾m E of Greenham, SO 505656; 50 acres of ancient deciduous woodland, close to Baynes Reserve (q.v.).

Bradenham Woods, Bucks: NT & BBONT: Bradenham Wood and Naphill Common lie between Bradenham and Naphill, SU 8397; Park Wood is ½m N of Bradenham,

SU 9298: a Grade 1 site for plateau and dip-slope Chiltern beechwood, with some oak on Naphill Common; BBONT manages a small chalk scrub reserve on the edge of Park Wood, open to members. Some sarsen stones with rare lichens are at 833973.

Braziers End Pits, Bucks: BBONT: 1m SW of Cholesbury, SP 926063, open to members: 4 acres of disused brickpits on the Clay-with-flints, with a colony of green-winged orchids.

Buckingham Canal, Bucks: BBONT: 3m NE of Buckingham, SP 726354: a short stretch of the disused Buckingham Canal; an educational reserve.

Bullingdon Bog, Oxon: Oxford City Council & BBONT, open to members: in the Lye valley between Headington and Cowley, SP 548059: an acre of calcareous fen, probably the only such fen within a city's limits in Britain, still with a most interesting flora. Its fox population is being studied by the University Zoology Department.

Burghfield Common, Berks: *see* Wokefield Common.

Burnham Beeches and Dorneywood, Bucks: City of London Corporation & NT: ¾m W of Farnham Common, SU 9585: a Grade 2 beechwood on sand and gravel, famous for its ancient pollard beeches, also with much oak and birch. Neighbouring East Burnham Common still has a good heathland flora with lesser gorse *Ulex minor*.

Buscot Park, Berks/Oxon: NT: 1m SE of Buscot, SU 239973: has a heronry and an ornamental lake.

Buttlers Hangings, Bucks: BBONT: 1m NW of West Wycombe, SU 819961, public footpath: 10 acres of chalk grassland and scrub, with good chalk flora and butterflies and a colony of the great green bush-cricket *Tettigonia viridissima*.

Calvert Jubilee Reserve, Bucks: BBONT, permit required.: ¼m N of Calvert Brickworks, SP 683248: a 95-acre reserve with a 50-acre flooded brick-pit and 7 acres of disused railway line, with interesting winter wildfowl, wild flowers and butterflies.

Chawridge Bank, Nuptown, Berks: BBONT: 1½m NW of Winkfield, SU 894738: 8 acres of neutral grassland and scrub, with an interesting flora.

Chequers, Grange Lands and Pulpit Hill, Bucks: BBONT: ½m SE of Great Kimble, SP 8305, public footpath: mainly Grade 1 chalk grassland and scrub, with boxwood in Happy Valley, which has spread from Ellesborough Warren, one of only three natural boxwoods in Britain; also a small beechwood on Pulpit Hill. Excellent chalk flora, including musk orchid, and butterflies; outstanding for mosses.

Chinnor Hill, Oxon: BBONT: on the Ridgeway Path ½m SE of Chinnor, SP 7600, public footpaths: 69 acres of chalk grassland and scrub on the steepest part of the Chiltern escarpment, with frog orchids, good juniper and small areas of beechwood.

Church Hill, West Wycombe, Bucks: NT: ¼m W of W. Wycombe, SU 828950: a steep hill, covered with chalk grassland and scrub, with many old yews and some interesting plants.

Church Wood, Hedgerley, Bucks: Royal Society for the Protection of Birds: ¼m E of Hedgerley, SU 975875: an outlier from Burnham Beeches with some fine old beech trees and good woodland birds.

Clipper Down, Bucks: *see* Ivinghoe Beacon.

Cliveden, Bucks: NT: 2½m N of Taplow, SU 913856: besides the well-known house and gardens has some fine hanging beechwoods on the steep cliffs above the Thames.

Cock Marsh, Berks: NT: 1m N of Cookham, SU 886868: 132 acres of flat marshy meadows by the Thames with a good flora, including water violet, and steep chalk slopes with a good chalk flora.

Coleshill Fritillary Meadow, Berks/Oxon: NT & BBONT: ½m W of Coleshill, SU 2393: a 6-acre fritillary meadow by the River Cole, recently transferred from Wiltshire following a boundary adjustment.

Cookham Dean Common, Berks: *see* Maidenhead Thicket.

Cookham Moor, Berks: NT: between Cookham Church and Station, SU 895853: 9 acres of marshy grassland in the middle of Cookham, with a flora similar to Cock Marsh, but less rich.

Coombe Hill, Bucks: NT: 1½m N of Wendover, SP 849066: 106 acres of Grade 2 chalk grassland and scrub, with heathland on the Clay-with-flints at the top; at 852ft, the highest point in the Chilterns.

Cothill Fen and Parsonage Moor, Berks/Oxon: NNR, NT & BBONT, permit required: ¼m W of Cothill, SU 463998: a Grade 1 calcareous fen, the best such fen in Central England, with a rich flora, including several marsh orchids. Parsonage Moor is the site of Professor E. B. Ford's important research on the genetics of the scarlet tiger moth *Panaxia dominula* and its variety *bimacula.*

Cowcroft, Bucks: BBONT, open to members: 1½m E of Chesham, SP 986018: a small 1½-acre grassland reserve.

Crog Hill, Berks: BBONT, permit required: 3m N of Lambourn, SU 323834: a 4-acre chalk grassland reserve with good flora and invertebrates.

Dancers End, Bucks: Royal Society for Nature Conservation & BBONT: 2m SW of Tring, Herts, SP 902096: 78 acres of beechwood, chalk grassland and scrub, with a very rich insect fauna and good flora, including wood vetch and Chiltern gentian.

Dorneywood, Bucks: *see* Burnham Beeches.

Dry Sandford Pit, Berks/Oxon: BBONT, permit needed for inner reserve: ¼m S of Dry Sandford, SU 467995: 19 acres of a disused sandpit, including a geological SSSI, where the full Corallian succession in the Oxford area is exposed; also a fen with a rich orchid flora and one of only two sites in southern England for variegated horsetail *Equisetum variegatum*, together with a stretch of limestone grassland with marbled white and other butterflies; very good for bees and wasps.

Ducklington Fritillary Meadow, Oxon: ¼m E of Ducklington, SP 3607: one of the best known fritillary meadows around Oxford, close to the River Windrush.

East Burnham Common, Bucks: *see* Burnham Beeches.

Ellesborough Warren, Bucks: *see* Chequers.

Englemere Pond, Berks: Bracknell District Council, managed with BBONT advice: 1½m W of Ascot, SU 906686: an acid pond with a good aquatic flora, surrounded by pinewoods.

Eversdown, Oxon: BBONT, permit required: 2½m NW of Henley-on-Thames, SU 7485: a 14-acre chalk bank, with grassland and scrub, and good flora and invertebrates.

Finchampstead Ridges, Berks: NT: ¾m W of Crowthorne Station, SU 808634: 107 acres, including Heath Pool and Simons Wood, of mainly coniferous woodland and heather-covered heathland.

Foxcote Reservoir, Bucks: Anglian Water Authority & BBONT: 2m NE of Buckingham, SP 712363, access restricted, but visible from Maids Moreton-Leckhampstead road: an important wildfowl refuge.

Foxholes, Bruern, Oxon: BBONT, open to members: 3m S of Kingham, SP 250205: 160 acres of oakwood, with plantations of beech and conifers, and a marshy meadow by the Windrush; nightingales and a good flora, some of it, including lichens and fungi, acid-loving.

Frilford Heath, Berks/Oxon: 1m N of Frilford, SU 4498: now mainly a golf course, but still has an outstanding beetle fauna and many interesting fen and heathland plants, with some affinities to the Breckland of East Anglia.

Gomm Valley, Bucks: BBONT, open to members: ¾m E of Wycombe Marsh, SU 898922: a 10-acre educational reserve of chalk grassland and scrub.

Grange Lands, Bucks: *see* Chequers.

Great Meadow Pond, Berks: *see* Windsor Great Park.

Happy Valley, Bucks: *see* Chequers.

Hartslock, Oxon: BBONT, open to members: 1½m SE of Goring, SP 617795: a 12-acre patch of chalk grassland and scrub with an extremely rich flora, good butterflies and an extensive view over Hartslock Woods and up and down the Thames.

Headington Wick, Oxon: *see* Sydlings Copse.

Heath Pool, Berks: *see* Finchampstead Ridges.

Henry Stephen/C. S. Lewis Reserve, Risinghurst, Oxon: BBONT, open to members: 1m SE of Headington Roundabout SP 562065: an important educational reserve with 7 acres of mixed woodland and a flooded claypit with a good freshwater fauna.

High Standing Hill, Berks: *see* Windsor Forest.

Hitchcopse Pit, Berks/Oxon: BBONT: 1m W of Cothill, SU 453996, open to members: a 2-acre sandpit, exceptionally rich in bees and wasps (70 species) and with an interesting flora.

Hodgemoor Wood, Bucks: Forestry Commission & BBONT: 1m W of Chalfont St. Giles, SU 9693, public footpaths: an extensive dry oakwood with a good deal of birch, containing three small nature reserves, one of them including a swallow-hole.

Hogback Wood, Bucks: NT: 1m W of Beaconsfield Station, SU 927912: 23-acres of deciduous woodland.

Hollybank Marsh, Oxon: BBONT: ½m E of Wootton, SP 4432094: a 4-acre wetland meadow, with a colony of reed warblers and interesting marsh plants.

Holtspur Bank, Bucks: BBONT: 1m NE of Loudwater, SU 916908: a steep 3-acre chalk bank with scrub and an interesting flora.

Hook Norton Railway Cutting, Oxon: BBONT, open to members: ½m S of Hook Norton, SP 360323 & 357313: 19 acres, in two sections divided by a tunnel, of disused railway cutting, with some limestone grassland and patches of incipient oakwood.

Horley Reserve, Oxon: BBONT, open to all: ¼m S of Horley, SP 417434 to 407427: 30 acres of mixed habitat, formerly ironstone workings and railway track; an educational reserve.

Hurley Chalkpit, Berks: BBONT: 2m SE of Hurley, SU 813820: 3½ acres of chalk grassland, scrub and beechwood, with a good flora.

Iffley Meadows, Iffley, Oxon: City of Oxford & BBONT, open to all: ¼m W of Iffley, SP 5203: a well known fritillary meadow.

Inkpen Common, Berks: BBONT 1½m E of Inkpen, SU 382640: 26 acres of heathland with some small bogs and an excellent flora, including the north-easternmost site in Britain for the pale dog violet *Viola lactea*, and good birds, e.g. nightingale and nightjar.

Ivinghoe Beacon, Steps Hill and Clipper Down, Bucks: NT: 1½m NE of Ivinghoe, SP 961169: a fine stretch of Grade 2 chalk grassland with a good flora.

Langley Park, Bucks: *see* Black Park.

Lardon Chase and Lough Down, Berks: NT: ¼m NW of Streatley, SU 588809: 66 acres of downland with good views across the Thames valley.

Lewknor Copse, Oxon: All Souls College & BBONT, open to members: ¾m E of Lewknor, SU 725975: a 2½-acre beechwood, on the Icknield Way opposite Aston Rowant NNR, with a fine display of spurge laurel *Daphne laureola*.

Littleworth Common, Bucks: SU 935863: 1m NW of Burnham Beeches: heathland, now much overgrown, with some acid ponds and interesting plants.

Lodge Hill, Bucks: 1½m S of Saunderton, SP 794001, astride the Ridgeway Path: an isolated hill in the Princes Risborough gap in the Chiltern escarpment with the flora and butterflies associated with good chalk turf and scrub.

Lodge Wood, Whistley Green, Berks: BBONT, open to members on 2 open days a year: ½m W of Whistley Green, SU 786737: a small wood with one of the best sites in Britain for Loddon lily *Leucojum aestivum*, also wild daffodils.

Long Grove Wood, Bucks: BBONT, open to members: ½m S of Seer Green, SU 963915: a 4-acre fragment of old coppiced beechwood.

Long Herdon Meadows, Bucks: BBONT, open to members: 1½m S of Marsh Gibbon, SP 648202: 11 acres of unimproved alluvial meadow by the River Ray with a rich flora typical of neutral grassland.

Lough Down, Berks: *see* Lardon Chase.

Magdalen Meadow, Oxford: Magdalen College: SP 524063: still one of the best surviving fritillary meadows; the adjoining park has had a herd of fallow deer since the 17th century.

Maidenhead Thicket, Pinkney's Green and Cookham Dean Common, Berks: NT: ½-1m W & NW of Maidenhead, SU 855810, 860825 & 863843: 613 acres of woodland, scrub and neutral grassland, with good birds.

Matthew Arnold Field, Boars Hill, Berks/Oxon: Oxford Preservation Trust and BBONT: ¼m E of Boars Hill, SP 483023: a grassy field, the poet's favourite haunt, and now an educational reserve for Matthew Arnold School, Cumnor.

Menmarsh, Oxon: BBONT, permit required: 1¼m S of Horton-cum-Studley, SP 590110: a small marshy area with sphagnum moss, formerly a site for fen violet *Viola persicifolia*.

Millfield Wood, Hughenden Valley, Bucks: BBONT, public footpath: ¼m E of Hughenden Church, SU 870954: 19 acres of ancient mixed deciduous woodland, with a fine flora, including coralroot *Cardamine bulbifera*, herb Paris and Solomon's seal.

Moor Copse, Berks: BBONT: ¼m SE of Tidmarsh, SU 637742: 56 acres of mixed deciduous woodland with a short stretch of the River Pang; interesting birds and plants and important Lepidoptera.

Moorend Common, Bucks: 1m SW of Lane End, SU 803905: a Chiltern common with good oakwood, scrub and damp grassland communities, managed by local trustees with BBONT advice.

Munday Dean, Bucks: BBONT: 2m NW of Marlow, SU 8288: a meadow with a good population of green-winged orchids.

Naphill Common, Bucks: *see* Bradenham Woods.

Northerams Wood, Berks: Bracknell District Council & BBONT: 1m SW of Bracknell, SU 856682: 6 acres of mixed deciduous woodland, with good bluebells.

North Leigh Common, Oxon: BBONT: 1m NE of North Leigh, SP 402140: 41 acres of heathland and scrub with good birds, a sphagnum bog and an interesting flora; it is the only site in the region for western gorse *Ulex gallii*.

Oakley Hill, Chinnor, Oxon: BBONT ¼m S of Chinnor, SU 757995: 12 acres of chalk grassland and scrub.

Obelisk Pond, Berks: *see* Windsor Great Park.

Old Slade, Bucks: formerly BBONT: 2½m S of Iver, TQ 039781: a group of disused gravel pits by the M4 motorway with good aquatic birds; an important educational reserve, now destroyed by the owners, a gravel extraction company.

Otmoor Rifle Range and the Spinney, Oxon: BBONT, permit required: 1m NE of Beckley, SP 5712: 56 acres of damp grassland on clay, with good butterflies and an important sample of the flora that has become extinct over almost the whole of the rest of Otmoor. The rifle range is still in regular use.

Oxford Lane, Kingswood, Waddesdon, Bucks: BBONT: SP 696186: a green lane with an old pond, good for butterflies and dragonflies.

Owlsmoor, Berks: 1m SE of Crowthorne, SU 860627: one of the very few remaining true bogs in the three counties.

Park Wood, Bucks: *see* Bradenham Woods.

Parsonage Moor, Berks/Oxon: *see* Cothill Fen.

Pangbourne Meadow, Berks: NT: just below Pangbourne Bridge, SU 640768: 7 acres of Thames-side meadow.

Pilch Field, Bucks: BBONT: 1¾m NW of Great Horwood, SP 747322: 22 acres of old ridge and furrow grassland with a marshy area and an interesting flora.

Pitstone Fen, Pitstone, Bucks: BBONT, permit required: 1m E of Tring Reservoirs, SP 936143: a chalk quarry, derelict since 1945, in which a calcareous fen rich in wildlife has grown up.

Pitstone Hill, Bucks: Bucks CC: 1½m S of Ivinghoe, SP 950145, astride Ridgeway Path: Grade 2 chalk grassland with good flora and butterflies.

Pixey and Yarnton Meads, Oxon: ½m SW of Yarnton, SP 4711: a stretch of neutral grassland on both banks of the Thames, classified Grade 1 because it has been managed in the same way for many centuries, being annually cut for hay, the various strips being redistributed among the owners by lot each year. Flora very good, especially for dandelion microspecies; also very rich in molluscs.

Port Meadow, Oxon: Freemen of Oxford & Wolvercote Commoners: 1½m N of Carfax, Oxford, SP 4908: another Grade 1 neutral grassland, complementing Pixey and Yarnton Meads because it has been grazed uninterruptedly for perhaps 1,000 years. Flora also interesting, but restricted. Good birds when it floods in winter.

Pulpit Hill, Bucks: *see* Chequers.

Rack Marsh, Bagnor, Berks: BBONT, permit required, annual open day: 2m N of Newbury, SU 456690: a 14-acre marshy wetland by the River Lambourn.

Rammamere Heath, Bucks: *see* Stockgrove Park.

Risinghurst: *see* Henry Stephen/C. S. Lewis Reserve.

Robertswood, Bucks: BBONT, permit required: 2m SE of Wendover, SP 884056: 37 acres of *c*30-year-old beech plantation, with an interesting chalk flora.

Rushbeds Wood, Brill, Bucks: BBONT, open to members: 1½m NE of Brill, SP 6615: a 107-acre ancient coppice oakwood with a fine woodland flora and butterflies: a SSSI.

Salcey Forest, Bucks: *see* The Straits.

Seven Barrows, Berks: BBONT, open to members: 3m N of Lambourn, SU 329829: a 3-acre group of at least 24 round barrows with excellent chalk plants and butterflies.

Short Heath, Bucks: BBONT, open to members: 3m N of Chesham, SP 959060: a 10-acre educational reserve of typical Chiltern woodland and chalk grassland.

Shotover Plain Country Park, Oxon: Oxon CC: SU 5606: includes a brackeny hillside with some oakwood. Nearby are The Coppice and The Dingle, Shotover Park, SP 576063: BBONT: 50-acres of deciduous woodland and acid grassland.

Simons Wood, Berks: *see* Finchampstead Ridges.

Sinodun Hills, Berks: *see* Wittenham Clumps.

Snelsmore Common, Berks: Newbury District Council: 1½m N of Newbury, SU 460710: a fine stretch of heathland and bog, with good plants and birds; now a country park.

Sole Common Pond, Berks: BBONT, open to members: 1½m S of Boxford, SU 413707: a small acid pond with a sphagnum bog, where sundew, cottongrass and bogbean grow, surrounded by mixed woodland.

Somerton Meads, Oxon: ¾m NW of Somerton, SP 492302: an important local wildfowl haunt with a good aquatic plant list.

The Spinney, Shotover, Oxon: BBONT, permit required, 2 open days a year: 1½m NW of Wheatley, SP 5706: a wooded valley with a series of ponds made by damming a stream.

Stockgrove Country Park, with Rammamere Heath, Bucks: Bucks CC: 1½m SE of Great Brickhill, SP 928300: mixed woodland and lakes on acid sand with a rich flora.

Stoke Common, Bucks: managed by local trustees with BBONT advice: 1m NE of Stoke Poges, SU 9885: a stretch of overgrown heathland.

Stoke Hammond Fen, Bucks: protected by BBONT by agreement with the owner: ½m E of Stoke Hammond: a small relict fen.

Stonesfield Common, Oxon: ½m S of Stonesfield, SP 392165: a patch of limestone grassland with a good flora, including bastard toadflax *Thesium humifusum*.

Stonor Park, Oxon: ¼m NE of Stonor, SU 740890: an ancient park with a herd of fallow deer, a rich chalk grassland flora and very good lichens.

Stony Stratford Wildlife Conservation Area, Bucks: Milton Keynes Development Corporation & BBONT: ½m N of Stony Stratford, SP 785410: 55 acres of artificial wetland, from which gravel has been removed; formerly a meadow by the River Ouse.

Stowe Park, Bucks: 3m NW of Buckingham, SP 6636: the school grounds include a 25-acre woodland nature reserve and a trout hatchery, and have good lichens.

Stow Wood, Oxon: *see* Sydlings Copse.

The Straits, Salcey Forest, Bucks: Forestry Commission, BBONT & Northamptonshire Naturalists' Trust, open to members: 2½m E of Hartwell, SP 813513: 33 acres of oakwood in this ancient forest, planted in 1847, with first-class butterflies and interesting plants.

Sutton Courtenay Field Centre, Berks/Oxon: Central Electricity Generating Board: 1½m S of Sutton Courtenay, SU 500920: a 15-acre educational reserve, including fresh water, in the grounds of Didcot Power Station, which the CEGB has made available to BBONT and other bodies to carry out field studies and courses.

Swains Wood, Bucks: BBONT, permit required: 2½m NW of Turville, SU 740920: 41 acres of beechwood, chalk grassland and scrub with an excellent chalk flora and butterflies.

Swyncombe Downs, Oxon: 2½m E of Ewelme, SU 673912: a well known viewpoint over the Thames valley, with good chalk flora and some juniper.

Sydlings Copse, Oxon: BBONT, open to members: 1½m N of Headington, SP 555096: 49 acres of mixed habitats, including deciduous and coniferous woodland, valley fen and both limestone and acid grassland, with a very interesting flora and fauna. It is part of the area (Headington Wick and Stow Wood) described by G. C. Druce in the *Flora of Oxfordshire* (1932) as 'perhaps the most interesting portion of botanizing country in central England', known since Gerard, Ashmole and other 16th and 17th-century botanists. Stow Wood has unfortunately been largely replanted with conifers.

Taynton Quarry, Oxon: 1½m N of Taynton, SP 239150: old limestone quarries, from which much of medieval Oxford was built, with a rich flora and good butterflies.

Thatcham Reedbeds, Berks: 2m W of Thatcham, SU 500668: an area of reedbeds, important for birds, plants and insects, partly designated as an official Local Nature Reserve.

Tuckmill Meadow, Watchfield, Berks/Oxon: Vale of White Horse District Council & BBONT, open to members: ¼m SW of Watchfield, SU 241900: a 13½-acre unimproved pasture, with interesting plants of both limestone and damp grassland.

Vicarage Pit, Oxon: Oxon CC & BBONT, open to members from September to February: 1¼m W of Stanton Harcourt, SP 401057: a flooded gravel pit, made a Local Nature Reserve to mark the European Wetland Campaign in 1976.

Virginia Water, Berks: *see* Windsor Great Park.

Warburg Reserve, Bix, Oxon: BBONT: 1¾m N of Bix, SU 720880, public footpaths: 253 acres of beech and other woodland, chalk grassland and scrub: see Chapter 12.

Warren Bank, Oxon: BBONT, open to members: 1¼m N of Ipsden, SU 720880: 7 acres of chalk grassland and scrub, with an interesting flora and good butterflies and grasshoppers.

Watchfield Common Wood, Berks/Oxon: BBONT: 2m S of Coleshill, SU 230920: an educational reserve with 22 acres of mixed deciduous woodland.

Waterperry Wood, Oxon: *see* Bernwood Forest.

Watlington Hill and Park, Oxon: NT: 1m SE of Watlington, SU 702935: 150 acres of beechwoods surrounding Watlington Park and 96 acres of chalk grassland and scrub, with numerous old yews, on the Chiltern escarpment; good chalk flora, notable mosses and very good butterflies.

Wendlebury Mead NNR, Oxon: 1½m N of Charlton-on-Otmoor, SP 5617: Grade 1 lowland meadow by a tributary of the River Ray, with an exceptionally rich flora.

Westend Hill, Bucks: BBONT, permit required: ½m S of Cheddington, SP 914169: a small chalkpit with good flora. Outside the reserve are some much overgrown lynchets or medieval cultivation terraces.

Weston Turville Reservoir, Bucks: BBONT, permit required away from public footpath: 1½m SW of Halton, SP 864095: a canal reservoir, with a calcareous fen on the W side, good for water birds and marsh plants.

Whitecross Green and Oriel Woods, Bucks and Oxon: BBONT, permit required: 1¼m W of Boarstall, SP 603144: 156 acres of ancient deciduous woodland, with good butterflies, birds and plants.

White Horse Hill, Berks/Oxon: NT: 2m S of Uffington, SU 300867: 235 acres of chalk downland and farmland with an outstanding chalk flora; includes the well known, probably 1st century AD, white horse figure cut in the turf.

Widbrook Common, Berks: NT: 1m S of Cookham, SU 897840: 65 acres of grazed marsh and grassland with good aquatic plants.

Willen Lake, Bucks: ¼m S of Willen in Milton Keynes, SP 8740: first-class winter waterfowl resort.

Winchbottom, Bucks: BBONT, open to members: 1½m S of High Wycombe, SU 863903: 11 acres of chalk turf and scrub, with good flora.

Windsor Forest, Berks: Crown Estates: 2½m S of Windsor, SU 9373: an important Grade 1 fragment of ancient oak forest, with an especially rich fauna of beetles and other insects. It includes 45 acres of High Standing Wood as a FNR.

Windsor Great Park, Berks: Crown Estates: 1m S of Windsor, SU 97: an extensive stretch of acid grassland, bracken and deciduous woodland, with some fine old oaks and three good waterfowl sites, Great Meadow Pond (965710), Obelisk Pond (977703) and Virginia Water (970690). The introduced mandarin duck breeds.

Windsor Hill, Bucks: 2m E of Princes Risborough, SP 827028: a Grade 1 Chiltern beechwood, which contains, as a BBONT reserve (open to members), 17 acres of Grade 2 chalk grassland and scrub, with good juniper and other chalk flora, and the Black Hedge, a medieval hedge mentioned in a charter of AD 900.

Wittenham Clumps, or Sinodun Hills, Berks: 1m SE of Little Wittenham, SU 570925: a well known viewpoint over the Thames valley, but with a rather uninteresting flora.

Wokefield (or Burghfield) Common, Berks: 1m N of Mortimer, SU 635662: a fine stretch of heathland with alder gullies and good fungi and butterflies.

Woolhampton Reedbed, Berks: BBONT: adjacent to Woolhampton, SU 5766: a reedbed of exceptional entomological interest.

Wychwood Forest and Ponds, Oxon: NNR: 1m NE of Leafield, SP 3316: a remnant of a once extensive ancient forest, still with some fine patches of old Grade 1 oakwood and limestone grassland, with a rich flora and fauna; far the best site in the region for old forest lichens. The Grade 2 ponds are spring-fed artificial marl-ponds with crayfish and a good calcareous aquatic flora.

Wytham Estate, Berks/Oxon: University of Oxford: 1m W of Wytham, SP 4608: a stretch of woodland and grassland on limestone, much used for research by the University biological departments.

Yarnton Mead, Oxon: *see* Pixey Mead.

BIBLIOGRAPHY

Chapter 1

Bilham, E. G., *The Climate of the British Isles,* London, 1938.
Fitter, R. S. R., *Wildlife in Britain,* Harmondsworth, Middx., 1963
Sherlock, R. L., *British Regional Geology: London and the Thames Valley,* 2nd ed. H.M.S.O., London, 1947
Stamp, L. D., *Britain's Structure and Scenery,* London, 1946
Walker, J. J. (Ed.), *The Natural History of the Oxford District,* London, 1926

Chapter 2

Benson, D. and Miles, D., *The Upper Thames Valley, an Archaeological Survey of the River Gravels,* Oxford, 1974.
Bradley, R. and Ellison, A., *Rams Hills, a Bronze Age defended enclosure and its landscape,* British Archaeological Reports, 19, Oxford, 1975.
Brodribb, A. C. C. *et al., Excavations at Shakenoak* 5 vols., Oxford, 1968–75.
Emery, F., *The Oxfordshire Landscape,* London, 1974.
Harvey, N., *The Industrial Archaeology of Farming in England and Wales,* London, 1980.
Havinden, M. A., *Estate Villages,* London, 1966.
Lambrick, G. and Robinson, M., *Iron Age and Roman riverside settlements at Farmoor, Oxfordshire,* Council for British Archaeology, London, Report 32, 1979.
Martin, A. F. and Steel, R. W. (eds.), *The Oxford Region,* Oxford, 1954.
Parrington, M., *The Excavation of an Iron Age settlement, Bronze Age ring ditches and Roman features at Ashville Trading Estate, Abingdon, 1974–6,* Council for British Archaeology, London, 1978.
Reed, M., *The Buckinghamshire Landscape,* London, 1979.
Richards, J., *The Archaeology of the Berkshire Downs,* Reading, 1978.
Rowley, T. (ed.), *The Oxford Region,* Oxford, 1980.
Steane, J. M., 'Medieval forests, woods and parks of Berkshire', *Arboricultural Journal,* 5, 189-200, 1981.
Thirsk, J. (ed.), *The Agrarian History of England and Wales IV 1500–1640,* Cambridge, 1967.

Chapter 3

Baker, H., 'Alluvial meadows: a comparative study of grazed and mown meadows', *Journal of Animal Ecology,* 25, 408-20, 1937.
Church, A. H., *Introduction the Plant Life of the Oxford District*, Oxford Botanical Memoirs, nos. 13-15, Oxford, 1922–5.
Dimbleby, G., *Plants and Archaeology*, London, 1967.
Dony, J. G. *et al., English Names of Wild Flowers*, London, 1974.
Elton, C., *The Ecology of Invasions by Animals and Plants*, London, 1957.
Godwin, H., *History of the British Flora*, Cambridge, 1977.

Lloyd, P. S. and Pigott, C. D., 'The influence of soil conditions on the course of succession on the chalk of southern England', *Journal of Animal Ecology*, 55, 137-46, 1967.

Pollard, E., Hooper, M. D. and Moore, N. W., *Hedges*, London, 1974.

Ratcliffe, D. (ed.), *A Nature Conservation Review*, Cambridge, 1977.

Smith, C. J., *Ecology of the English Chalk*, London, 1980.

Tansley, A. G., *Britain's Green Mantle*, (2nd ed.), London, 1968.

Woodell, S. R. J., 'The flora of walls and pavings', *Nature in Cities*, ed. I. C. Laurie, Chichester, 1979.

Chapter 4

Bowen, H. J. M., *The Flora of Berkshire*, Oxford, 1968.

Druce, G. C., *The Flora of Buckinghamshire*, Arbroath, 1926.

Druce, G. C., *The Flora of Oxfordshire*, Oxford, 1927.

Frankum, R. G. and Frankum, M., *The Birds and Plants of Freeman's Marsh, Hungerford, 1970–4*; with *Supplement 1975-9.* Hungerford, 1975, 1979.

Perring, F. H. and Farrell, L. 1983, *British Red Data Book I. Vascular Plants.* 2nd ed. Nettleham, Lincoln.

Chapter 5

Carter, H., 'The present status of mammals in the Reading Area', *Reading Naturalist*, 1973.

Fraser, A. C., 'Mammals of the middle Thames', *Middle-Thames Naturalist,* 8: 7-10.

Chapter 6

Price, K., 'The birds of Buckinghamshire', *Records of Buckinghamshire*, 15: 20-31, 1947.

Radford, M. C., *The Birds of Berkshire and Oxfordshire*, London, 1966.

Sharrock, J. T. R., *The Atlas of Breeding Birds in Britain and Ireland,* 1976.

Chapter 7

Arnold, H., *Provisional Atlas of the Amphibians and Reptiles of the British Isles,* Abbots Ripton, Hunts, 1973.

Chapter 8

Banks, J. W., 'River Thames Fish Surveys', *Proc. First British Freshwater Fisheries Conference* 336-44, 1979.

Pitcher, T. J., *Population dynamics and schooling behaviour in the minnow* Phoxinus phoxinus *(L.)*, D.Phil. Thesis, Oxford, 1971.

Varley, M. E., 'British Freshwater Fishes—Factors affecting their distribution', *Fishing News* (Books) Ltd., 1967. 1967.

Wheeler, A. C. and Maitland, P. S., 'The scarcer freshwater fishes of the British Isles. 1. Introduced species', *Journal of Fish Biology* 5, 49-68, 1973.

Williams, W. P., 'The growth and mortality of four species of fish in the River Thames at Reading', *Journal of Animal Ecology* 36, 695-720, 1967.

Yoxon, M., 'Survey of the fish population of the Grand Union Canal and Mount Farm Lake', *Ecological Studies in Milton Keynes* XI, Milton Keynes, 1965.

Chapter 10

Faunal Lists

Bowen, H., 'Molluscs found in the Reading Area', *Reading Naturalist,* 1975.

Ellis, A. E., *The Non-marine Mollusca of the British Isles,* Oxford 1969.

Fonseca, E. C. M.d'A., *H.I.B.I.* Vol. 10, pt 4(b). *Diptera: Cyclorrhapha (Muscidae),* 1959.

Fraser, F. C., *H.I.B.I.* Vol. 1, pts 12 and 13. *Mecoptera, Megaloptera, Neuroptera,* 1959.

H.I.B.I.: Handbooks for the Identification of British Insects. Royal Entomological Society.

Hobby, B. M. *et al.*, 'Fauna' in A. F. Martin and R. W. Steel (eds.), *The Oxford Region,* Oxford, 1954.

Jones, R., *The Country Life Guide to the Spiders of Britain and Northern Europe,* London, 1983.

Joy, N. H., *A Practical Handbook of British Beetles,* 2 vols., London, 1932.

Kimmins, D. E., *H.I.B.I.* Vol. 1, pt 9. *Ephemeroptera,* 1950.

Kimmins, D. E., *H.I.B.I.* Vol 1, pt 6. *Plecoptera,* 1950a.

Lambrick, G. and Robinson, M., *Iron Age and Roman riverside settlements at Farmoor, Oxfordshire,* Council for British Archaeology Report 32, London, 1979.

Macfadyen, A., 'The small arthropods of a *Molinia* fen at Cothill', *Journal of Animal Ecology* 21: 87-117, 1952.

Mosely, M. E., *The British Caddis Flies (Trichoptera): a collector's handbook,* London, 1939.

Ragge, D. R., *Grasshoppers, Crickets and Cockroaches of the British Isles,* London, 1965.

Smith, K. G. V., *H.I.B.I.*, Vol. 10, pts 2 and 3. *Diptera: Lonchoperidae and Conopidae,* 1969.

Southwood, T. R. E. and Leston, D., *Land and Water Bugs of the British Isles,* London, 1959.

Taylor, E., 'A note on Dutrochet's leech, *Trocheta subviridis* Dutrochet, and its occurrence in Oxford', *Annals and Magazine of Natural History,* (11) 10: 431-42, 1943.

Todd, V., 'Key to the determination of British Harvestmen (Arachnida: Opiliones). *Entomologists' Monthly Magazine,* 84: 109-13, 1948.

Victoria County History of Berkshire, London, 1906, pp. 71-120.

Victoria County History of Buckinghamshire, London, 1920, pp.6 9-119.

Victoria County History of Oxfordshire, London, 1939, pp. 60-191.

General Natural History

Bristowe, W. S., *The World of Spiders,* London, 1971.

Cain, A. J. and Sheppard, P. M., 'Selection in the polymorphic land snail *Cepaea nemoralis,*' *Heredity,* Vol. 4, Pt. 3, 1950.

Colyer, C. N. and Hammond, C. O., *Flies of the British Isles,* London, 1968.

Corbet, P. S. *et al., Dragonflies,* London, 1960.

Darlington, A., *The Pocket Encyclopaedia of Plant Galls in Colour,* London, 1968.

Evans, G., *The Life of Beetles,* London, 1975.

Oldroyd, H., *The Natural History of Flies,* London, 1964.

Stubbs, A. and Chandler, P. J., (Eds.), 'A dipterist's handbook', *Amateur Entomologist,* 15: 1-255, 1978.

Todd, V., 'The Habits and Ecology of the British Harvestmen (Arachnida, Opiliones), with special reference to those of the Oxford District', *Journal of Animal Ecology* 18: 209-29, 1949.

Identification Guides

Blower, J. G., *Synopses of the British Fauna No. 11: Millipedes (Diplopoda),* Linnean Society of London, 1958.

Chinery, M., *A Field Guide to the Insects of Britain and Northern Europe,* London, 1973 (and references therein).

Eason, E. H., *Centipedes of the British Isles,* London, 1964.

Ellis, A. E., *British Snails: the Non-marine Gastropoda of Great Britain and Ireland,* Oxford, 1969.

Kerney, M. P. and Cameron, R. A. D., *A Field Guide to the Land Snails of Britain and Northern Europe,* London, 1979.

Locket, G. H. and Millidge, A. J., *British Spiders,* Vols. 1-2, Ray Society Monographs, 1951, 1953, 1974.

Sankey, J. H. P. and Savory, T. H., *Synopses of the British Fauna* No. 4: *British Harvestmen (Opiliones),* Linnean Society of London, 1974.

Sutton, S. *et al.*, *Woodlice*, London, 1972.

Chapter 11

Bowen, U., *How to Make a Small Pond*, BBONT Oxford, 1977.

Department of the Environment: The Welsh Office, *Report of a river pollution survey of England and Wales*, London, 1970.

Goriup, P. D. and Karpowicz, Z., *River Surveys Report*: NCC South Region, 1976.

Hattey, R. P., *Survey and classification of rivers for nature conservation*: NCC South Region Report, 1977.

Hobby, B. M., *et al.*, 'Fauna' in A. F. Martin and R. W. Steel (eds.), *The Oxford Region*, Oxford, 1954.

Jordan, D., *A study of four small stony streams in Wychwood Forest National Nature Reserve, Oxfordshire*, B.Sc. honour, project, Department of Biology, Oxford Polytechnic, 1979.

Kelcey, J. *et al., Ecological Studies in Milton Keynes*, A series of reports, Milton Keynes.

National Water Council, *River Quality: the 1980 survey and future outlook*, 1981.

Ratcliffe, D., (ed.), *A Nature Conservation Review*, 1977.

Street, M., 'The food of mallard ducklings in a wet gravel quarry and its relation to duckling survival', *Wildfowl* 28, 113-25, 1977.

Chapter 12

Bowen, U., 'Field studies on a power station site', *Natural Science in Schools*, 8: 72-4, 1970.

Bowen, U., *Projects for Environmental Studies*, BBONT Oxford, 1972.

Bowen, U., *How to Make a Small Pond*, BBONT Oxford, 1977.

Gardiner, P. *et al., BBONT 1959–69*, Oxford 1970.

Nature Reserves Investigation Committee 1945. *National Nature Reserves and Conservation Areas in England and Wales*, London, 1945.

Ratcliffe, D. A. (ed.), *A Nature Conservation Review*, 2 vols., Cambridge, 1977.

Wildlife Conservation Special Committee (England and Wales), *Conservation of Nature in England and Wales*, Cmd. 7122, London, 1947.

Chapter 13

Clapham, A. R. *et al., Flora of the British Isles*, 2nd ed., Cambridge, 1962.

Hubbard, C. E., *Grasses*, Harmondsworth, Middx., 1954.

Lange, M. and Hora, F. B., *Collins Guide to Mushrooms and Toadstools*, London, 1963.

Summerhayes, V. S., *Wild Orchids of Britain*, London, 1951.

Walker, R., *The Flora of Oxfordshire and Contiguous Counties*, Oxford, 1833.

Watson, E. V., *British Mosses and Liverworts*, 2nd ed., Cambridge, 1968.

INDEX